Scared
Straight

Scared Straight

The Panacea Phenomenon Revisited

James O. Finckenauer
Rutgers University

Patricia W. Gavin
Anna Maria College

with

Arild Hovland
NOVA Norwegian Social Research

Elisabet Storvoll
NOVA Norwegian Social Research

WAVELAND
PRESS, INC.
Prospect Heights, Illinois

For information about this book, write or call:
Waveland Press, Inc.
P.O. Box 400
Prospect Heights, Illinois 60070
(847) 634-0081

ISBN 1-57766-035-8

Printed in the United States of America

7 6 5 4 3 2 1

Contents

Preface

There seem to be certain enduring beliefs about why children go wrong and what ought to be done about stopping that from happening. This book is about one of those beliefs and its actualization. It is about a program that is known around the world as Scared Straight. Scared Straight was the Hollywood name given to the Juvenile Awareness Project. That project embodied a simple concept: employing fear to deter youth from committing crime. In 1976, prison inmates formed the Lifers' Group and brought teenagers into prison to participate in depictions of the ghastly realities of prison life. The intent of the experience was to discourage these teens (and sometimes pre-teens) from behaving in ways that might lead them down the path to crime and prison. The implicit underlying belief motivating the effort was the belief in deterrence, specifically the deterrent value of fear and aversion.

In the first edition, *Scared Straight! and the Panacea Phenomenon* (originally published in 1982), I examined and critiqued the Scared Straight project at New Jersey's Rahway State Prison. Drawing upon this case study, I described a pattern of failure that seemed to be associated with other efforts to deal with juvenile delinquency. This pattern appeared to result from a futile but nevertheless seemingly persistent quest for simple remedies or cure-alls. It was this pattern that I referred to as the "panacea phenomenon."

It was my conclusion that the belief in deterrence as delivered by the Rahway Lifers was unfounded; that the Juvenile Awareness Project, aka Scared Straight, could not and did not accomplish the lofty purposes claimed for it. Nevertheless, for twenty years now the project has continued to confront thousands of youngsters with prison horror stories. During these twenty years, there have also been innumerable spin-offs and clones of the original Scared Straight program, not only in the United States, but abroad as well.

A revisit seems called for. Much of the original content of *Scared Straight! and the Panacea Phenomenon* is still applicable today, but some deserves reconsideration. The purpose of this revisit is to update the evidence, and to extend the discussion both into the present and across the oceans.

Patricia Gavin, whose interest in juvenile corrections complements my own, has been a valued collaborator on this new edition, which we open by examining anew the panacea phenomenon—but this time yoking it to the vague notion of myths. Myths are widely accepted beliefs that give meaning to events; they are socially cued, whether or not they are verifiable. As such, myths appear to play a very significant role in governing some people's ideas about how to deal with youthful offenders. Although generally unsupported (and insupportable) by fact, myths seem to have the function of offering simple explanations for complex, often otherwise unexplainable issues and problems. Juvenile delinquency is one such problem. Myth-based explanations are sometimes accepted out of ignorance or misunderstanding, but not exclusively so. Some myths survive in the face of overwhelming evidence to the contrary. Why is this? And, what does it have to do with panaceas in general and the Scared Straight panacea in particular?

This background will be followed by a reiteration of the original Scared Straight case study. Next, Patricia Gavin and I will take advantage of the research and other developments since 1982, both with respect to the original project and with as many clones as we can find. We will move to the broader stage of developments over the years since 1982. What has happened with the Rahway project? What has been happening elsewhere with respect to this approach? Has there been any research and evaluation, and if so, what have been the results? Is "Scared Straight" alive and well?

We will then be joined by two colleagues as we turn to a new case study that offers us the latest example of the phenomenon. Modeled on its U.S. precursor, Norway's Ullersmo project operated from 1992 to 1996. In chapter 8–11, Arild Hovland and Elisabet Storvoll will take us on a fascinating look at the history of that project, how and why it came to be, and what happened to it. Hovland and Storvoll's study not only gives us the opportunity to reexamine many of the issues raised fifteen years ago, it also permits us to do so in an international, comparative context. The possibilities for comparison are truly exciting.

We will close by returning to the broad issues posed at the outset. The ideas embodied in Scared Straight have not died, despite a considerable battering by contrary evidence that they do not work. We will offer our thinking on why that is so. In this, we are indebted to Elaine Duxbury and Ted Palmer of the California Youth Authority for their insights with respect to the staying power of Scared Straight and other like programs that survive despite their ineffectiveness. Finally, we will try to discern what the myth and panacea framework portends for some other popular ideas for dealing with juvenile delinquency.

James O. Finckenauer

chapter one

Dealing with Delinquency
Myths and Panaceas

Just as it was a generation ago, and for generations before that, serious juvenile crime is one of the more complex and intractable problems facing many countries in the world today. Nowhere is this more apparent than in the United States. Despite thousands of programs and the expenditure of millions of dollars on juvenile justice and delinquency prevention in the previous two decades, arrests of juveniles for violent crimes increased more than 50 percent between 1988 and 1994. Although there was a welcome downturn in 1995, juvenile arrests for violence are projected to climb again, doubling by the year 2010. This troubling situation led the U.S. Office of Juvenile Justice and Delinquency Prevention to open a recent report as follows:

> Over the past few years, juvenile crimes have made television and newspaper headlines nationwide, fueling public perceptions of a juvenile crime "epidemic" and prompting public outcries for swift, decisive action to stop it. Policymakers, practitioners, and scholars have called for a juvenile justice system that is tougher on that small percentage of hardened, violent, youthful offenders who are responsible for a large majority of juvenile crime.[1]

The key words suggesting the ever popular response to crime are "epidemic," "swift and decisive," "tougher," and "hardened and violent." That very same sense of urgency and deep concern about a youth crime plague prevailed in 1976. That was the year a group of inmates at New Jersey's Rahway State Prison, known as the Lifers' Group, began what later became known around the world as the Scared Straight program. Groups of boys and girls were brought into the prison. Once inside, menacing prison inmates subjected them to threats, intimidation, emotional shock, loud and angry bullying, and persuasion. The purpose? To

1

deter them—literally to scare them out of delinquency. After careful examination of this program, Finckenauer concluded that deterrence was not being achieved. He also concluded that despite the cold reality of there being no simple answers to the perplexing problem of juvenile delinquency (à la Scared Straight), this probably would not keep some people from seeking them.[2]

Because it was a prime example of the panaceas for delinquency, seemingly born of a search for the magic bullet, we want to revisit Scared Straight—both the original program and its offspring. What has happened in the years between then and now? We will look anew at the panacea phenomenon in delinquency prevention, seeking to explain the apparent staying power of panaceas like Scared Straight. Our thesis is that this steadfastness might be traced to a reliance upon myths as the foundation for at least some of these programs.

We will also take a global perspective in our return visit. Other countries too are struggling to cope with increases in juvenile delinquency and violence. In England, for example, two ten-year-old boys kidnapped a two-year-old boy from a shopping center and murdered him. A Japanese boy murdered a younger schoolmate and cut off his head. Three Brazilian youths doused a sleeping man with gasoline and killed him by setting him aflame. Each of these vicious crimes caused considerable soul-searching in their respective countries. Because youth crime and violence does not respect national boundaries, the United States is not alone in its concern with delinquency. So too has it not been alone in succumbing to the seductiveness of the Scared Straight idea as a way of responding to this concern.

Let us begin with some context for our discussion. A critical element of that context is the very nature of juvenile delinquency. That nature is complex in a way that makes both understanding and coping difficult. Why is delinquent behavior so complex? Because there are innumerable combinations of individual and social factors that go into explaining why any individual child might become an offender. Just so, there are various combinations of conditions and circumstances that increase or decrease any child's odds of offending. Many of those conditions and circumstances can be consciously manipulated in an attempt to change the odds. What and how we choose to manipulate—and why—is also part of the context for our discussion here.

Human behavior is infinitely diverse, hard to predict, and equally hard to control. Youthful misbehavior is no exception. At the same time, our tools for understanding—the science of human behavior—is far from being an exact science. There is much we cannot explain. As a result, our choice of tools to shape youthful behavior is subject to severe limitations. But because behavior problems are real, they cannot be ignored. They cannot be put aside until we have the perfect explanation and solution. We must sometimes proceed in ignorance, and often with less than complete understanding. How do we then decide what to do, and why?

Let us take the example of a learning-disabled child. That child may have difficulty learning to read. This is a difficulty that could spring from a variety of causes—physiological, psychological, and social. Without fully comprehending the causes of the reading disability, experts nevertheless can experiment with various teaching techniques to see what might help in any particular instance. Presumably the techniques will be selected on the basis of informed assumptions about what is causing the problem and what might solve it. What distinguishes this form of behavior from the behavior that interests us—juvenile offending—is that the former is not seen to be blameworthy. Having poor reading skills is not a free-will choice, and it does not victimize others. The choices of possible solutions will be made (except perhaps in rare and bizarre cases) in a morally neutral environment.

Yet, like a learning disability, delinquency too has causes that are physiological, psychological, and social. But unlike it, delinquency can be judged by standards of right and wrong and good or evil. When blameworthy deviant behavior is also attributed to a rational choice, other assumptions with respect to causes and solutions may enter in. These other assumptions have to do with the fundamental beliefs, morals, and values of those making the assumptions. Why does a child choose to commit evil deeds? What can be done to stop him or her from making those choices? We are interested in the answers to these questions and from whence they come. This leads us to myths and, in particular, to the possibility that myths may provide the roots for certain delinquency prevention efforts like Scared Straight.

The Mysteries of Myths

We begin by considering just what is a myth. Let us make clear that what we are talking about here are not myths about, for example, Greek gods or other supreme beings. Instead, we are referring to those much more personal beliefs that mediate between humans and nature, that determine how we perceive, experience, and interpret the world.[3] Some scholars, for example Bartollas and Miller, refer to what we are talking about as ideology.[4] Without getting into a debate about semantics, we prefer the term myth.

Myth has most often been used to refer to some false belief or illusion. For example, historians Gerster and Cords defined myths as false beliefs "which have traditionally been accepted as 'true' and taken to be 'real.'"[5] But there is much more to it than that. Gerster and Cords also said that myths are "both true and false simultaneously. . . . there is a point at which myth and reality intersect; at that given point, they become one and the same. Myth becomes reality precisely when people act as if the myth were true and their beliefs and attitudes are based upon it. . . ."[6] This blurring of the distinction between what is true and what is false is one of the more intriguing aspects of myths. It is also an aspect that may help account for their persistence and their influence.

Some argue that because myths provide contexts for defining rationality and truth, they do not themselves have to be either true or false. According to Gerster and Cords, for example, point out that "myths have a real existence in the minds of their believers and thus are psychologically true even though factually false."[7] If we act on the basis of something we erroneously believe to be true, our action is obviously no less real. But to complicate matters further, myths are not always "factually" false. Or at least not completely so. The most enduring myths are those that have elements of truth to them. As Edelman pointed out, such myths are not synonymous with fiction; instead they are "a widely accepted belief that gives meaning to events and that is socially cued, whether or not it is verifiable."[8]

It seems to us that as society goes about trying to understand and shape youthful misbehavior it runs into two broad types of myths. The first consists of false beliefs that are held out of simple ignorance or misunderstanding. These can be thought of as "pseudo" myths. We call them pseudo because they refer to some subject about which there is a clearly relevant body of information, such that it is not necessary to rely simply on belief. In the case of pseudo myths, it might be supposed that reasonably open-minded people, given evidence that contradicts what they previously held to be true, could be expected to alter their opinion. If they are ignorant of any contrary information they naturally have no reason to change their opinion.

Some examples of the continuing pseudo myths about juvenile crime as recounted in a leading text include: "juveniles account for the bulk of serious crime in the United States; . . . juveniles are more likely than adults to victimize the elderly; . . . juveniles commit more serious violent crimes than adults."[9] A variety of sources, including the FBI's *Uniform Crime Reports*, show that none of these statements are true. Take for example the belief that juvenile offenders are responsible for much of the violent crime in the United States. Arrest data show the opposite to be true. Over 81 percent of the violent crimes of murder, rape, robbery, and aggravated assault (as measured by arrests in 1996) were committed by adults.[10] Juvenile delinquency, in fact, is overwhelmingly nonviolent. Nevertheless, people believe the opposite.

Because not everyone is open-minded, and because there is usually plenty of room to attack the evidence against the pseudo myths, only some of them will be dispelled. In the examples just cited, one line of attack could be to criticize the arrest data used to refute them. After all, arrest data represent just the tip of the iceberg and do not show how much actual serious crime and violence juveniles commit.

With the second type of myths (what we call the "real" myths), there is even less possibility for refutation. This is because the myths are not completely false beliefs. They may not only have some factual basis, but more importantly, they provide explanations in situations where there are otherwise none or where there is a need to create and maintain a certain image of reality. They go beyond facts and data to fill in the gaps in our knowledge. This means they will not be readily dismissed with the limited factual information available. Whereas we may be able to falsify pseudo myths with hard evidence, real myths are much more likely to survive no matter what the evidence.

So what are "real" myths? The best way to think of them is as jumbles of basic beliefs—combinations of facts, prejudices, values, pictures, memories, and projections. This montage helps us explain our world to ourselves. Once we have our own set of myths, we become comfortable with them. We resist giving them up. It is for this reason that myths can be thought of as gnarled thickets of sometimes dubious ideas that do not yield readily to contrary evidence.

One of the functions of myths in general seems to be to reduce complex problems to simple terms. One such complex problem, of course, is that of juvenile delinquency. The very simplicity of myths in turn adds to their appeal. Simple explanations, derived from or cued to prevailing myths, make sense to their audience. Anthropologist Claude Levi-Strauss argued that myths help people live with uncertainty and ambivalence. "The purpose of myth," he wrote, "is to provide a logical model capable of overcoming a contradiction."[11] Myths help explain that which is otherwise unexplainable; they help resolve that which is otherwise unresolvable; they get rid of unwelcome contradictions. They do all this by offering an acceptable approximation of the facts.

The idea that myths may give meaning and direction to reality, and help govern our perception of the world, has very significant implications. It means, for example, that we may accept, modify, or reject new information depending upon how well it fits with the myths in which we believe. This is why new knowledge or evidence will not necessarily dispel belief in myths, whether they are pseudo or real. According to Edelman, "large numbers of people . . . cling to myth, . . . and reject falsifying information when prevailing myths justify their interests, roles, and past actions, or assuage their fears."[12] Beliefs in myths seemingly help us to avoid cognitive dissonance and to maintain cognitive integrity. Such beliefs also might support our self-interest. This too could account for the fact that people hang on to pet ideas often in the face of overwhelming contrary information. The opposing information is simply disparaged or ignored.

In their book, *Myths That Rule America*, London and Weeks pointed out that numerous public policies have been developed on the basis of myth. Such policies, they said, are typically unsuccessful because they are ill-conceived. "They are ill-conceived because they rely so heavily on erroneous assumptions."[13] We know that for a variety of political reasons, solid analyses of social problems are rarely the chief influences upon solutions for them. Addressing this issue, Edelman concluded that validity is neither a help nor a hindrance to the employment of rationalizations for individual beliefs and the public policies that are derived from them.[14] This might be especially true of programs for juvenile offenders, where we run into issues of good and evil, as well as heated emotional debate about what is wrong and what should be done about it.

Bernard, who offered a compatible argument to ours, believes delinquency is a subject about which people have strong beliefs but little information. There are, he said, a number of myths about juvenile delinquency, and these myths are not necessarily false. "People generally just don't know or care whether they are true or false. They hold the belief because it is convenient to do so."[15] It is inconvenient to have one's basic beliefs and self-interest undermined.

To the extent that efforts to deal with delinquency are grounded in myth, it would seem that they are headed for failure. Or at least they are if their effectiveness is measured in empirical terms. "Empirical" simply refers to hard data on matters like recidivism and cost-effectiveness. Casting efforts in terms of myth, however, appears to have another rather anomalous feature, namely that they don't have to "work"—they really don't have to be effective—as long as those efforts provide useful and acceptable ways of thinking about the problem. The constituents of such programs (the true believers) are rewarded not by substantive changes, but by symbolic reassurance that needs are being attended to and problems are being managed.

On one level then, simplistic solutions to complicated problems like delinquency are doomed to failure because they are inadequate. But panaceas derived from myths may also be more symbolic than real—more concerned with how the solutions appear than with whether they actually accomplish anything. Thus, despite the fact that they could well waste time and effort, divert attention from reality, and objectively result in failure, depending upon the strength of the belief and the reasons for that belief, we might nevertheless see these panaceas survive—and even thrive.

Bennett developed what he called a "policy as myth" perspective that illustrates the power of myths in this respect. Bennett said that the point of many government policies is not really to solve problems. The policies are not the real political ends, but only a means—a means not to the solution of problems, but to the creation of certain public images of society and politics.[16] Myth-based programs may thus ultimately persist because they reinforce societal traditions and values. The area of juvenile justice would seem to be particularly ripe for this approach.

Efforts to combat juvenile crime are grounded in an incompletely understood problem; yet, practically everyone believes that he or she has the expertise to solve it. This contradiction is compounded by the high visibility of the problem and the enormous pressure to do something about it. Thus, it is not surprising that there might be a readiness to grasp simplistic explanations and solutions.

Panaceas derived from mythical assumptions could be expected to be grasped by a public and public officials who are looking to find fast, familiar, and comfortable ways of dealing with problems. After all, they do not wish to be troubled with solutions that are complicated on the one hand or modest on the other. More importantly, they especially do not want solutions that challenge or are dissonant with their basic beliefs. Bennett concluded that: "In most policy areas it is more acceptable to suffer failure based on [politically] correct theories than it would be to achieve success at the price of sacrificing social values."[17]

Political scientist Stuart Scheingold argued that in the United States there is a myth of crime and punishment that is composed of "traditional beliefs about the nature, consequences, and appropriate responses to crime. This belief system has powerfully punitive overtones and deep roots in American culture."[18] In arguing that crime became particularly politicized during the 1960s and '70s, Scheingold said that politicization should be thought of in cultural and personal terms, rather than simply as a response to a rising crime rate. The public became receptive to a hard line on crime because the public's more punitive attitudes are a reflection of its basic values. Scheingold asserts that: "whether we respond punitively or nonpunitively to our fears is culturally determined—attributable, that is, to the values and emotions which we bring to our thinking about crime rather than to a reliable demonstration that one approach actually works better than the other."[19] In other words, he suggests responses to crime are driven more by beliefs than by results, particularly by a belief in individual responsibility and in holding criminals accountable for their actions through punitive consequences.

The Myth of Deterrence

One of the beliefs that plays a very powerful role in crime control is the belief in deterrence. Deterrence is based upon the fundamental view that people ponder taking certain actions by weighing the risks and benefits. According to this understanding, we are all rational beings who seek pleasure and avoid pain and who exercise free will in making behavior choices.

One of the appeals of deterrence is that it emphasizes individual responsibility—that individuals should be held responsible for their criminal behavior. This is linked to the opinion that offenders make a free-will choice to commit crimes. Obviously, if offenders engage in deviant behavior because of a rational choice, and if this choice is determined by a weighing of the risks and benefits, then it follows logically that a way to deal with crime is to increase the risks and decrease the benefits. This is the kind of deterrence model for dealing with crime that is embodied in Scared Straight.

To citizens who are fearful and angry about crime, intimidating potential criminals is a very attractive idea, as well as a very logical one. "It is a common sense idea that some people, who otherwise would break the law when doing so was to their advantage or when it seemed for some other reason desirable, would nevertheless resist temptation and stay on the right side of the law because of the living example of what can happen to those who commit crimes."[20]

Edelman dichotomized the ways in which people respond to their fears about crime into two opposing myth patterns. In the dominant myth pattern, he believes people see the criminal "as responsible for his own plight (authorities and concerned professionals help while protecting the rest of society against irresponsible and dangerous people)."[21] According to this view, the basic social structure of society is sound. We are OK; it is the criminal who is not OK! We need not feel sympathy for people who choose to commit crimes.

There would seem to be several implications associated with this myth pattern. If the delinquent is responsible, then it follows that he or she ought to be held accountable. Accountability means consequences, and the main consequence is punishment. Punishment has been shown to affect behavior through a combination of swiftness, severity, and most importantly, certainty of application. All criminal behavior is assumed to wax and wane in response to punishment. Because punishment is undesirable, and harsh punishment is the most undesirable of all, it will serve as a deterrent, or so it is believed. It will deter both the one punished (special deterrence) and other would-be criminals (general deterrence).

A second implication of Edelman's myth has to do with the "authorities and concerned professionals." These are the folks who are doing the helping and protecting. It is generally the social service employees who are doing the helping and the law enforcement authorities who are doing the protecting. By defining delinquency in accordance with this particular myth pattern, both of these groups create a situation that calls for the skills and authority they have—and that they wish to maintain. They present themselves as legitimate authorities on the causes of delinquency and on how to deal with it. This is one way that self-interest sustains support for a myth.

In the case of Scared Straight, many social welfare agencies and criminal justice agencies embraced the idea and adopted its use as an extension of their own efforts. To subsequently reject it would mean giving up their belief in this special kind of deterrence, admitting they were wrong, and denying themselves an attractive and popular option.

A third aspect of Edelman's thesis is that since the social structure is assumed to be sound, one can neither blame the exploitative capitalist nature of society for causing delinquency, nor, as is more commonly done, attribute delinquency to poverty, discrimination, unemployment, racism, and poor schools. None of these causes are readily solvable, certainly not by child welfare or the police. It is much more comforting to believe that it is the young criminal who is at fault, and it is youthful predators who need and deserve to be frightened and intimidated out of their crime.

Viewed in terms of a simple risks/benefits or pain/pleasure equation, deterring delinquency (or any other behavior for that matter) appears rather simple. It makes sense that if we increase the risk-of-pain side of the equation enough we can tip the balance in favor of deterrence. As we indicated, this belief in deterrence demands the related belief that people (including children) are logical creatures who decide to do or not do something based upon rational deliberation. It also assumes that pain and pleasure influences are clearly identifiable and separable. However, even deterrence advocates admit to problems with that assumption: "The stimuli confronting an individual can rarely be partitioned neatly into things tending to produce pain and those likely to produce pleasure; most situations in which we place persons, including criminals, contain elements of both."[22]

Do people make behavior choices by weighing the consequences? Yes! How do we know this? If from nowhere else, from personal experience. We don't put our hand back on the hot stove if we have previously been burned by it. We slow down when we see a police patrol car. This mass of personal experiences, absent any other information, can support an individualized belief in deterrence. We know that we can be deterred and what deters us. It is not hard to see how we could then project this onto other people, and into other situations. It is this process that contains the ingredients of a myth—some factual evidence, some valuation of pain and punishment, some judgment about how other people think and behave, some memory, some hope—and the message is that deterrence works. This simple belief in deterrence underlies much of the support for harsh punishment as the answer to crime. It also underlies support for Scared Straight as a specific way to prevent delinquency.

The realities, particularly in the context of Scared Straight-type programs, are much more complicated. Hard evidence supporting the belief in deterrence is difficult to attain. A leading text in criminal justice recently concluded that the belief in deterrence is largely based on "conjecture, faith, or emotion, with little or no empirical data."[23] Earlier the highly prestigious National Academy of Sciences panel that studied deterrence concluded that "we cannot yet assert that the evidence warrants an affirmative conclusion regarding deterrence."[24] In other words, they found no evidence that deterrence works.

It seems, therefore, that in order to hold on to the myth of deterrence, people must either be ignorant of the realities and complications, or ignore or dismiss them. We will not get into what all the complications are here, but just briefly sketch why deterrence efforts of the Scared Straight kind are built upon a simplistic idea and erroneous assumptions.

Deterrence and "Scared Straight"

Let us begin with the perception of the risks and benefits of delinquency. Contrary to a simplistic notion that youngsters are homogeneous in this respect, their perception differs from one young person to another. "Deterrence" is especially effective with those who are already deterred. It works best with those whose moral commitment to law or fear of disapproval constrain them from law-breaking in the first place.

Then there are the many benefits of delinquency that may not be perceived by adults. Besides any material rewards, these include social acceptance by peers, enhanced self-esteem, excitement and adventure, and thumbing your nose at the adult establishment. In addition to the fact that what may be perceived as a benefit by the young may not be so seen by adults, what adults see as risks may not be so perceived by the young. This means the adult supporters of Scared Straight programs—who think like adults and not children—may underrate the benefits and overrate the risks.

Deterrence is based upon threat, and that threat has to be credible to be a deterrent. Scared Straight programs are premised upon the belief that prison inmates are more credible messengers than other adults—parents, teachers, probation officers, or the police. Who better to convey a message about the consequences of breaking the law than those who are serving time? But whether the inmates make the impression they intend on the youths is open to question. For example, the prisoners portray themselves as poor, downtrodden, powerless persons not to be emulated; whereas the youths might perceive them as very powerful and frightening. Clearly there is a mixed message. In addition, as you will see, some youths believe the prisoners are only acting and role playing. This too would seem to undermine their credibility. Some observers have criticized what they call the exploitation of inmates in this manner. According to one critic, "he [the inmate] is used in the program in much the same manner as the hide of the dead coyote, strung on a barbed wire fence by the frustrated rancher in hopes of deterring other coyotes from raiding his stock."[25]

Factors other than benefits and risks also enter into juveniles' behavior choices. These too are not constants—either across youth or within the same youth across time and situations. Emotional state or consumption of alcohol and drugs, for example, can alter rational deliberation.

The kind of deterrence exemplified in Scared Straight is an unusual mixture. It is a very particular kind of deterrence, a repressive deterrence. Repressive deterrence is the product of an aversive experience—in this case being confronted with the harsh, degrading, dehumanizing, and life-threatening conditions that await in prison. Interestingly, the original Scared Straight experience was both direct and vicarious. Youths who physically entered the prison to be confronted by inmates were directly experiencing the fearful effects of punishment. But the fact that it was not real—that they were not really being punished—made it also vicarious. Elements of both specific and general deterrence were there. In some of the Scared Straight clone programs this mixture is not found. The experience in those programs, as we will see, is purely vicarious.

Some of the critics of the original Finckenauer research accused him of misinterpreting the Lifers' Group program as a "product of straight deterrence theory."[26] We will take up this criticism in examining the evolution of this and other programs over the past twenty years. Perhaps the goal is no longer deterrence?

Myths and Delinquency Prevention

It seems to us that the belief in certain myths (whether deterrence or something else) will determine receptivity to and interpretation of new information. Every person who attempts to prevent juvenile delinquency does so with a set of beliefs, based on both real and pseudo myths. This person may be a judge, a lawmaker, a social worker, a teacher, or simply a parent or sibling, or, as it turns out, a prison inmate. Their myths are composed, to a greater or lesser degree, of facts, as well as of values, biases and prejudices, personal experiences, and hopes and fears. Once established, however, the gnarled thicket endures, and it is out of this that each person makes judgments about what is causing juvenile crime, and what will cure it.

Let us offer an example, drawn from the Scared Straight context, of how a strongly held belief can endure despite an experience that contradicts and discredits that belief. In a study of youth perspectives on possible solutions to delinquency, 250 delinquents in residential facilities, group homes, and aftercare agencies were interviewed.[27] Asked what might be done to combat delinquency, one of these incarcerated youths argued as follows: "I say the best thing you could do is just like let them talk to people who are going through or having the same problems that they are having. Let them know what that person experiences, because I see now like a lot of little kids say jail is so awful but they don't really know until they went there. The school took me up to Sing Sing Prison, and I ain't going to lie, I got kind of scared in there because the men, they would have beat you up and not cared because they're already there for life, so they have nothing to lose."[28] This was spoken by a young man who somehow managed to get himself locked up after his scare. We guess it is supposed to work with other kids! You can see that it is not just adults who perpetuate this myth; youths also get caught up in it.

The Panacea Phenomenon

The argument we are developing is an amended and expanded version of that first set out by Finckenauer in 1982. We still concur with Daniel Glaser that the highway of delinquency prevention history is paved with punctured panaceas.[29] Indeed, the panacea phenomenon seems to characterize many efforts to prevent and control juvenile delinquency that have been carried out over the years. We agree that panaceas have been punctured, but that puncturing does not guarantee their demise. This conceptual theme underlies our examination of the history of the Scared Straight idea.

We argued earlier that one of the simultaneous causes and effects of the failures and frustrations in dealing with juvenile crime has been the refueling of a continuing search for the cure-all. This search is conducted, encouraged, and exploited not only by the general public and politicians, but also by juvenile justice officials and social scientists as well. We still believe that to be the case—and offer current examples of the rush to juvenile boot camps, to Project DARE (Drug Abuse and Resistance Education), and even to juvenile curfews. Both boot camps and DARE, not coincidentally, have many of the same deterrence aspects that make Scared Straight appealing.

Finckenauer argued that the panacea phenomenon seemed to have spawned a particular pattern in the battle with juvenile crime. First, a certain approach is posed as a cure-all or becomes viewed and promoted as a cure-all—as an approach that will have universal efficacy and thus be appropriate for nearly all youths. The approach may be promoted and sold as the all-encompassing solution to the delinquency problem. Think big! is the watchword. Each promoter/salesperson believes, or at least behaves as if, his or her idea is effective in saving youths and "hypes" it accordingly. Unfortunately, the approach, no matter what it is, almost always fails to deliver. It fails to live up to the frequently unrealistic or unsound expectations raised by the sales pitch. As this failure slowly becomes apparent, frustration usually sets in and the search for the next panacea or "answer" begins anew. This cycle of futility is illustrated in the figure on the following page.

We still believe this is an accurate depiction, but that it is incomplete, because it implies that the ostensibly failed panacea is discarded and rejected. Based upon the thesis we have outlined here, we are now suggesting that this will not necessarily be so.

Because we are focusing on the ideas and the thinking upon which delinquency programs are based, it is worthwhile to reiterate the discussion of the role of faulty theorizing in explaining why programs may

---

The Panacea Phenomenon

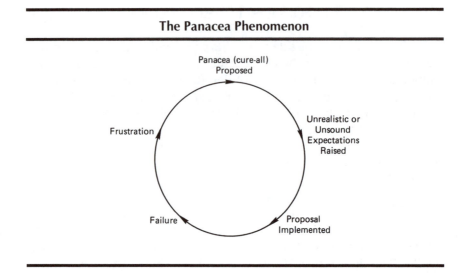

go wrong. We should point out that theoretically sound programs may fail for other reasons, such as being poorly implemented, under resourced, or wrongly targeted, but our interest here is in the role of faulty theory. If you begin with a flawed theory, it makes no difference how well it is implemented, resourced, or targeted. At this point in the discussion we would like to make it clear that theory is not something that should be limited to academic discourse. It is invaluable to practitioners operating in the real world of crime policy. Nearly every effort to prevent juvenile delinquency is premised on there being some connection between what is done for purposes of prevention on the one hand, and the delinquent behavior itself on the other. The idea for this connection comes from some theory, no matter how informal or poorly thought out it may be.

Each delinquency prevention effort is based upon assumptions about why delinquent behavior occurs with Scared Straight, as we indicated, the goal is to instill or enhance the fear of consequences in order to keep young people from becoming or continuing to be delinquent. The implicit assumption underlying Scared Straight is that juveniles become delinquent because they do not fear the consequences of going to prison, and, if they are made to fear those consequences, they will cease and desist.

If these kinds of assumptions are not or cannot be made, the program lacks a rationale. It is most often the case that the assumptions (as in the Scared Straight example) are implicit rather than absent, usually surfacing if and when there is an evaluation. This is what happened with the original Scared Straight study.

As was true with the Lifers' Group, the rationale is not always or even usually made explicit by whomever is trying to develop and implement a delinquency prevention program. They do not indicate why they think what they are doing or propose to do should be expected to work. This violates the generally accepted adage that programs should have theoretical foundations, and further, that they should be applied to theoretically appropriate types of populations. The absence of a theoretical foundation can then lead to a program being viewed literally as a cure-all. In many cases, even good solutions are not appropriate for everybody.

Programs must have some theoretical grounding, and there should be evidence or at least a sound argument as to why what is to be done is expected to help the youths who are to be subjected to it. As already indicated, a review of the delinquency prevention literature shows that explicit theory is rare. The theory employed thus far is only implicit. Programs are conducted for no better reason than someone thought they seemed like a good thing to do at the time, perhaps on an ad hoc basis. They also may be founded upon so-called theories that are naive or already discredited.

Besides the pressure to "do something," there is another kind of pressure on program promoters to promise more than they can deliver. This pressure comes from the intense competition for scarce resources. Cautious proposals that promise only modest results are unlikely to compete effectively for the limited funding available. Overselling, hyping, is rewarded, especially when the program is based on "gut-level" beliefs (myths) held by those who control the purse strings.

Aside from financial incentives, there are other reasons for the persistence of the panacea phenomenon. In the late 1960s, Stratton and Terry wrote about what they called the "isms" fallacy as being characteristic of delinquency prevention. "Doism" is the naive and overly optimistic belief that it is better to do something than to do nothing.[30] This can lead us to plow ahead with good intentions, but perhaps with utter disregard for the possible consequences of our actions—consequences that can be negative and detrimental. With respect to children especially, a considerable degree of harm has been perpetrated upon them under the guise of doing something that is "good" for them.

"Newism" refers to the appeal of approaches just because they are new. "This orientation is reinforced by the failure of older programs and the continuing rise of delinquency rates. This results in the bandwagon effect of implementing new programs and policies without carefully assessing their validity or reviewing the history of similar types of programs that preceded them."[31] A new approach has the advantage of being associated with progress. However, the fact that it is a new approach can also mean that there has not been sufficient time to evaluate it, and thus it can ride the tide of the attractiveness of the underlying idea for awhile.

In some instances there is ignorance of the "past," of the fact that certain ideas have already been discredited. This is especially so if the past has taken place in another country and word of failure has not gotten out. But in other cases, consistent with our thesis, the past is known but is ignored. Why? That is the tantalizing question to which we believe we have proposed an answer.

The third kind of "ism" is "faddism." It refers simply to the attractiveness of fads, whether they be in hairstyles, underwear worn on the outside, pants worn down around the thighs, or in ideas, as in boot camps for juvenile offenders. Delinquency prevention fads consist of programs that are often cheap, simple, and short in duration, as Scared Straight demonstrates. They may also come and go quickly, but not necessarily so; again as witness the Scared Straight example. It is the staying power of some that may be explained by their links to myth.

In the chapters that follow immediately, we will go back to the 1970s to trace the original case study of Scared Straight. That study will then be used as a baseline against which to examine developments over the ensuing generation. Next, we travel not only forward in time, but across the Atlantic to Norway. Here we find our second case study. Finally, we will return to our overarching questions: What has happened to this unusual effort at delinquency prevention? Why has it happened? And, what are the implications for some other ideas for combatting juvenile crime?

Notes

[1] U.S. Department of Justice, Office of Juvenile Justice and Delinquency Prevention. *1996 Report to Congress: Title V Incentive Grants for Local Delinquency Prevention Programs* (Washington, DC: U.S. Government Printing Office, 1997), p. 3.

[2] J. O. Finckenauer, *Scared Straight and the Panacea Phenomenon* (Englewood Cliffs, NJ: Prentice-Hall, 1982).

[3] R. M. MacIver, *The Web of Government* (New York: New York Free Press, 1965).

[4] C. Bartollas and S. J. Miller, *Juvenile Justice in America* (Englewood Cliffs, NJ: Prentice-Hall, 1998).

[5] P. Gerster and N. Cords, *Myth in American History* (Encino, CA: Glencoe Press, 1977), p. xiii.

6 Ibid., p. xiii.

7 Ibid., p. xiii.

8 J. M. Edelman, *Political Language: Words That Succeed and Policies That Fail* (New York: Academic Press, 1977), p. 3.

9 I. M. Schwartz, *(In) Justice for Juveniles: Rethinking the Best Interests of the Child* (Lexington, MA: Lexington Books, 1989), pp. 27–28.

10 U.S. Department of Justice, Bureau of Justice Statistics, *Sourcebook of Criminal Justice Statistics* (Washington, DC: U.S. Government Printing Office, 1997), Table 4.7.

11 C. Levi-Strauss, *Structural Anthropology* (New York: Basic Books, 1963), p. 229.

12 J. M. Edelman, *Political Language*, p. 3.

13 H. I. London and A. L. Weeks, *Myths That Rule America* (Washington, DC: University Press of America, 1981), p. ix.

14 J. M. Edelman, *Political Language*.

15 T. J. Bernard, *The Cycle of Juvenile Justice* (New York: Oxford University Press, 1992), p. 11.

16 William Bennett, *Public Opinion in American Politics* (New York: Harcourt Brace Jovanovich, 1980).

17 Ibid., p. 397.

18 S. Scheingold, *The Politics of Law and Order: Street Crime and Public Policy* (New York: Longman Publishing Group, 1984), p. 59.

19 Ibid., p. 56.

20 H. Gross and A. von Hirsch, *Sentencing* (New York: Oxford University Press, 1981), p. 181.

21 J. M. Edelman, "Language, Myths and Rhetoric," *Society* 12, no. 5 (1975): 15.

22 J. Q. Wilson, "What Works? Revised: New Findings on Criminal Rehabilitation," *The Public Interest* 61, no. 3 (1980): 17.

23 S. T. Reid, *Crime and Criminology* (Madison, WI: Brown and Benchmark, 1997), p. 90.

24 Cited in Gross and von Hirsch, *Sentencing*, p. 231.

25 R. L. Keller, "Ideological Underpinnings and Policy Implications of Juvenile Awareness Programs" (Unpublished manuscript).

26 M. Israel, The Rahway Lifers' Group: The Politics of Being My Brother's Keeper. *New Jersey Monthly* (November 1980): 98.

27 A. P. Goldstein, *Delinquents on Delinquency* (Champaign: Research Press, 1990).

28 Ibid., p. 117.

29 D. Glaser, "Achieving Better Questions: A Half Century's Progress in Correctional Research," *Federal Probation* (1975): 3–9.

30 J. R. Stratton and R. M. Terry, (Eds.), *Prevention of Delinquency: Problems and Programs* (New York: The Macmillan Co., 1968).

31 Ibid., pp. 2–3.

chapter two

The Juvenile Awareness Project

In December, 1975, a small group of inmates serving sentences of twenty-five years or more in New Jersey's Rahway State Prison formed what they called the Lifers' Group. The Lifers' Group was created in part to counteract what these inmates saw as a stereotyped, Hollywood-type image of prisons and convicts held by the general public. This image, they felt, stigmatized convicts as immoral and inhuman. In order to dispel what they saw as a false image, the Lifers wanted to try to prove that they could be useful and worthwhile people even though locked up in a maximum-security prison. One of their early activities in pursuit of this objective was to obtain, repair, and gift-wrap Christmas toys for needy children.

Among a number of committees formed among the Lifers was one called the Juvenile Intervention Committee. This particular committee was largely the brainchild of the then president of the Lifers, Richard Rowe. Rowe was serving a double-life term for rape, kidnapping, and armed robbery. He was personally motivated to try to do something for kids over concern for his own then twelve-year-old son who was getting into trouble on the outside. Rowe said: "We were looking for something we could do to keep kids out of trouble, and I thought: . . . bring them in and let them find out what a life of crime is all about, straight from us. A lot of us have kids of our own, and we were worried what was going to happen to them."[1]

The idea of having young delinquents or potential delinquents visit the prison can also be traced to the observation of groups of college students on prison tours. The Lifers thought that if this could be done with college students, it could also be done with younger groups of juveniles. This belief becomes very important because it represents a subtle but significant shift in what would be the purpose of the prison visits. The college tours were intended to be little more than educational. The ulti-

19

mate purpose of the juvenile visits, on the other hand, was to be something very different. The purpose, as it turns out, was much more complex and difficult—namely to deter or scare delinquency out of the kids.

This shift from an educational, consciousness-raising type of endeavor to an endeavor aimed at changing attitudes and behavior was an enormous leap into an arena which had witnessed almost nothing but failures. In addition, deterring juveniles could be measured; its success could be tabulated; and, the measuring rod used could become the petard upon which the Juvenile Awareness Project might be hoisted.

The Lifers quickly developed their plan for bringing youngsters into Rahway so that these young people could hear about life there from those who knew it best—the convicts who were forced to live it. There were two important steps which had to be taken before the plan could be implemented, however. Because the Lifers were convicts, they were by definition unable to proceed with any activity in an independent fashion. They could not, on their own, simply bring kids into the prison. First, the then superintendent of the prison, Robert S. Hatrak, had to agree to permit youngsters to tour the prison and meet with the Lifers. Second, some official or agency had to be willing to bring the kids to Rahway.

Rowe's wife communicated the plan to a local police chief and a juvenile court judge. The judge, George Nicola, was receptive because he had become a firm believer in deterrence, in what he called "the need for youth to understand and appreciate the nonrewards of juvenile delinquency." Judge Nicola had indicated his support for approaches to controlling juvenile crime that use "shock experiences" to convince youngsters that "crime doesn't pay."[2] Together these officials, impressed with the possibilities, convinced Hatrak to open the door. Hatrak said yes, but he was apprehensive, "It was risky, to bring in kids with murderers and robbers. If something had ever happened to one of those kids, it would have been all over, not only for the Lifers, but for a lot of other things here as well."[3]

The Beginning

In September, 1976, the first group of youngsters entered the prison. That same month, the very first piece of publicity about the program appeared in a New Jersey newspaper, the *Hackensack Record*. Entitled "Rahway Lifers Give Juveniles the Unvarnished Facts—Youths Get Lowdown on Jail," the article stated that "The juveniles are the first under-eighteen-year-olds to be allowed into a maximum security prison in the United States." We now know that this statement was not true. The article was cautious, but generally favorable to the idea.

In the beginning, the plan called for admitting only one group a week. But by January, 1977, the idea had become so popular that the number of visits was increased to two a day, five days a week. Police departments and other youth-serving agencies in New Jersey and elsewhere began clamoring to bring their kids to Rahway in order to get the "cure." Rowe's son was among the first to attend.

At first, the Juvenile Awareness Project was relatively low-key. The stress is on the word relatively. The youngsters came into the prison, were briefed by a guard, passed through a metal detector, and then entered the interior of the prison where visitors were seldom permitted. There some of the Lifers at first "rapped" with them as a group or on a one-to-one basis. These rap sessions employed harsh language to discuss prison violence, including assault and murder, homosexual rape, suicide as a fact of prison life, inedible food, the impersonal atmosphere in which there is no unity among inmates, and the need to live "by the bells." The youngsters would ask questions and engage in discussion with the inmates. Finally, there was a brief tour and an opportunity to view the "Hole" or solitary confinement, where, the youngsters were told, inmates might be sent for such things as violating prison rules.

Over a period of time, the Lifers' approach evolved into a form of shock therapy rather than a form of counseling. This occurred because the inmates felt that with the low-key, big-brother approach, they were not really reaching many kids in the most effective way. There was no overt attempt to intimidate or terrorize the youngsters at first, but this later became a more prominent and dramatic feature of the project. Again, this proves to be a critically important turn of events. Not only were the Lifers going to attempt to alter the attitudes and behavior of the juveniles, but they were going to try to do it in a very special and spectacular way—by scaring them straight.

This shock-confrontation treatment was intended to enlighten youth about the effects of involvement in crime. It was authoritarian in style and was supposed to represent the most negative aspects of prison life. Thus, the basic idea guiding the project became the effort to deter juveniles from committing criminal offenses by means of an aversive-type of behavior modification technique. This technique was later approved and sanctioned by the Department of Corrections which said the purpose of the program was "to deter juvenile delinquency and subsequent criminal behavior." The Lifers described their project as follows:

> We are showing these young people that the stories about the big house (adult prison) being the places of bad men is in all reality the places of sad men. We are using ourselves as examples to prove the fact of what crime and its involvement is really all about.

We are far from being experts on life and its problems, but we do feel that our prison experiences put in the proper perspective just might turn a young person away from crime and the following in our poor footsteps. In using ourselves as examples we are showing and explaining to them what a life of crime is really all about. This is our main objective. We are explaining to these young people that we who have been through these difficulties and are paying for our misdeeds are both willing to help and are able to understand their problems.

Through our own experiences we feel that these young people might be apt to heed our advice where they might not listen to a parent or someone in authority. We can and do expound freely on this, and we are able to relate to their problems having lived them ourselves. Over fifty percent of our membership has been involved in a juvenile offense or has spent time in a juvenile prison. We are trying to destroy the peer relationship of offenders and non-offenders.

The young people are brought into the institution and are taken on a tour which consists of showing and explaining what an isolation cell is (the hole, used to house men who have committed rule infractions) and a showing of a regular cell block with explanation. Then they are escorted to the prison auditorium where we have a rap session in which we try to cover the full spectrum of crime and its non-rewards. In these rap sessions we explain, using ourselves as examples, about prison, crime and its ramifications. We have a group classification of the youngsters who may be taking part in our program. Our conversation is geared to our classification, or what we are told by the authority who may be escorting them.

The Good (those with no involvement in crime)—The Bad (minor infractions with the law or authority)—The Ugly (those who have been away or are borderline cases). Our language may be that of the street or prison language or a discussion in a question and answer talk with high school or college students.[4]

The early history of the Lifers and the Juvenile Awareness Project was described in detail by ex-Lifer Frank Bindhammer, a founder and officer with the Lifers' Group, in a 1979 interview. Portions of that interview follow:

Finckenauer: What was the original purpose of the Lifers' Group? How did it come about?

Bindhammer: OK. You know, everyone has the impression that the Lifers' Group originated at Rahway State Prison when in fact it did not! It actually originated at Trenton State Prison, and a gentleman by the name of Paul Fitzsimmons, I believe it is, and a couple of other convicts, Lifers, got together in an effort to form this organization to help convicts become motivated toward helping themselves. OK? I'm sure that you agree that there's no such thing as rehabilitation in our penal system. There is self-rehabilitation and these guys wanted to get other prisoners motivated towards helping themselves—make them consciously aware that they do need to make certain adjustment—get involved in education, vocational training, group therapy, whatever might be available to them—to help them with legal matters, to attempt to change certain laws regarding Lifers, and one in particular was to aggregate consecutive sentences. From there we contemplated fund-raising events for various organizations, but that never got off the ground because of the present administration. They were totally against it. When Richard Rowe, who was released from prison, came back on another charge, he was resentenced for . . .

Finckenauer: Meaning he had been paroled once . . .

Bindhammer: He had been paroled. He was, he had several indictments pending—he was found guilty on those charges and sentenced to, if I'm not mistaken, double life. When he returned to Trenton State Prison and became involved in the Lifers' Group he requested permission to be transferred to Rahway. That, it was granted. Shortly after he transferred he approached the superintendent of Rahway, who was Bob Hatrak, incidentally, and requested permission to initiate a chapter of the Lifers' Group. For whatever reason Bob Hatrak agreed to allow him to do this. And he did. The bylaws of the Rahway Chapter was basically the same as at Trenton. They were in the process of doing more or less the same thing insofar as changing certain legislation regarding the Lifers' work inside. But beyond that they weren't doing anything.

When I was transferred to Rahway the program was approximately four months old. Richard Rowe approached me and asked me to become involved in the program. When I say they weren't doing anything, I mean that they weren't becoming involved in community affairs—reaching out into the community attempting to initiate similar programs as, such as the Juvenile Awareness Project. I was involved in the program approximately a month when I talked to a person by the name of Robert Clements about becoming involved in the Lifers' Group. I explained to him what my ideas were insofar as expanding that program was concerned. He was reluctant to become involved because Robert Clements had been involved in other prisoner organizations that later on proved to be failures for one reason or another, whether it was because the administration deliberately did things to discourage them or because the prisoners themselves lost interest. However, Robert Clements decided that he would give it a try and he signed up to become a member and was immediately accepted, and between us we start talking about the possibility of initiating a voice tape project.

We wanted to produce voice tapes of various prisoners' experiences as juveniles—that is to say, their experience in crime, with crime, their institutional experiences. We would mail these tapes to law enforcement agencies, public schools—high schools, colleges—with little or no success. And I say that because the people that we were producing them for never gave us any feedback as to the number of juveniles that were getting to listen to them and what their reactions was. Well, we started producing the tapes before we actually secured permission from the present administration. Then we did in fact draw up a proposal; we requested a meeting with Superintendent Hatrak and his staff regarding this project.

The meeting was postponed on several occasions, and one day Chief Deputy James Ucci came into the inmate group center area. He was accompanied by Richard Kern, who was a captain at the time and who is currently Chief Deputy of Rahway. I had previous problems with Chief Ucci, so when the men informed me that they were going to speak to him about this proposal I decided to leave the room so as not to influence his decision. When I returned, Richard Rowe and Robert Clements and Robert Jones, who were all present told me, "Frank, I'm sorry but he knocked down the program." Well, I left the Lifers' Group to find Chief Ucci, and I approached him and I explained to him exactly what we wanted to do. He was totally against the idea and I asked him as a personal favor to give us the opportunity to prove ourselves. And he told me OK. He says, "You have this one chance. If you blow it, that's it!"

So, that's how we actually got permission to begin, officially begin, this voice tape project. But we weren't satisfied with that. We wanted to reach the juveniles directly. We did in fact, eventually meet with Robert Hatrak and Richard Kern and they liked the idea of a juvenile awareness program but they wanted us to confine ourselves to juv . . . well, to young people 18 years of age and up.

Finckenauer: You proposed to them at this time, to bring juveniles . . .

Bindhammer: Juveniles into the institution. And, they refused us to, refused to allow us to bring in juveniles, say, ten years of age and up. They wanted us to restrict ourselves to people eighteen years of age and up and over, and they would not allow us to bring them into the actual prison. They wanted us to meet with them in an isolated area. An area that was away from the general population and any activities. We were dissatisfied with that. Now Richard Rowe is from that area. His wife had read an article in a local newspaper regarding Judge George Nicola of Middlesex County and Chief Anthony O'Brien and their effort to help young people. He asked his wife to contact these people and determine whether or not they were in fact sincere about helping young offenders. She did contact Judge Nicola and Anthony O'Brien and they expressed an interest in becoming involved in what we were attempting to do. Judge George Nicola and Anthony O'Brien contacted Robert Hatrak after meeting with us and requested permission to make referrals to this program. And that's how we actually secured permission to initiate the Juvenile Awareness Program. I think I did get a little ahead of myself.

What motivated us to do this. OK. Speaking for Robert Clements and myself, I know what motivated us. Robert Clements and I have been involved in crime since we were young kids—eight years old. We've been sent to juvenile reformatories. We know exactly what they're like. We know that while we were in these places that they were nothing but schools of crime, homosexuality and hatred—and I'm not saying that the prison administration or the institution administration was responsible for this. I don't think that they set up all night contemplating devious ways of dealing with these young people. I think it was more the result of peer influence, pressures and so forth. It wasn't the administration that was ripping you off, although at that time, there were a number of sick people working in those institutions. They were sadistic, sick people. They were people that were raping young kids in these institutions. But the major factor in the whole thing, I would venture to say, was peer influence. It was your associates that ripped you off—exploited you emotionally, mentally, spiritually, physically—and kids were taught to distrust, to hate. And that's what happened to us. And it's out of genuine concern that we were interested in initiating this voice tape project and subsequently the Juvenile Awareness Program.

One day when we were in the office, in the Lifers' office, a group of college students, if I'm not mistaken they were from Rutgers University in New Brunswick, were touring the prison and the escorting officer, if I'm not mistaken, was a person by the name of Sergeant Summers, and he asked us to speak to this group regarding the functions of the Lifers' Group. As I recall it, Robert Clements told me, he says, "You know, this is your chance to learn to speak to people." Because I never really learned to communicate with people. He says, "You have the task of telling these young people what the Lifers' Group is about." I was pretty messed up about it. I really didn't know what to say to these kids. So after brief, giving them a brief outline of what we were trying to do, I start trying to give them some real insight into the realities of crime, institution life and everything. And, I wish you could have been there to see the effect that this was having on these young people. They were shocked! And these were straight kids! So when they left, we sat down and discussed the reaction of the students. And if this had that type of an effect on straight kids or allegedly straight kids, what might it do to youthful offenders? And there was no abuse involved—no profanity—none of those things. So that's when we actually start discussing the possibility of initiating a juvenile awareness program—bringing young people in and talking to them—explain to them what the realities of crime is—what institution life is about—discuss with them some of the problems that they're experiencing—try to give them some insight into how they might be able to deal with those problems.

We actually started off as being the good, big brother. No man, none of the prisoners, were allowed to use any type of abuse or anything like that. All that they were able to do was share their experiences. When the program was approved the first group of juveniles referred to the program was from Middlesex County, if I'm not mistaken. Middlesex or Woodbridge. Whichever the case. But they were referred by one of two people—George Nicola or Anthony O'Brien. If I'm not mistaken, it was at that time Bill Eastman from the Asbury Park Press was present, and we did nothing but share our experiences with these young people in an effort to give them some insight into what they were opening themselves up to experiencing should they decide to continue a life of crime. We were trying to emphasize the significance of education, vocational training, the necessity for law and order and, yes, we were using hypothetical situations to help these kids understand where we were coming from. Again, no one was allowed to abuse these kids—directly attack any juvenile.

We attempted to do this for quite some time as other police departments and youth service organizations became involved. We were doing sessions more frequently and during this period, the early stages of the program, we did not attempt to abuse these kids or humiliate them in any way. I think the program was in existence approximately nine months. When I went to attend a session in the auditorium, Sergeant August approached me. He had a young kid with him and the kid was maybe twelve, thirteen years of age, and he asked me if I recognized the boy. And I told him I didn't. He said, "Well, you should. He's been here four times." And I asked him, "How was he referred to this program four times?" He asked his youth counselor to bring him. So I asked the kid why. He said, "I think you guys are cool!" Come to find out, there were other young people requesting second, third and fourth visitations.

So, it was a result of this we decided to use a hard-core approach, more or less, break it down into groups—the good, the bad, the ugly—and stop being the big brother because we felt that we were defeating our purpose. We're trying to make ourselves appear to be the most despicable people imaginable in an effort to turn them away from us and here they're identifying with us. When they left the institution we wanted them to look toward the professional people that were referring them to the program in the first place—for advice, for guidance. Our intention was to destroy that Hollywood stereotype image of criminals and gangsters being cool, tough people, of prisons being the in thing—to attack these young people's own self-image, destroy that image of being a cool, tough person so that when they return to their respective communities they would be more susceptible to opening themselves up to their counselors—the professional people. And, judging from all the reports that we were getting, it did have a positive effect.

What we encouraged the various agencies that were making referrals to the program to do was follow-up counseling. Keep track of every juvenile that went through the program. They were supposed to provide whatever type of assistance that these young people required. We're not professionals, Jim, we can't do that. We can't even keep track of the juveniles that participate. From the inception of the program, we attempted to establish a community-based project for that purpose. To follow up on these juveniles that participate—find out whether or not the organizations that were making referrals were doing their job. Department of Corrections knocked the proposal down. They refused it.

Finckenauer: This was early on.

Bindhammer: It was early in the program—within the first year. They did not want us to establish an outside organization. And, to be perfectly honest, not to attack the Department of Corrections, I think they had reason for that—if you investigate the people that would have probably become involved outside. So from that point on is when we actually began to use that hard-core approach. But the purpose of using that was merely to get these young people's attention. Let them know how other people feel to be ripped off. Most of the kids that were being referred in the early stages, I would venture to say, were from local high schools and so forth. But, we were informed in advance that kids from a local high school would be participating in our sessions. So we geared the program towards rap sessions. They would be seated in an auditorium and it would be a question and answer situation.

Finckenauer: As opposed to being on stage?

Bindhammer: Exactly, Exactly. They would not go on a stage and it would be open to question and answer. Again, there was no abusive language and I think it gave a lot of the school counselors and principals some insight into the type of students that they were dealing with. A lot of them said, "These are all good kids. They've never been involved in anything." And then we would ask them, "OK. How many of you kids have actually done something that you could have been arrested for and possibly sent to jail?" Ninety-nine percent of the hands would go up. Whether it was pot, drinking, or, you know, petty theft, and the principals are generally shocked. "Not my kids!" OK? But that too was good.

But as the program expanded the demand became greater and greater and greater and we had to exclude school students—high school, grammar school students. As a matter of fact, we can no longer allow college students to come in and view the program because it's too much of a strain. So we confined ourselves to dealing with just juveniles that were adjudicated juveniles or what were supposed to be adjudicated juveniles. We later found out that some of these organizations were slipping in ringers, so to speak. The kids that had not had actual arrest records. And when we found out about it we would approach the escorting personnel and, you know, asked them, "What's going on?" "Oh, they haven't been caught yet but the parents know they're doing these things." Well, that's one thing for the police to refer somebody to us or youth services—kid, the kids from amongst those case loads—but to just take somebody that they're not actually working with and bring them in is another story. As a matter of fact, we had one group of kids come in that were medicated. They were all on some form of drug. How can you deal with that kid? We had to ask the escorting counselors to take them home! How can we deal with this type of kid? And then it's been my experience that many of the counselors should have been up on the stage instead of the kid. Honest to God! Some of these people are ridiculous.

Finckenauer: I won't ask you to name any of those . . .

Bindhammer: No, please don't. But, I'm telling you for a fact, I can't understand how some of these people become counselors in the first place. They're singling out kids. They're asking you to lean harder on this one and it seems like they're actually taking pleasure in what's going, happening to these young people. And it's not a joke!

Finckenauer: Were you or anybody else in the Lifers' Group, to your knowledge, aware of this kind of approach being used before in prisons? Or, was it something that, as far as you knew, was an original thought?

Bindhammer: As far as I know, Jim, no one was doing it exactly the way that we were doing it. I had heard later on that other prisons have made an attempt to do something like this.

Finckenauer: But you weren't aware of this at the time?

Bindhammer: No, I was not. Well, we weren't allowed to communicate with other prisoners. That is to say, in other states and so forth. So we had no way of knowing that this was being done.

Finckenauer: So as far as you knew, this was an original thought, original approach or effort to . . .

Bindhammer: Yes, it was. As far as I was concerned it was.

The Public Becomes Aware

As the Juvenile Awareness Project began to take off in early 1977, it attracted the attention of criminal justice and other public officials, also members of the media, and through the media—the public. As interest escalated, the measuring rod of success began to come into play more and more. Some newspaper stories during 1977 illustrated the height of success. For example, on March 17, 1977, the *Bergen Record* (a New Jersey newspaper) reported: "Since the program started seven months ago, the Lifers' Group has talked to six hundred juvenile exoffenders. Only nine have been arrested following the talks, all on minor offenses." On April 17, 1977, the *Trenton Times-Advertiser* reported: "Since last September, when the program began, fourteen hundred youths in trouble with the law have been through the program . . . only fourteen youths who went through the two-hour shock treatment have gotten in trouble with the law, only five seriously." The July 30, 1977, *Newark Star Ledger* indicated that 2,921 juveniles had visited the Project and that "A preliminary survey shows fewer than 10 percent have been in trouble since their visits."

At least one article in a professional publication was also very supportive and laudatory. New Jersey Criminal Justice Planner, James P. Murphy, writing in the July 1977, *Police Chief* magazine asked, "Does the shock therapy work?" His answer: "In less than six months, the lifers have met with over 155 juveniles. The young people come from urban and suburban areas of New Jersey. Only one has been taken into custody following the visit to Rahway."

Where did these figures come from? For the most part, they were much the same kind of information which was collected on similar programs in other states. One method of collecting follow-up information was through questionnaires sent by the Lifers' Group to parents or guardians of juveniles who have visited Rahway. The form for this letter follows.

Lifers' Group
Rahway State Prison
Lock Bag R
Rahway, New Jersey 07065

Date : _____

Re: Juvenile Intervention

Dear Parent/Guardian:

On _____, your son/daughter took part in our Juvenile Intervention Program here at Rahway State Prison. Would you please answer the below questions and return this questionnaire to the above address.

1)   Have you noticed a marked change in your child's conduct since their visit to the prison?
     Yes: _____ No: _____

2)   Has there been a slight change In their conduct since their visit to the prison?
     Yes: _____ No: _____

3)   Do you think that another visit is necessary for your son/daughter?
     Yes: _____ No: _____

4)   Are there any specific areas you think we might be of some assistance to you, or your son or daughter? Please explain:

We invite your questions or comments:

Signed: _____
                                                        Parent/Guardian

---

A second source of information was letters received from the sponsoring agencies that brought youngsters to Rahway. The results from these letters were generally very positive, and it was this information that was reported in the news media and other publications. The "numbers game" was being played very early, as illustrated in the above articles.

Once again Frank Bindhammer's comments:

Finckenauer: Where did these figures come from? Very early on, if one looks at, one follows the newspapers, the stories as they begin to appear, this is like late fall of 1976 now, the program has only been in operation for a short time, things begin to appear and immediately one begins to read success stories about this number of kids and this many have not been rearrested.

Bindhammer: I think if you investigate it, you find out that Judge Nicola, immediately after becoming involved, was communicating with any organization that made referrals to the program. OK? He was more or less gathering statistics in his own way. We had no actual knowledge . . .

Finckenauer: And he was giving these to the newspapers?

Bindhammer: Let me explain this to you now, Jim. He was writing to every organization that made referrals to our program, requesting a report on the number of juveniles that they referred, and what their reactions, reaction was to the program, and what recidivism rate was amongst the juveniles. Judge Nicola done this for quite some time and before the Lifers even received copies of any of the correspondence we had no idea what was being said to Judge Nicola—communicated to him from, by these various organizations. We had to rely on Judge Nicola to let us know how many juveniles were rearrested out of the number of juveniles that were referred. It's my understanding that the statistics quoted were the statistics of the organizations that were making referrals to the program, not from the Lifers. The Lifers had no control over that.

Finckenauer: What was the reaction when you began to hear about these figures?

Bindhammer: What is the normal reaction? You're elated about it. Here's, you know, you're talking about people, Jim, who have for the most part been taught to believe themselves to be no good, worthless human beings. People who have never really been involved in anything positive in their lives. Now they've been motivated to do something for somebody else—share their experience with other people in an effort that they might benefit. They see these things—it's the first time in their lives that they actually feel like useful, productive human beings. You throw statistics in front of them like that—80, 85 percent—what is it going to do to that type of person? They're overjoyed! They feel that, "Hey, I'm really doing something—something worthwhile." And who are convicts to question these professional people?

Finckenauer: That's true!

Bindhammer: And when we had requested copies of this correspondence it seems that there was always something coming up. I think the first time that we actually received copies of Judge Nicola's correspondence was some time in '78.

Finckenauer: So this might have been going on for, probably was going on for some . . .

Bindhammer: Exactly. Almost two years.

Finckenauer: Without your being aware of it?

Bindhammer: Oh, we were aware that he was communicating with these organizations, and whenever he appeared at a banquet or some type of social function he would recite the figures or make quotes from various correspondence that he received. But we never received any of this information.

Finckenauer: What is your feeling about that?

Bindhammer: What is my feeling about it? To be perfectly honest, I'm not taking anything away from Judge Nicola, but I think that all relative information should have been shared with everyone involved—all the organizations that were making referrals, the Department of Corrections, the prison administration, and, of course, the Lifers.

Finckenauer: But that wasn't happening?

Bindhammer: No, that wasn't happening.

What about these numbers—this seemingly incredible success rate? One conclusion seems clear: the figures were and are suspect. They may be so subject to error and inaccuracies as to render them totally unreliable and invalid.

To begin with, a large number of kids participating in the project had admittedly been neither delinquents nor even predelinquents (showing some indications of potential delinquency). Nondelinquents who remain nondelinquent after some treatment intervention—any treatment intervention—cannot be considered program successes.

The information that was collected by means of the form letter mentioned earlier is subjective, of the "to your knowledge" variety and is thus of questionable validity. Also, letter responses were frequently based upon follow-up periods of only a few days or weeks. Crime-free behavior over a short period of time is not unusual, even for the most hard-core delinquent. Follow-up periods this short are meaningless indicators. Finally, self-selection determined responses to the letters. Because only some parents and agencies responded, the subject juveniles cannot be considered a representative sample of the whole. Perhaps only those who had good things to say bothered to respond.

The scientific name for the measuring rod referred to earlier is, of course, recidivism. This is the "stuff" of the numbers game. In this case, recidivism was neither defined nor applied uniformly by those reporting. Whether it meant rearrest, reconviction, further school problems, or further incorrigibility was not and is not known. It probably meant some or all of these things. Further, recidivism is an inappropriate measure of the behavior of a youngster who has had no previous contact with the juvenile justice system.

Public Figures React

As the Juvenile Awareness Project attracted more and more public attention, it also attracted the attention of various public figures. New Jersey's Governor Brendan Byrne visited a Lifers' party at Rahway Prison in July, 1977. The governor was quoted at the party as saying, "The main thing in evaluating it is to determine if it works. That kind of orientation for young people has to have an impact." He seemed to concur with the claims of success, telling reporters, "more and more of our problems are with youth." Byrne credited the Lifers' insight and experience in crime as a valuable tool in "helping us all to learn how to deal better with society." The governor characterized his visit to the prison by saying it was "exciting to be here to witness, firsthand, the results of some imaginative thinking . . . making the next generation better than ours." Another official, Robert Mulcahy, who was corrections commissioner at the time, was reported as saying, "We are very excited about the program. This is one time when men on both sides of the bars are working together and accomplishing something beneficial to everyone."[5]

Many police officers, judges, and juvenile corrections officials were in agreement that the program was an effective deterrent to juvenile crime. Juvenile justice officials from many states visited the program or wrote asking for information about it. Superintendent Hatrack and Corrections Sergeant Alan August, who was appointed liaison officer to the Lifers' Group, began to travel around speaking to various audiences about the Juvenile Awareness Project.

Perhaps the most outspoken and vigorous supporter of the program in the criminal justice community was the juvenile court judge who had been one of its founders, George Nicola. Some of his reported comments are indicative of his enthusiastic support. "It's a project worthy of effort. The bottom line, of course, is the rate of recidivism. That's what counts." Of a group of "revolving door delinquents" who were constantly in trouble, Nicola said, "less than 1 percent have gotten into trouble again" after visiting the prison. He said, "New Jersey is becoming a model for the rest of the nation. I am receiving calls from all over the country about the program. I'm thankful for this program, as should the people of New Jersey be thankful."[6] Judge Nicola's philosophy which governs his handling of juvenile offenders is unusual. It is also critically important in explaining his strong support of the Lifers' approach. Some of his comments reported in *Youth Forum*, the newsletter of the National Council on Crime and Delinquency, are instructive in this regard.[7] Discussing his view that locking up juveniles for short periods is the best way to rehabilitate them, Nicola said, "I send them there for shock experience. . . . We know what the problems are in the reformatories. Kids come out worse than when they go in. All I want that kid to realize is that crime doesn't pay. Now you're in hell. Now, do you want to be with them or outside?"

Nicola's judicial strategy called for sending four-time losers (kids appearing in juvenile court for the fourth time) to an institution. The purpose was to shock the delinquent, and any followers and companions. The judge insisted that he utilize the recall process to bring out any incarcerated juvenile who showed good progress in a couple of months. The success of this approach was extolled by Nicola's court administrator, Dr. James S. Winston:

> Since January of 1975, approximately 105 juveniles have been sent to institutions. Of these juveniles, thirty have been recalled after serving a brief period of time, only five of which have engaged in subsequent delinquent behavior. Many of these recalled juveniles, who once were considered revolving-door delinquents, have remained out of trouble for periods exceeding nine months since being recalled. This has been due to the rapid shock of the incarceration immersion technique which seems to be working quite well in the case of serious offenders.[8]

Judge Nicola's belief in and use of shock treatment to achieve deterrent effects comes through clearly. Also hinted at is his somewhat indiscriminate use of various figures to support his claims of success. But Judge Nicola also showed that he recognized the difficulty which the Lifers faced in trying to scare crime out of the kids they talked to. He said, "Memories can be short. Peer pressure is by far the most powerful force at work in juvenile crime. And the Lifers have a hard time fighting that from behind bars."[9]

The First Evaluation

In July, 1977, Deputy Corrections Commissioner William H. Fauver directed that an evaluation of the Juvenile Awareness Project be conducted.[10] This task was undertaken by two departmental interns, Lawrence Gilman and Richard K. Milin, over a period of several weeks during that summer. The purpose of the evaluation was: "to determine the program's strengths and weaknesses; to assess its impact on the youngsters who participate in it; to gain an understanding of its organization and operation; and to evaluate its effectiveness from the point of view of the attitudes of the adults who bring the juveniles to the institution in order to expose them to the unique experience the Lifers' Group offers them."

In their own words, they were not able "to undertake an exhaustive and comprehensive analysis of the Lifers' Group program due to staff limitations and time constraints." They were only able to make "a limited attempt" to evaluate the effect of the program on recidivism. However, they did review literature on the program, conduct interviews and a telephone survey, observe sessions in the prison, and consult with department of corrections officials.

Gilman and Milin recognized the kinship of the project with both shock therapy and deterrence theory. About the former they said, "'Shock therapy' has a long history, but it has been controversial for most of that history. Some psychologists have challenged its effectiveness on the grounds that a single frightening experience cannot change an individual's lifestyle. . . . Even if 'shock therapy' can have positive results, the criticism that it uses bad means to good ends must be answered." On its relation to deterrence, the researchers said: "Since the Lifers' JA Program conveys information specifically aimed at increasing the perceived magnitude of the probability and losses of imprisonment for juveniles, the deterrence theory provides it with a strong theoretical basis."

After their rather brief and limited survey, the two researchers reported a number of findings and recommendations. Some of these findings included the following:

> Only 43 percent of the group leaders surveyed agreed that juveniles in their groups saw inmates as heroes before attending the Lifers' program. However, of those who did agree, all felt that the Lifers' destruction of this hero image had a favorable effect in changing the juveniles' behavior. Unfortunately, there is no hard data on this point . . .

The most prevalent reaction to the program among the juveniles interviewed was that they "did not want to end up in prison," which suggests that the Lifers' successfully increased the juveniles' perception of the losses they would suffer if they were imprisoned. Some juveniles also seemed to have been convinced that they would inevitably be caught and imprisoned if they continued their criminal activity, suggesting that the Lifers successfully increased some juveniles' perception of the probability of arrest and incarceration as well.

Eighty-six percent of the group leaders surveyed thought that the effort to frighten the juveniles increased program effectiveness. . . . The leaders' support was not based on hard data, and few leaders offered theoretical grounds for their belief. . . . Since actual costs of scare tactics have been demonstrated [reference here is to some children reportedly being unable to sleep after visiting the prison] while benefits are only believed to exist, concern over these costs must take precedence. These costs may be eliminated by temporarily discontinuing the use of scare tactics pending a demonstrable loss of program effectiveness. If the use of scare tactics is to continue, it should at least be demonstrated that the juveniles will not listen unless threatened, and that there are significant reductions of the recidivism rate as a result of the effort to frighten the juveniles.

The current screening and classification of groups by Lifers and group leaders does not appear to be sufficient . . . the Lifers tend to gear their presentation towards the "hardest-core" members of each youth group. An improved screening and classification procedure could greatly diminish the adverse effects of the JA Program.

For the most part, the group leaders surveyed were enthusiastic about the overall effectiveness of the JA Program. . . . Those respondents who saw no change in behavior felt that the effects of the program wore off within a few days. Two respondents who did notice a change in behavior expressed the same concern. Although little "hard" recidivism data were available, 57 percent of the respondents stated that the recidivism rate of the juveniles who attended the program was lower than they ordinarily would have expected . . .

Gilman and Milin concluded their report by saying, "Although there is no conclusive data, the program seems to be effective in changing juveniles' behavior, and few modifications seem necessary."

This evaluation was a commendable effort despite its recognized deficiencies and shortcomings. The report raised a number of pertinent and important issues. One was the recognition that the program could have adverse and counterproductive effects because of its scare tactics. Their recommendation that the use of these tactics be suspended, at least temporarily, was never followed. Another issue raised was the inadequacies in the screening and classification process (a practically nonexistent process). This too became an issue which was never addressed. Finally, the emotional commitment to the program on the part of its sponsors came through very clearly in the report, but in almost every instance there were no data to support their belief and their enthusiastic support. It was almost as if people wanted so much to believe it was so, that therefore it was so. Even among professionals who might have been expected to be more skeptical, there was unquestioning support. The researchers themselves seemed to get caught up in this euphoria when they concluded that the program was effective in changing the youngsters' behavior, despite the absence of any data to support their conclusion. There were, however, some undercurrents of doubt and some second thoughts that came out in the report for the first time; these doubts became more prominent in the following months as events unfolded in 1977 and early 1978.

Some Other Thoughts

Not all the media coverage was as glowing as mentioned previously in this chapter. For example, on April 19, 1977, the *Home News* of New Brunswick, New Jersey, described a visit to Rahway by some high school boys who had previously been to the juvenile court. It said, "Although some of the students later conceded somewhat half-seriously that they were frightened by the presentation, few appeared to be really disturbed by the vivid description of prison life the program depicted." A December, 1977, article in *Corrections Magazine* quoted from a letter to the inmates from a fourteen-year-old girl which closed with the following: "P.S. Y'all didn't scare me because I already knew what was going to happen." This made apparent the dangers of overexposure of the Juvenile Awareness Program on TV and in the newspapers which could reduce the factor of fear of the unknown and lessen the program's potential for scaring kids.

Corrections Magazine referred to the Department of Corrections evaluation report and the problems disclosed in it. One of the problems mentioned was the lack of effect (however measured) upon the hardcore, "ugly" juveniles. Yet these kids were the most obvious and intended targets. The article also referred to reports that some less-mature kids seemed to be affected too much in that they had trouble sleeping for weeks after their experience.

A troubling incident occurred in November of 1977—troubling more in terms of its implications than in what actually happened. On

November 16, 1977, a group of twenty-two eighth-grade boys was taken to Rahway to participate in the Juvenile Awareness Project. Following the boys' participation, complaints were received from parents that several boys had been kissed and fondled by the Lifers. This incident was extensively investigated by school authorities and by the Internal Affairs Unit of the Department of Corrections. The department report concluded that it was possible that some of the boys were kissed and one may have had his long hair touched by an inmate. It also agreed with parents' complaints that the school authorities had not properly informed them (the parents) of what the project was all about and what the sessions entailed. Finally, the report indicated that nothing more happened in the session than usually happens. "In fact, less happened than usual," the report said. "All this could have been avoided if . . . the students had been selected more appropriately. . . ." We should keep in mind that this *happened* some four months after the department's evaluation report which addressed the inadequate selection and screening process.

An investigation by the principal of the school which the boys attended concluded that there was "a foul-up in communication with the prison concerning the type of youngsters being brought in that morning." He said, "The boys on this trip were very frightened by what they experienced and when they returned to school . . . stories became exaggerated." His recommendation was that the school not continue that program, "not because I do not believe it has value for our students, but because I felt it could create further turmoil in the community which has already produced elimination of certain aspects of the Lifers' program which were extremely vital to its success in steering youngsters from pursuing criminal activities." In other words, this was a potential "hot potato" which should be left untouched.

The Department of Corrections promulgated program modifications after this incident. Among them was the following rule which we should file away for future reference:

> Only juveniles with a criminal or police problem background will be permitted to participate in the sessions on the auditorium stage. Juveniles that do not have a previous criminal or police problem background will observe the session in the audience with the adult escorting personnel.

Several implications can be drawn from all this. First, this is a sensitive and volatile technique which can be easily abused, with possibly negative consequences for children inappropriately exposed to it. Maybe it didn't really happen that time, but certainly the potential was there. Second, the department was either ignoring its own report or the

Lifers were operating autonomously, out of the control of the corrections authorities. In either event, the scare tactics and the lack of classification and screening were obviously still present.

January, 1978, saw the third major turning point in the developing history of the project. Comparable in importance to the decision to run a program whose acknowledged purpose was to deter juvenile delinquency and the decision to try to accomplish this purpose by scaring kids, was an article which appeared in that month's edition of *Reader's Digest (Reader's Digest* sells thirty million copies monthly in twelve languages). This was not a local newspaper story, nor even an article in *Police Chief* magazine. This was the big time. The article, by Roul Tunley, was entitled, "Don't Let Them Take Me Back!"[11] One of the millions of readers of Tunley's article was one Arnold Shapiro, director of motion pictures and special projects for Golden West Television in Los Angeles, California. It was this article which planted the seed that was to become the famous television documentary *Scared Straight!*

Because of its important pivotal role, and because it provides a concise, but informative description of a Lifers' session, Tunley's article is reproduced here in its entirety.

Don't Let Them Take Me Back!

Roul Tunley

Nine youngsters stood outside the main gate of Rahway State Prison. Aged twelve to seventeen, none had seen the inside of a maximum security lock-up before; until recently, in fact, no minor was ever allowed in one. But these kids had all been in some trouble with the law—car theft, mugging, arson, shoplifting, drugs. So they were literally perched on the door step of prison, ready to go in either direction.

But today they weren't worried about that. The 2 $^1/_2$-hour prison visit meant a full day off from school. They joked and feinted blows at each other, cocking their hats at rakish angles. They were sure it was going to be fun.

At the sound of an earsplitting bell, the main door swung open. The kids filed through and into a long corridor the color of sour cream. "Line up against the wall!" ordered a sergeant. They obeyed.

"You may think this is a sightseeing trip," he continued. "It isn't. When you went through the door, the man who brought you lost jurisdiction over you. You're in our hands. You'll do as we say. The first thing is to stop smoking! And don't chew gum! And take off those hats!"

The festive air vanished.

Another buzzer; another door opened. They filed into a small, concrete room, deeper into the prison. The door banged shut. "Take a look through here at our game room," invited the sergeant. The boys peered through a glass opening at an arsenal packed with the instruments of riot control: guns, gas, truncheons, helmets. Another officer told them to empty their pockets of cigarettes, knives, metal, anything "contraband." One by one, they filed through a metal detector. The sergeant stamped each wrist with a color-coded, invisible ink.

Then came more doors, leading ever deeper into the prison. Each one clanged behind them with a steel finality that echoed through the building. Now they were passing the "hole"—a wing lined with tiny cells, each windowless, with metal walls, a cot, a toilet bowl. From one, a man yelled: "Get me outa this place!" A guard told him to shut up.

The boys climbed steep, steel steps to yet another barred door—the seventh. It too banged shut behind them. They found themselves in a small auditorium, where they were led to a stage and seated on a hard bench. In front of them were eight of the toughest convicts in the prison system—men serving life or "life plus" for murder or other major crimes.

A black inmate, his arms like tree trunks, stepped to within several feet of the boys. They squirmed uneasily as he peered into each face without saying anything. Finally he spoke:

"We're gonna tell you turkeys what prison life is really like, not what you've seen in the movies or on TV. These men are gonna tell you things that are not easy to tell. If I find any of you smiling or looking around or not paying attention, I'll break your goddam jaw."

Not a foot shifted. And for ninety minutes the "Lifers" described existence behind the thirty-foot walls.

"Do you know how I got here?" asked a thirty-one-year-old con who'd been in Rahway for thirteen years. "Doing the same crap you're doing. At eight, I stole bikes. By ten, I was shoplifting. In my teens, I was breaking into houses. I thought I was too smart to get caught. I wanted to be like the older guys in my gang, my heroes. One day I went with one of them to break into a house. We'd rung the doorbell and the phone. There was no answer and we thought we were safe. But when we got upstairs, we found the owner facing us with a pistol. We ended up killing him. That's why I'm here, and it could happen to any of you punks."

Another inmate then took over. "You're scared all the time in prison," he said. "Nobody on the outside ever tells you about the things that go on here—the murders, the suicides, the rapes. Sure, the rapes."

He pointed to a fair-skinned boy with long, blond hair. "You're good-looking," he said. "We like boys like you. You'd be raped within twenty-four hours of landing here, and I'd be the first to try. And there's nothing you could do about it."

The boy looked as though he were going to be sick.

"Oh, sure, you could rat and go to the Man and tell him what happened," the prisoner continued, "and for your own sake you'd be put into Protective Custody. We call it Punk City. From then on, there'd be no visits, no movies, no association with any other prisoner. You'd be locked up twenty-two hours a day, allowed out only to exercise by yourself. You'd never go back to the prison population. Because if you did, you'd be dead."

"Of course there is another alternative. You could become some strong con's 'woman.' But you'd have to have sex whenever he wanted, wash his socks and underwear, clean his cell and run errands. And when he wanted to share you with someone else, you'd have to do it."

As the boy began to cry, the con sneered. "You wouldn't like that, huh?" he asked. "My, oh, my. And I thought you was a real hard guy."

Another prisoner stepped forward. He told the boys they hadn't seen the real "hole," just the double-lock cells. He'd been sent to the real one: no light, no bed, one tray of food a day, and no one to talk to. After a few days, he reached a point where he'd do anything to get out, and one night he tried.

"I banged my head against the wall until it was a bloody mess," he said, "all the while yelling for the guard. But he didn't come until he was good and ready. I was handcuffed and carried to the prison hospital. The doctor sewed me up as though he were trussing a chicken. Then I was carried right back to solitary, only this time to a padded cell where I couldn't injure myself. I still had to do my time."

The smallest boy in the group—a twelve-year-old whose feet didn't touch the floor—was told to stand up. A convict then ordered him to tell the biggest boy to stand with his nose against the wall. The small boy hesitated, then gave the command. The convict told the big boy to obey. Then the youngster was told to order another boy to get down on all fours. The order was given, and the second boy also did as he was told. Another youngster was ordered to crawl under the bench. When all had been given and obeyed some command, and were finally back in their seats, the convict asked each one how he liked it. They all shook their heads.

"Well," said the inmate, his voice rising to a yell, "that's what it's like in here every day! I'm forty-five years old. How do you think I like it when some punk eighteen-year-old guard tells me to clean out a filthy toilet? But I do it."

The average pay at Rahway is $1.25 a day—for work in the laundry, the shops, the yard. A man is rich if he has two dollars in his prison account. "Do you know what my most precious possession is?" asked a convict. He extracted a metal spoon from his rear pocket and held it up. "This. I eat with it, sleep with it, go to the shower with it." He explained that prisoners aren't allowed knives and forks, and that when a man loses his spoon, he eats with his fingers until the guards, convinced he has not made a weapon of it, issue him another.

The last speaker was tall, thin, unsmiling, and his blue eyes blazed like laser beams. He told the boys he'd give anything to change places with them. They could go home at the end of the morning. He had to stay at least twenty more years.

A fourteen-year-old shifted uncomfortably on the bench and looked away for a second. The con turned on him. "I don't think you believe what we've told you," he said. "You think you're too smart to get caught." The con's face almost touched the boy's. "But let me tell you something," he shouted. "You're one of the stupidest guys I've ever seen!"

Suddenly, unexpectedly, the boy spat in the prisoner's face. And time stopped on that stage in Rahway. No one moved. Not a sound was heard. The boy on the bench sat frozen, his eyes wide with the horror of what he'd done. Like everyone else in the room, he knew that the prisoner had killed for less. Finally, spittle running down his face, the con stepped back. He took a handkerchief from his pocket and wiped his chin. Then he spoke in a low voice:

"If that's what it takes to get through to you, to make you realize what a mess you're making of your life, I'll take it. At least it shows you have guts. Why not use them for something better?"

The session was over.

Without a word, the boys got up and filed out one by one through the seven steel doors, through the room where the invisible ink on their wrists was checked with black light to make sure it matched the day's code, through the corridor past the riot equipment room. Finally, they emerged into blinding sunlight.

There were green trees in front of the prison—a sight some convicts hadn't seen in decades. The twelve-year-old impulsively threw his arms around the juvenile officer who'd brought them. "Don't ever let them take me back there!" he pleaded.

No one was embarrassed by this. Walking silently to the bus, the boys showed no jauntiness, no joking. Later, the driver who took them back to their community said it was the quietest bunch of teen-agers he'd ever taken anywhere.

This dramatic and powerful depiction of the Lifers so impressed Shapiro and his California colleagues that it stimulated the initiation of a series of events resulting in a film, in numerous awards, but finally in controversy.

Notes

[1] Kevin Krajick, "To Scare the Crime Out of Juveniles," *Corrections Magazine* (December 1977): 22.

[2] *Youth Forum*, 1 (June 1977): 3.

[3] Krajick, *Corrections Magazine*, p. 22.

[4] *Lifers' Group Brochure*, Juvenile Awareness Project Help.

[5] *Newark Star Ledger* (10 July, 1977).

[6] *Youth Forum*, 1 (June 1977): 3.

[7] Ibid., p. 3.

[8] Dr. James Winston, "Reducing Juvenile Delinquency by Judicial Action in New Jersey," *Journal of Juvenile and Family Courts* (February 1978): 23.

[9] Krajick, *Corrections Magazine*, p. 23.

[10] *An Evaluation of the Lifers' Group Juvenile Awareness Project*, New Jersey Department of Corrections, Trenton, NJ (July 1977).

[11] Roul Tunley, "Don't Let Them Take Me Back!" *Reader's Digest* (January 1978): 96–100.

chapter three

Scared Straight
The Making of a Myth

Newspapers and magazines were not the only media to become involved in disseminating information about the Juvenile Awareness Project. Perhaps the most powerful medium of all, television, soon became interested. Television crews from the major networks, other U.S. stations, and overseas networks visited the prison. It was quickly recognized that the Lifers' project would make for great television viewing. It was appealing, dramatic, and exciting. Viewer appeal seemed to stem in part from the obscene language, the erotic and explicit sexual references, and the sado-masochistic content. In mid-1977 Channel 13, the New York Public Broadcasting System affiliate, aired a documentary film on the project.

Sometime after reading the *Reader's Digest* article, Arnold Shapiro conceived the idea of producing his own documentary film about the Juvenile Awareness Project.[1] He contacted the Lifers at Rahway Prison and did some preliminary research to familiarize himself with the subject of juvenile crime. Shapiro reviewed materials sent to him by the Lifers. He was also informed by them of the earlier television documentaries which had been shown by New York area television stations. One of the best of these was produced by Richard Hughes for WPIX-TV. Shapiro requested a video cassette tape of the film, which was entitled *I Am My Brother's Keeper*, from WPIX. This moving and informative documentary had been first shown in New York in December, 1977.

Arnold Shapiro showed the *Reader's Digest* article and the cassette tape to his colleagues and superiors at Golden West Broadcasters and television station KTLA in Los Angeles. He was given permission to visit New Jersey and interview the Lifers, Rahway officials, and some

45

youth agency representatives to determine the feasibility and the possible cost of making a documentary film.

In April of 1978, Shapiro met with Superintendent Hatrak and Sergeant August at the prison. He accompanied a group of youngsters into the prison and got a firsthand taste of what a Lifers' session looked, sounded, and felt like. At a meeting with the Lifers after the session, Shapiro determined that they would cooperate and participate in the filming of a documentary.

Ex-Lifer Frank Bindhammer described this meeting as follows:

Finckenauer: How did the movie come about?

Bindhammer: What actually happened was Arnold Shapiro requested an interview with the Lifers' executive staff to discuss the possibility of his, for making or producing a documentary.

Finckenauer: You did not know who he was at this time.

Bindhammer: Oh yes. Yes. He had communicated with one of the staff members for some time before he actually came in to meet with us. So we did have some insight into who Arnold Shapiro was. When Arnold Shapiro visited Rahway he explained to us what he would like to do. The Lifers agreed to allow him to film the sessions and to work with him. And, that's how he actually became involved. After talking with Arnold Shapiro I learned that he did in fact read an article that appeared in *Reader's Digest* and this article stimulated his interest and that's why he contacted us in the first place.

Finckenauer: Well, what did he tell you that he wanted to do?

Bindhammer: He told us that he did, in fact, want to do a documentary based on the program. And, of course, we cooperated with him. He felt that he could, in fact, produce a quality film. He had, if I'm not mistaken, already contacted the various TV stations that had done documentaries and had an opportunity to view their work and felt that he could do something that was superior to that. And at the same time do the program some type of a justice.

Arnold Shapiro met with several persons from agencies that were routinely referring youngsters to the Juvenile Awareness Project. All, according to Shapiro, were cooperative, helpful, and even enthusiastic about the idea of his making a film. Two of them (Det. Sgt. Charles Martini of the Ridgefield Park Police Department and Tony Rivera, a youth counselor from Passaic, New Jersey) agreed to propose to juveniles with whom they were working that they consent to be filmed for the documentary. Martini and Rivera were confident that their youngsters would cooperate.

Shapiro planned his filming for early May. Filming was to include showing the faces of the juveniles—which had not been done before— and interviews with them. It would portray them before, during, and after their Rahway visit. One potential problem discussed at Golden West during the planning was the realization that the film would proba- bly have to contain explicit language never before heard on Los Angeles television. For that matter, with few exceptions, such language had never been heard in any telecast anywhere. It was decided, according to Sha- piro, that the public interest potential of the film would outweigh its necessarily coarse language.

This issue of language was not only a sensitive one because of the possible repercussions from censors or from religious or conservative figures, but it was also an attractive one because it could be anticipated that it would add to the shock effect of the film. Obscene language is shocking to those who are not used to it; and, if nothing else, it gets just about everybody's attention.

Shapiro maintained telephone contact with the Lifers, and with Martini, Rivera and others during April. He also spent some time in Pas- saic, Ridgefield Park, and again at the prison during this period. Sergeant Martini described his involvement with the documentary at that time as follows:

> In April of 1978 I received a phone call from Mr. Shapiro. Mr. Sha- piro gave me an indication of the idea that he had perceived in read- ing this article in *Reader's Digest*. At that time I explained to Mr. Shapiro that the only way I can get involved in such a program of film- ing that would be that he would have to contact the juvenile presiding judge who would have to give permission to me to be allowed to have the kids filmed and taken to Rahway.

> At that time Mr. Shapiro to my knowledge contacted Judge Harvey Sorkow, presiding juvenile judge in my county, and with his permis- sion we took thirteen kids from our community to Rahway. Parental permission was signed for myself and Mr. Shapiro. My involvement with the parental permission for Mr. Shapiro, he sent me a folder of permission slips with the letter statement or release form. At that time I had handed them to the kids that had been chosen to go to Rahway. I told them to take them home, to review them with their parents and return them as soon as possible as Mr. Shapiro will be in town two weeks later.

> Approximately April 28, 1978, Mr. Shapiro appeared in my office. We rode around and he viewed areas of the county he wanted to film.

On April 30 he filmed the thirteen juveniles which are in that *Scared Straight!* documentary.[2]

Arnold Shapiro says he had no responsibility for choosing the particular youngsters who appeared in *Scared Straight!* In fact, he says he did not actually meet them until the day they were filmed. He does claim that a stipulation was made to Martini and Rivera that each juvenile to be filmed must have "broken the law." They did not necessarily have to have been arrested, just have broken the law. Shapiro also says he wanted a mixture of kids—by age, race, sex, and offense type. As it worked out or was planned to work out, Ridgefield Park—a suburban, mostly white middle-class community—provided the white kids, boys and girls who were less serious "law breakers." Passaic, an urban community, provided the black kids who could be considered "hardcore." Shapiro distinguishes between what he calls softcore and hardcore juvenile offenders.

Shapiro says he did not have access to the police records of any of the juveniles, but he was given assurances by the people in Passaic and Ridgefield Park that each of the juveniles was a lawbreaker. This assurance was reinforced, says Shapiro, when he personally interviewed all the kids on film. He states that no juvenile told him that they had not broken the law, although some did say they had not been arrested.

The film interviews were conducted on April 29 and 30. According to Shapiro, the youngsters were not told how to act, what to say, or what to do. He says they were told only to answer his questions in complete sentences and to be totally honest. Neither the youngsters nor their counselors were given any of the questions beforehand, says Shapiro. He is also of the opinion that the kids did not exaggerate their crimes or their attitudes during the filming in order to display a more bravado image. To the contrary, he thinks that if anything the kids were conservative, cautious, and generally "toned down." The filming of the kids brazenly entering Rahway State Prison, the actual session, and of the contrite departure took place on May 1, 1978.

To accompany the showing of the film, a brochure and other publicity materials were prepared for distribution. These materials included the following statements:

- Fact: Half of all serious crimes in the United States are committed by Youths 10 to 17! Violent juvenile crime between 1960 and 1975 tripled!
- Fact: Existing deterrence programs or punishments seem ineffective as the number of juvenile crimes increases every year—twice as fast as adult crime!
- Fact: "Kiddie crime," as it's sometimes called, includes murder, rape,

armed robbery, violent assault, mugging, robbery, arson, vandalism—hardly "kids stuff."

- Fact: Virtually all adult criminals were juvenile offenders. IF ONLY THEY COULD HAVE BEEN STOPPED THEN!
- Fact: 80–90% of the kids in THIS unique program are Scared Straight. Take an hour and watch this powerful approach work.[3]

And the following:

Scared Straight

A most unlikely group of men has begun a most unusual program to combat the alarming epidemic of juvenile crime.

The unlikely group of fifty men—calling themselves "the Lifers"—are all hardened criminals serving life sentences for murder and other major crimes. And the program they started is unusual and different because it works!

. . . This "shock therapy" approach is frightening, yet compelling to watch, most importantly—it's effective.

The cameras follow and profile a group of seventeen juvenile offenders—aged 14 to 18—before, during, and after their half-day at Rahway. All their experiences, emotions, and attitude changes are captured on film. Full-face to the camera, these kids are candid in describing their criminal ways and equally candid in relating how they felt after their grueling hours inside the prison. The content is startling and powerful. There's even a three-month follow-up on the remarkable progress of the kids.

Crime-fighting convicts are unique, and so are the results they're achieving: 80 to 90% of the kids who visit Rahway go straight! It's a startling and encouraging statistic. If just one child were "scared straight," the program would be worthwhile, but thousands of young criminals have already experienced "the Lifers'" program, and most of them have reformed![4]

These promotional statements can be read in the context of the characteristics of the panacea phenomenon, described earlier. We should ask ourselves if they seem to fit the definition of such a panacea. The particular antidelinquency program—in this case the Juvenile Awareness Project—is promoted as a cure-all, as some kind of magic answer to the delinquency problem, and it is "hyped" accordingly. The fit would seem to be reasonably good.

More important and influential evidence suggesting that *Scared Straight!* exemplified the panacea phenomenon is heard in the narrative of the film itself done by actor Peter Falk. Some examples follow:

Over eight thousand juvenile delinquents have sat in fear on these hard wooden benches. And for the first time they really heard the brutal realities of crime and prison. The results of this unique program are astounding. Participating communities report that 80 to 90 percent of the kids that they sent to Rahway go straight after leaving this stage. That's an amazing success story, and it's unequalled by traditional rehabilitation methods. . . .

The Lifers' program is saving many kids from a life of crime. And at the same time it's helping the convicts too. . . . America has 450 prisons but only a handful of programs like this one. It's not easy to make allies of convicts and those people who locked them up, but in New Jersey former enemies now work together. . . .

But while we're attacking the causes of crime, we can still allow those convicts who care about kids to start programs inside their own prisons. It doesn't cost the taxpayers any money, and it can stop thousands of prison-bound delinquents in their tracks. For that, parents, police, judges, victims and all the rest of us will be very grateful. Prisoners can help in the fight to save today's children from becoming tomorrow's convicts.

Finally, the film closed with this statement from Judge George Nicola:

When you view the program and you review the statistics that have been collected, there is no doubt in my mind, and in the mind of anybody who has seen this program, that the Juvenile Awareness Project at Rahway State Prison perhaps is today, the most effective, inexpensive deterrent in the entire correctional process in America.

There is little way that these statements can be misinterpreted or misunderstood. They clearly promise a new "cure" for juvenile crime.

Scared Straight! Goes Public

The film was first aired on November 2, 1978, by KTLA, Channel 5 in Los Angeles. *TV Guide* for that evening carried the following blurb: "SCARED STRAIGHT!" Special: Inside a maximum security prison. This hour-long program follows seventeen juvenile offenders as they learn, at firsthand, about the realities of prison life. Using brutally frank and frequently obscene language, 'Lifers' at Rahway (NJ) State Prison tell the young people about the ultimate pay-off for their criminality." Actor Peter Falk's narration of the documentary seemed to enhance the authenticity and drama of the film. After all, would Columbo mislead his audience?

Scared Straight! was received by a large and very enthusiastic audience. There had been few, if any, television documentaries like it. It not only had "street" language, but it had vivid descriptions of sex and violence, powerful and frightening caged men, and the sights and sounds of a fortress prison. It was, in short, a sensational media event. The elements of "good" television—stimulating color, emotion, and sound—were there in dramatic abundance.

Some mental health professionals—psychiatrists and psychologists—are of the opinion that a major part of the mass appeal of this film rested in its sexual content. This content is explicit in its descriptions and threats of sexual violence such as homosexual rape. The language is sexual and shocking. But this content is also implicit or present on a subconscious level as well! The film is very physical, and it portrays human relationships in which powerful figures emotionally and physically subjugate those who are powerless. The inmates do not come across as sad or weak creatures. Instead, they are very dynamic and super-masculine. The subtle effects of these images on the undeveloped or confused sexual identities of adolescents are open to speculation.

Scared Straight! became an overnight smash. Its success was recorded by the Los Angeles press. For example, the *Valley News* called it "One of the most riveting hours of television ever produced!"[5] Los Angeles' most influential newspaper, the *Los Angeles Times*, said it was "One of the most unusual and powerful television programs ever broadcast!"[6] KTLA was quickly flooded with over two thousand letters, almost all of them supportive, including one from the mayor of Los Angeles.

After the film's overwhelming success in Los Angeles, The Signal Companies, Inc., which sponsored the film as a public service, decided to show it nationally. Thus, during the week of March 5, 1979, *Scared Straight!* was shown in two hundred major cities from coast to coast. Many local television stations also aired a half-hour sequel to the film hosted by Dick Cavett. Cavett discussed the Juvenile Awareness Project with Frank Bindhammer, Robert Hatrak, Alan August, and three juveniles who had visited Rahway. S. James Coppersmith of WNEW-TV in New York described the reaction to that station's broadcast:

> *Scared Straight!* was broadcast on our Station WNEW-TV on March 8, 1979. . . . The overwhelming reaction we received from our viewing audience certainly supported our judgment. Seldom have I known a program to receive as much favorable comment, to wit, almost 700 letters, of which approximately 94 percent were laudatory. . . .
>
> The size of WNEW-TV's audience was another interesting phenomenon. According to the Nielsen Rating Service, on March 8 from 10:00 to 11:00 P.M., *Scared Straight!* was the highest rated show in

the time period—39 percent of the total viewing audience. . . . Translated into numbers, that means over 3 million people in the New York/Northern New Jersey metropolitan area were watching. . . .[7]

Not all the reaction to the documentary was favorable, however, as witness this commentary from a reviewer for the *Kansas City Raytown News*:

> If you like filthy language and think convicts are glamorous, you'll like *Scared Straight!* If you think juvenile delinquents should be treated "like the animals they are," you'll love *Scared Straight!* If you believe criminals are the best doctors for a sick society, *Scared Straight!* is for you.
>
> This is a propaganda presentation which sets forth a persuasive argument for the setting up of a "Lifers" program in your state. . . .
>
> The program is shocking—not because of dirty language; we've all heard that. It's shocking to realize that we have so many crime-hardened children in our society and yet have no more effective way to reform them than with what amounts to emotional electroshock.[8]
>
> Bald and bare as it is, the language isn't even the most offensive part of *Scared Straight!*, which purports to offer news of an almost surefire panacea for juvenile delinquency: convicts.
>
> Confronted with a phenomenon, the American instinct is to institutionalize it.[9]

Still, *Scared Straight!* had an impressive array of influential supporters. It was endorsed and recommended by the National Education Association. The vice president for Mental Health Materials Center gave his endorsement: "This strong film deserves wide use by educators, guidance counselors and others who work with potential delinquents. A powerful and convincing argument for this treatment of juvenile delinquency."[10] A film reviewer for the *Saturday Review* called it "One of the most powerful and disturbing documentaries to hit the screen. It has a raw eloquence no viewer will forget."[11]

Scared Straight! also reaped a number of prizes and awards. These included the George Polk Award for television, the Gold Camera Award, and the choice as best film of 1979 by the National Council on Family Relations. The prizes were capped in April, 1979, when it was awarded an Oscar by the Academy of Motion Picture Arts and Sciences as Best Documentary Feature for the year. This was followed by a prestigious Emmy award later in the year.

The Critics Surface

Despite the accolades from the entertainment world, and a great deal of interest and support in the criminal justice community, not everyone was sanguine about *Scared Straight!* or the Juvenile Awareness Project. It was at this point that it became increasingly difficult to separate the two. The Lifers' project had in effect become the "Scared Straight" program.

Perhaps the most persistent and ultimately telling criticism of *Scared Straight!* came from the Washington-based National Center on Institutions and Alternatives (NCIA) beginning in March, 1979. The NCIA President, Dr. Jerome G. Miller, was the respected former commissioner of youth services in Massachusetts who made his reputation by closing down that state's juvenile institutions. Writing in the NCIA investigative newsletter for March, Miller said:

> We followed the documentary first with curiosity and interest. But as the claims, testimonials, and true believer simplicity developed, our curiosity turned. Indeed, there has not been such a "successful" program in the last one hundred years of treatment of juvenile delinquents as this "Scared Straight." One becomes inured to hearing such claims from assorted religious zealots and the occasional reformed addict, but here we are hearing claims of historic consequence made for a program in delinquency treatment—claims "hyped" to a degree unprecedented with an audience of tens of millions.

> But it didn't stop there. The program was followed by discussion groups virtually unanimous in their praise. Normally incisive interviewers, such as Dick Cavett, seemed totally enthralled and titillated with the program. . . . It was a fitting culmination to the hype, the result of highly professional press agentry. . . .

> Ultimately the program tells us more about ourselves and the current state of our society than anything else. Having been deluged for the last number of years with media events depicting children as devils, witches, and anti-Christs, it should not be surprising that we now bless a panacea designed to scare the hell out of our children.[12]

Jerry Miller says he became interested in *Scared Straight!* because of the publicity and notoriety promoting the film; publicity which turned a relatively obscure project—obscure at least on a large scale—into a national panacea. Miller and his associates conducted an investigation of *Scared Straight!* and reported the following:

> The film and promotional materials surrounding it give the misleading impression that the youth pictured are "chronic, life-long hell-

bent offenders." On the contrary, the group had "relatively minor or non-existent involvement with the law."

At least one of the youngsters appearing in the film had visited Rahway previously, contrary to impressions given in the film.

The filmmakers perceived the youngsters as being more delinquent than was actually the case. Some reported having committed some minor offenses, including setting off firecrackers, smoking marijuana, and filching cookies and candy bars. They were not, however, "hard core" delinquents by any stretch of the imagination.

There were indications that the youngsters were encouraged to act in a particular manner, i.e., boisterous and cocky going in, but contrite and scared coming out.

Permissions were obtained from parents who were told that the film would be shown on the West Coast and thus not subject their children to ridicule or stigmatization.[13]

Miller's criticisms were widely reported by the media, raising a storm of controversy. Newspaper accounts of the charges used such words as misleading and faked to describe the documentary. For example, the TV Screen Editor for the *Milwaukee Journal* wrote the following:

I'm afraid we've all been had with the recently shown documentary *Scared Straight!* . . . a "documentary," produced for profit, that probably had no particular social significance, undoubtedly scared no one straight, unfortunately got a lot of people planning cuss sessions to scare their delinquents with and, for the most part, tediously assaulted the ears with the kind of language that TV stations, in saner moments, wouldn't dream of permitting.[14]

These charges against the film culminated in the filing of a ten million dollar lawsuit against Arnold Shapiro, Golden West Broadcasters, Peter Falk, Police Sgt. Charles Martini, and New York's WNEW-TV in September, 1979. The suit asked for punitive and compensatory damages on behalf of a majority of the Ridgefield Park juveniles appearing in the film. The lawsuit contended the youngsters and their parents were misled; that the youths were wrongly portrayed as juvenile delinquents; that they suffered permanent psychological damage; and that the families suffered mental anxiety.

The Film's Defenders Respond

Producer/Director Arnold Shapiro defended *Scared Straight!* in an April, 1979, interview with the *New York Times*.[15] He denied charges that the documentary misrepresented the youngsters' degree of criminal involvement or the success rate. Shapiro formally responded to the charges at congressional hearings before the House Subcommittee on Human Resources on June 4, 1979. He said:

> From the very beginning of this project, I have understood my responsibility as a communicator of information to be as honest and accurate as possible. I did not want to make the Rahway program something that it wasn't. I also did not want to underplay what it was. My initial production research convinced me that the program was effective and did work, and, therefore, we were presenting an important documentary. We said that this program is effective. We do not say in the script or anywhere else in the documentary that every juvenile should go through this program, that it works for every juvenile. Nor do we say that it has a one hundred percent success rate. . . .

> I have produced numerous informational and documentary television programs over the last fifteen years. I have received five Los Angeles area Emmys for other programs I have done. I am known by my colleagues as a very responsible and cautious documentary producer who will often avoid a dynamic piece of material if I feel that it is sensationalistic or inaccurate. There is nothing in *Scared Straight!*, either visually or in the narrative, that I feel is inaccurate, irresponsible, misleading or that I would want to change if I were rewriting the script today.[16]

Mr. John T. Reynolds, Executive Vice President of Golden West Broadcasters, also defended *Scared Straight!* at the congressional hearings. He said:

> When we decided to produce *Scared Straight!* we didn't do it frivolously or with a feeling this was something that would be exploitable because obviously we knew we were going to produce a very controversial film. We did it because we believed as broadcasters we have a responsibility to communicate to the world some of the things that go on in the world. . . .

> We decided to make this product and to do this film and to put it on the air after much thought because we thought it was an important message. The matter of degree of success is why we are here to discuss it today. If nothing else, people all over the country are talking about juvenile delinquency.[17]

Later in an article published in *P.D. Cue* magazine, Mr. Reynolds accounted for the massive public response to the film as follows:

> . . . after much review and discussion, it is our conclusion that the country was ready for and receptive to a television documentary dealing with the terrible increase in juvenile crime. In addition, contrary

to most documentaries, *Scared Straight!* had a beginning, a middle and a positive ending. It had an ending which left viewers fulfilled and with a feeling of great hope that indeed there may be a means of effectively deterring the youth of America from a life of crime.[18]

One of the girls in *Scared Straight!* also testified at the hearings in defense of the documentary. She denied that there was any fabrication in the film and described her initial reactions as follows:

> . . . when they said—you know, we were told to act and we had to— I ain't an actor, you know, that is what I am trying to say. That is why I got so mad when all that stuff came up because the only thing that was repeated because they wanted to film us walking in. We got there and they were not even ready for us yet. They didn't know we were there when we got there so that is the only thing we filmed over. When we walked in I thought, you know, this is great but what am I doing here. You know, I am never going to go to no prison.

When asked what she thought of the program she said:

> A lot of them said that, you know, they saw it on TV. See, in our town at 10 o'clock the parks close and the night that *Scared Straight!* was on the police didn't even have to chase no one, they all ran home at 9:30 to watch it. But they said like you have to watch it, it was a put-on. Who are you kidding?

> You can ask them now and they will tell you it was not a put-on because, see, if they thought—a lot of people think that maybe we were told to do certain things and how to act and what to say and all but when you go there and you are not on film and it is the same thing, then they know the truth. So you just have to go there, experience it and then you will know. . . .[19]

Finally, I asked ex-Lifer Frank Bindhammer about his own involvement with the film. That portion of our interview went as follows:

Finckenauer: What's been the aftermath of the film both in terms of your own involvement and in a kind of general sense?

Bindhammer: It was shown in Los Angeles the first time. If I'm not mistaken that was in October of '78 and the response was so overwhelming that they decided to attempt it here nationally.

Finckenauer: You mean that was not an original purpose?

Bindhammer: No. Oh no! Not that it wasn't the original purpose, but they simply did not believe that they could sell it to other markets. OK? It was only after it was aired in LA that they approached the Signal Company.

Finckenauer: You're not involved in this lawsuit, by the way, are you?

Bindhammer: Not to my knowledge.

Finckenauer: Because I want to ask questions about things that have to do with . . .

Bindhammer: You can ask, Jim. If I can't answer the question, I can't answer it.

Finckenauer: One of the issues has to do with the location or the areas in which the film was shown. I've not seen the briefs, but it's my understanding one of the complaints being made against the film people is that they were given assurances it would not be shown—

Bindhammer: No, that's not true, Jim. That is not true. I distinctly remember talking with Arnold Shapiro about that prior to the, his making this film. And the Lifers had inquired about it. Would this program be aired nationally or in any other area and Arnold's response to the best of my knowledge was, "It will probably only be shown in California because the New York markets and so forth have produced documentaries on this program, so there's a possibility that it will not be shown there." But the man did not make a commitment to the Lifers. There's absolutely, honestly, Jim, I'm not lying to you when I say this. I don't know what the Lifers said, I don't know what the parents or anyone else says, but I know for a fact that Arnold said this. I was present. And, you know, I can understand someone attacking the man if they have some justification but, and in that regard they do not. Now, I can only speak for what was said in my presence. Whatever happened with the parents or somebody else outside of that institution, I have no knowledge of that. But I know for a fact that he did not promise that the film would not be shown nationally.

Finckenauer: At what point in there did you leave the institution and become involved with that?

Bindhammer: Well, I was released September 19, 1978.

Finckenauer: So the film was actually completed?

Bindhammer: It had been completed. As a matter of fact, not only had it been completed but Arnold Shapiro brought the film into the institution to give a premiere and shortly thereafter I was released. When Arnold Shapiro found out that I was in fact released from prison, he contacted me and he asked me if I would be willing to come out to California to do a screening of *Scared Straight!* and to talk about crime, institutional life, etc. and I agreed to do that. Golden West held the screening on their lot and I did in fact address a pretty large audience after viewing

Scared Straight! and their response was really tremendous. The president and vice president of Golden West was rather impressed with my presentation and the following day when Arnold Shapiro drove me to the airport he mentioned that they expressed an interest in possibly asking me to come back to do some promotional work, and wanted to know if I would agree to do that. And I told him I would. Ten days later, I believe it was, I returned to California to do promotional spots for *Scared Straight!* And, it was at that time that the management of Golden West and Signal Company asked me if I would, in fact, be interested in working with Golden West and I agreed to do that. As a result of, well, you're aware of the fact that I had traveled around the country promoting *Scared Straight!* and talking to various people about initiating some of the programs in correctional institutions. As a result of the congressional subcommittee hearing, the Signal Companies and Golden West decided to, not to promote the Juvenile Awareness concept. So, I wrote to John Reynolds, who is executive vice president of Golden West and explained to him exactly what my situation was—what my thoughts and so forth were regarding the program, and we agreed that I should do my own thing—which is to promote similar programs. So, I left their employment to do exactly that.

Finckenauer: In the period then, between roughly September and June, you were then traveling to various cities and the film was being shown and you were speaking to organizations and groups around the film as portraying the program?

Bindhammer: Well, my purpose of, yes, was to fill in all the gaps that *Scared Straight!* left out.

Finckenauer: What kind of reaction did you get? Were you surprised at the reaction that this film got? And that you got?

Bindhammer: I think that most people are really ignorant to what crime and institution life like this is really about, Jim. And to hear somebody get up and talk about it, not simply attack Department of Corrections, but to try to be objective about it and give them some real insight into what it's about. It's something that they never heard before and they do respond favorably. I think that people should be made educated or they should be enlightened as to what is actually happening in these places.

Finckenauer: What was their reaction to the film? You saw people's original reactions?

Bindhammer: They were shocked! Because again, they were ignorant to what institution life is really about. They never heard anybody talk about these type of things.

Finckenauer: But they got the impression that this would be a thing to do?

Bindhammer: Not simply based on the film. Again, because there's so much more to the program than the documentary *Scared Straight!* And that, I think, is what they were responding to more readily than to *Scared Straight!*

Finckenauer: By and large they were supportive?

Bindhammer: Yes.

Finckenauer: What kinds of groups? College groups?

Bindhammer: No. No. These were all professional people. You're talking about youth services organization, law enforcement, juvenile judicial system, attorneys, mental health.

Finckenauer: What do you think is going to happen now? And when I say that, I mean, what do you think is going to happen in terms of the film, because I think a lot of people's knowledge about this whole thing has to do with the film. It doesn't go a lot beyond that.

Bindhammer: With regards to the film?

Finckenauer: Yes, what do you think is going to happen to that?

Bindhammer: I would personally like to see it back on the, I'd like to see it shown a number of times in every area with explanations. I think that if it is shown and the public is given a bit more insight into what the program is about, how the program, the faults of the program as well as the benefits, and let them decide whether or not the programs like this should be initiated in other institutions. I think you should share with the public not only your success but your failures. Let them know what the pitfalls of the program are.

Finckenauer: But I guess now if your judgment is correct, that they're now not advocating showing this film?

Bindhammer: As far as I know, they're not going to show it again. I don't know.

The lawsuit was ultimately dismissed. What cannot be dismissed is the conclusion that the documentary misled the American public into thinking this was some kind of miracle cure for juvenile crime. The scare tactics in the Juvenile Awareness Project were overemphasized. This has resulted in encouraging the brutalizing, terrorizing, and traumatizing of youngsters across this country and elsewhere. Inmates have been exploited, and other kinds of inmate efforts to prevent delinquency have been discouraged or destroyed. For example, shortly after *Scared Straight!* was shown in California for the first time, inmates in San Quentin's SQUIRES Program complained to KTLA about their program not being chosen as the subject for the documentary, since theirs is a

California program. Inmates from a Rahway-type project at the Susan-ville prison in California criticized the publicity surrounding "*Scared Straight!*" for undermining the effectiveness of their own Dead-End Center program. Inmates from both California institutions indicated that the glare of publicity and controversy would severely damage the spontaneity, credibility, and authenticity of their own efforts.

Almost simultaneously with the events just traced in this chapter, other activities were taking place not far from the walls of Rahway State Prison. The location was the Rutgers University School of Criminal Justice in Newark. These activities, comprising my evaluation of the Juvenile Awareness Project, are detailed in the following three chapters.

Notes

[1] U.S., Congress, House, Subcommittee on Human Resources of The Committee on Education and Labor, *Hearings, Oversight on Scared Straight*, 96th Cong., 1st Sess., June 4, 1979, p. 52.

[2] Ibid., p. 117.

[3] Ibid., p. 213.

[4] Ibid., p. 214.

[5] National Center on Institutions and Alternatives, *Scared Straight: A Second Look* (n.d.), p. 4.

[6] Ibid., p. 4.

[7] U.S., *Hearings, Oversight on Scared Straight*, p. 183.

[8] Patricia Levine, "Scared Straight: Bad Language, Glamorous Cons," *Kansas City Raytown News* (21 February 1979): 5.

[9] Patricia Levine, "Caution: Contains Explicit Balderdash," *Kansas City Raytown News* (21 February 1979): 5.

[10] Jack Neher, in *Film News* (n.d.).

[11] Pyramid Films, *Scared Straight!*, film advertisement (n.d.).

[12] U.S., *Hearings, Oversight on Scared Straight*, pp. 9–17.

[13] Ibid., pp. 3–7.

[14] Wade H. Mosby, "Questions Won't Scare Channel 4 Straight," *Milwaukee Journal* (6 May 1979).

[15] Arnold Shapiro, "Producers Defend Scared Straight," *The New York Times* (29 April 1979).

[16] U.S., *Hearings, Oversight on Scared Straight*, pp. 45–46.

[17] Ibid., p. 67.

[18] John T. Reynolds, "The Scared, Straight Phenomenon," *P.D. Cue* (August/September, 1979): 20–22.

[19] U.S., *Hearings, Oversight on Scared Straight*, pp. 99–100.

chapter four

How to Find Out If the Project "Works"

My evaluation of the Juvenile Awareness Project was conceived in the late spring of 1977. The JAP had been in operation for some eight or nine months at that time, and approximately two thousand kids had participated in it. Public awareness of the project was still rather limited—this was before the extensive newspaper and magazine coverage; before the TV coverage; before the Department of Corrections' study; before the somewhat infamous "fondling incident" described earlier; before the *Reader's Digest* article; and before *Scared Straight!* The idea for the study came to me from the Assistant Dean of the School of Criminal Justice, who relayed a conversation about the Lifers' project between New Jersey's Chancellor of Higher Education and the then commissioner of the Department of Corrections. Corrections Commissioner Mulcahy expressed interest in there being an outside study or evaluation of the project. I was asked if I would be interested in such an undertaking, and, finding the idea fascinating, I readily agreed.

Since one can study little without financial support, my first step was to seek money to support the research. In order to present my ideas for evaluating the project, I decided to prepare a brief concept paper and a proposed budget. Before writing the paper, I arranged to visit Rahway Prison. There I spoke with Richard Rowe, who was the president of the Lifers' Group, observed a session while sitting on the stage, and discussed the project at length with Sergeant Alan August. I was also given descriptive information about the Lifers and about the project.

My first impressions from this visit remain vivid in my mind. I had been in the prison a number of times, so this part was not new. I had also worked in a juvenile correctional facility which used group confrontation techniques and was thus very familiar with "shock-confrontation" as a treatment mode. Still, the Lifers' session made me uneasy. The particular group which I observed consisted of eight to ten girls and one boy. They all seemed to be very young (eleven to thirteen years old) and did not fit my conception of "hard-core" delinquents. The disturbing parts of the session were the unrelieved harshness of the inmates' approach and the belittling and berating of individual kids; but above all there was the sexual nature of the inmates' message to the girls. The latter consisted of explicit descriptions of the homosexual attacks which would be made upon these girls once they were confined in a female prison. The value to the girls of repetition of these scenes seemed debatable; further, I recall thinking that I would not want my own teenage daughter subjected to this sort of treatment. I left the prison somewhat troubled and admittedly somewhat skeptical, but still intrigued with the idea of determining whether or not it "worked," and whether or not the claims of success were valid. Sometime later, I also attended a meeting of police juvenile aid officers at which Judge George Nicola described the project and expressed his belief in its effectiveness.

The concept paper stressed that "the basic idea guiding the project is an effort to deter certain juveniles from committing offenses." I pointed out that the Juvenile Awareness Project would provide an excellent opportunity for trying to test the efficacy of the deterrence concept. The size of the sample of kids to be studied would be determined by the availability of resources and to some extent the length of the funding period. The questions that could be addressed in the proposed study were:

1. How is the "shock-confrontation" treatment modality received by the youths?
2. Which youths are deterred, if any?
3. Are any youth negatively affected with regard to both psychological effects and future behavior patterns?
4. Does the experience have a lasting, constructive influence on the participating juveniles?
5. What contributing factors such as age, sex, race, socioeconomic status, criminal history, peer influences, etc., influence receptivity to this approach?
6. Is there a typology of juveniles which can be defined in accordance with potential amenability to involvement in the project?

The proposal was sent first to the Victoria Foundation, Inc. and The Fund for New Jersey on July 28, 1977. The Victoria Foundation response was unpromising. The response from the Fund for New Jersey was equally unpromising, but did raise some interesting points. The answering letter said in part:

> I have one major problem with the proposal and that is whether the questions you seek to answer can be answered in any reliable manner. . . . It is not clear to me that there is anything in your proposed research design which is capable of establishing a connection between a two- or three-hour visit to Rahway prison and the avoidance of arrest in the months and years which follow the visit. Conversely, it would be equally difficult to trace a subsequent arrest to the experience at the prison.[1]

The perceptiveness of this letter rested in its questioning of the implicit causal assumptions of the JAP linking the prison visit to subsequent delinquent behavior.

The proposal was also sent to New Jersey's State Law Enforcement Planning Agency in the summer of 1977. This agency provided federal money for a variety of projects in law enforcement and criminal justice, including projects pertaining to juvenile delinquency and juvenile justice. SLEPA's first informal reaction to funding the study was also negative. The stated reason was that SLEPA was not mandated to support what they called pure research projects. Subsequent to this initial response, however, the Lifers' Group also submitted a proposal to SLEPA for funding of the JAP itself. This action placed the agency (SLEPA) in a difficult position. There were those in SLEPA who were not enamored with the idea of giving public funds to a group of inmates, no matter how ostensibly worthy the cause. Resistance in some law enforcement circles was adamant. At the same time, SLEPA officials recognized that the Juvenile Awareness Project had become very popular and that the Lifers had many influential supporters. Thus, a flat turndown also did not seem particularly palatable. Financial support of my study, on the other hand, was seen as defensible because it was a necessary step before any consideration of direct funding could be given. This move would permit SLEPA to do something without treading into a potentially risky area.

This link which developed between my proposal and the Lifers' proposal was to cause later problems in the evaluation. The denial of funding directly to the Lifers, coupled with approval of my application, left the impression that I had, in effect, gotten their money. Although it seems clear that the Lifers had little or no chance of receiving funds, whether or not there was an evaluation, they and their supporters saw things differently. This did not make for a smooth working relationship, and it made the necessary cooperation that much more difficult to achieve.

During the preparation of the application, questions arose about what agency should actually receive the funds, that is, Rutgers University or the Department of Corrections. SLEPA preferred the Department of Corrections, and the department agreed to house the study for administrative purposes. This decision also had implications for the study and its aftermath. Several were immediately clear. The department was going to be responsible for a study which it had not designed and maybe only partially understood, which was physically located in a university and run by university personnel, and which was going to be independent and autonomous in its implementation.

SLEPA approved the grant on October 27, 1977, after budget revisions to bring the SLEPA share below $20,000, which seemed to be some kind of necessary ceiling. The final total budget, including matching funds, was $21,272 for ten months (December 1, 1977–September 30, 1978).

It is important to note that neither SLEPA nor the DOC is a research-oriented agency. In neither agency was there much consideration of the design of the research, of the possible findings, nor of their potential implications. Also, there was no clear understanding of the possible pitfalls confronting the study. These and the failure to comprehend the fact that research is often a high-cost, high-risk activity were to bring problems later on. These problems were in part due to inadequate communication on my part, but they also seem to be inherent in evaluations undertaken in conjunction with operational criminal justice agencies.

Dealing with the Courts

One objective of the research was to secure information regarding arrests and adjudications of juveniles in the study sample. In accordance with the provisions of the New Jersey juvenile code, juvenile court judges in those counties which were the biggest referral sources to the Lifers' project were immediately contacted by letter to gain permission for access to the desired information. This occurred at the end of October. In early November, one judge agreed to meet with me and Ms. Janet Storti, who was to be the full-time project specialist. (Janet was a second-year graduate student in the School of Criminal Justice.) The judge who asked for the meeting was somewhat suspicious of the Juvenile Awareness Project because the fondling incident described in chapter 2 had just recently occurred and involved children from his jurisdiction. The judge was very supportive of our evaluation. However, he and several other judges indicated that we should gain the formal approval of the New Jersey Administrative Office of the Courts for the study. This body is the administrative arm of the New Jersey Supreme Court.

On November 16, 1977, a letter making such request for approval was submitted to the chief of the Juvenile and Domestic Relations Court Services of the AOC. The request included the SLEPA-approved privacy certification protecting the confidentiality of the juvenile subjects. There was no formal response to the request. There was a telephoned suggestion that we meet with Judge Nicola to introduce ourselves and brief him on the nature of the evaluation. This suggestion was made in the context of the Juvenile Awareness Project being Judge Nicola's "baby."

After several delays and problems with scheduling, the meeting with Judge Nicola took place in his office on December 19, 1977. He was, to say the least, not supportive of the study. He felt the Lifers should have gotten the SLEPA money. He was critical of the academic community which, according to him, knows little or nothing about the "real world." He saw no need for an evaluation since he already had collected hundreds of letters attesting to the success of the Juvenile Awareness Project. Judge Nicola offered us his letters, and he offered to pick the sample which should be studied.

Several days later, the AOC juvenile chief requested a written plan for gaining parental/guardian permission for sampled juveniles to participate in the evaluation. This plan was sent to them on December 23, 1977.

Over a month later, on January 25, 1978, I was advised by telephone and later by letter that the Supreme Court had met in administrative conference on January 19th. The Court had "requested that Judge Nicola discuss the . . . proposal with the other . . . judges and then submit to the Supreme Court for its approval a plan agreeable to all the judges for you to access the juvenile records."[2] The letter went on to suggest "that Ms. Storti cease attempting to obtain lists of the juveniles who attended or who will attend the Lifers' program unless and until the Supreme Court approves your proposal."[3]

I spoke with Judge Nicola about the so-called plan on January 31, 1978. He invited Janet and me to the monthly dinner meeting of the juvenile judges to be held the following February 8th. The purpose of this was to explain what we were doing and answer any questions. The judge indicated he had confidence in his program and that not to do an evaluation would be a mistake. He conceded that Rutgers University was a "pedigree" institution. He said he endorsed the evaluation, and he felt the dinner would speed up the process for the plan to be presented to the state Supreme Court. He added, significantly, that he was not stalling the procedures. Nicola did question again my "theory hypothesis" that the program does not work (he was referring back to my earlier discussion with him of what my null hypothesis was). He said other judges would question this as well.

Janet and I attended the judges' dinner and meeting. Judge Nicola, acting as host, was charming and supportive. One might have gotten the impression that this whole thing was his idea. He presented the proposal; we said nothing; there were no questions; the judges approved overwhelmingly.

Despite surmounting what I thought was the final obstacle, nothing happened for the next six weeks. Then on March 21, 1978—exactly three months and three weeks after we were into the preliminary phases of study, and exactly four months and one week since the first request was made—a letter was received indicating that " . . . the Supreme Court has granted your request . . ."[4] This meant that the sample selection originally scheduled for January could finally begin in full in April. It meant that nearly 40 percent of the allotted time and almost that much of the budget had been expended, but the real work of the study had not begun.

Whatever the cause or causes of the delays, and whether or not they were justified, the effects were not helpful—to say the least.

The Study Design and the Reality

The Plan

The research design proposed to evaluate the Juvenile Awareness Project was explanatory; through an analysis of relationships among various aspects of the project and its results, it would be possible to find reasons why particular events and reactions occurred. The specific goals of the research were to evaluate the psychological and behavioral reactions the juveniles experienced as a direct result of their involvement in the project, the recidivism rate of these juveniles, and the extent to which the initial exposure and the effects therefrom were manifested in the lives of the participants. These were to be quantitatively and qualitatively measured to demonstrate both short- and long-term results.

The objectives of the approved study plan were as follows:

1. Select and interview a random sample of approximately fifty juveniles who had participated in the project since its inception in September, 1976. These interviews would have two components: (1) administration of an anonymous self-reported delinquency instrument, of which there are a number available, e.g., Porterfield, Short and Nye, and Gold; and (2) structured questions to ascertain impressions of and reactions to the project. Some of the juveniles in this sample would have attended the project more than a year before.

2. As a supplementary verification of the self-report information, efforts would be made to secure information regarding arrest and adjudication of the sampled juveniles. Section 24 a. (6) of L. 1973, c. 306 provides that "records shall be made available to any person or agency interested in a case or in the work of the agency keeping the records, by the order of the court for good cause shown." The appropriate courts would be petitioned for access to the desired information.

3. Correlation of the dependent variable of outcome measures, obtained as indicated above, with the independent variables of age, educational level, sex, race, socioeconomic status, and previous criminal history.

4. Selection of a sample of approximately one-hundred juveniles designated for attendance at the project. Random assignment of fifty of the juveniles to an experimental group and fifty to a control group. The experimental group would attend the project; the control group would not.

5. Standardized psychological tests would be administered to both the experimental and control groups on a before and after basis. The only intervening variable not controlled for by random assignment would be attendance at the project. Possible tests for this purpose were the Attitude Toward Punishment of Criminals scale developed by Thurstone and Wang, and the Attitudes Toward Any Institution scale developed by Kelley. These scales were used in a study by Stanley Brodsky of attitude changes among delinquent and predelinquent groups who were exposed to a "Prison Profiles" program at Illinois State Penitentiary. Other possibilities included the California Personality Inventory or a semantic differential measure.

6. Self-report delinquency instruments would be administered to both the experimental and control groups from four to six months after the experimental group had visited Rahway. The experimental group would also be questioned about impressions of and reactions to the project.

7. Other behavioral measures for both groups would be sought as described above.

8. Correlations of dependent and independent variables would be made as described in (3) above.

The plan also included a discussion of alternative methods to be followed if the original design had not worked out for some reason. The possibilities were outlined as follows:

- Alternatives to the proposed classical experimental design included a quasi-experimental design, in which a similar comparison group—but not a control group—was to be tested and assessed. This type of design is less rigorous in that the absence of random assignment leaves open the possibility of other uncontrolled variables entering into the outcome. Comparability of groups can also be a problem. It is, however, probably the best alternative method that could have been used if necessary. It is relatively convenient, flexible, and can allow for quick decisions by working backward in time.

- Another alternative was an ex post facto or "after only" design. This type of design does not employ control or comparison groups and, therefore, limits the confidence that can be placed in any findings and conclusions.

- A combination of the before/after and after only designs could also have been used. The juveniles attending the Rahway sessions could have been pre- and posttested to give a before/after psychological measure. A sample could then have been followed up in the community to obtain an after-only behavioral measure. The absence of a control or comparison group would again have limited the validity of any findings.

The experimental design was considered to be the best and most rigorous method of conducting evaluative research. It was the research design of first choice, but if for some reason had it proved to be infeasible, a quasi-experiment would have been designed and implemented.

Adjustments in the Plan

As indicated, one objective of the evaluation was to select a sample of approximately one hundred juveniles designated for attendance at the Juvenile Awareness Project. These juveniles were to be randomly assigned to experimental and control groups—fifty youths to each.

In order to select a sample representative of the type of juveniles attending the project, monthly reports of sponsoring agencies visiting Rahway during September, October, and November, 1977, were obtained from the Lifers. Out-of-state agencies and agencies serving a national population, such as the Job Corps, were excluded. The remaining forty-nine agencies were classified by agency type. These types were: counseling (youth services bureaus, Big Brothers, family services, etc.), police, educational (high schools, etc.), drug treatment (NARCO, Inc., DARE, etc.), employment (youth employment services, vocational rehabilitation, etc.), and recreational (YMCA, YWCA, Boys Clubs, etc.). It should be noted that only one of these agency types (the police) is a law enforcement agency. Only two (the police and drug treatment) could be expected to be handling almost exclusively juvenile offenders. The others (with the exception of probation departments, which were classified as counseling agencies) handle all kinds of kids, most of whom are nondelinquent.

A stratified random sample of twenty-eight sponsoring agencies was selected to represent agency type. I wanted to ensure that the agencies were represented in our sample in the same proportions in which they were represented in the total referral group of forty-nine. The reason for this was a suspicion that the types of kids being referred to Rahway were in part dependent upon the types of agencies which were referring them. In other words, I suspected that the police might be referring a different type of kid than the YMCA was referring, and that a probation department might be referring a different type of kid than a high school was.

Each of the agencies in the sample was contacted and asked if it would be willing to participate in the evaluation. Those willing, were asked to provide the names of juveniles proposed to visit Rahway. The agencies were told to use whatever selection procedures and criteria they were normally and routinely using to select juveniles for participation in the Lifers' project. The juveniles nominated were not to include any who had already visited Rahway.

The above process began in December, 1977, but was seriously stymied and delayed by the court permission problems described previously. From the agency sample, only eleven agencies (two cooperatively) actually provided us with the names of juveniles who were included in our sample. This represented a comparatively large attrition problem, the reasons for which were numerous and varied. These reasons included:

1. Agency refusal to cooperate with no particular reason given.

2. Agency advised not to cooperate with the evaluation. An example of this was the fact that no agencies in Judge Nicola's jurisdiction were willing to work with us. A probation officer from Judge Nicola's county asked for a private meeting. He explained that he had serious questions about the Lifers' project and Judge Nicola's role in it, but said he could not cooperate with us because it might jeopardize his employment.

3. Personnel problems, that is, the agency had no one to transport the kids to the prison.

4. Failure to gain parent/guardian permission before releasing names of juveniles to us. Two police departments had this problem. Our letter to the particular parents asking for signed consent came as a great surprise and shock to some previously uninformed parents. They became angry about what they viewed as an unauthorized dis-

closure of their child's name and refused permission. The police departments asked us to destroy the lists and to forget the whole thing.

5. Provided names of juveniles who had already attended the Juvenile Awareness Project. This was discovered accidentally in a review of the attendance rosters at Rahway. Although this could have been done inadvertently (which says something about the referring agency's record-keeping system), I suspect that in some cases it could have been done purposely. Knowing that this was an evaluation, some agencies—wanting the project to look good—simply gave us a sample of known successes. In any event, each name had to be checked against the roster at the prison.

6. Inability or unwillingness to go along with the need for random assignment of some juveniles to a control group. This is not an atypical or unusual problem in criminal justice research. It often militates against the use of pure experimental designs. Some agencies had participation in the project mandated by the court as a condition of probation for their clients. Thus, they could not hold back any kids to be used as controls.

This agency attrition problem consumed a large amount of Janet's time, in particular. Numerous and repeated telephone contacts were made with sponsors; letters describing the evaluation were sent; copies of the privacy certification were sent; and meetings were held. More often than not, after a considerable investment of time and resources, the sponsoring agency did not come through for the reasons already enumerated.

The eleven agencies that ultimately participated included six counseling agencies, two police departments, one high school, one neighborhood employment service center and a YMCA. The kids came from urban areas, for example, Newark and Trenton, as well as from smaller communities. One agency participating was the Ridgefield Park Police Department, which also furnished subjects for the *Scared Straight!* documentary.

The design called for random assignment to experimental and control groups within the designated lists received from each agency. This was done by simply alternating assignment of subjects to the two groups. Two pairs of agencies made joint referrals because they had a cooperative arrangement. This meant that eleven agencies in effect made nine sets of referrals.

Attrition continued to be a nagging problem. Once the names were obtained, all of the parents or guardians had to be contacted to give informed, written permission for their child to participate in the study. Only a few overtly refused, but many simply failed to respond, which meant these kids could not be included. It also meant considerable lost time waiting to see whether or not they would respond and how. Human-subjects concerns such as this are another common problem in criminal justice research, particularly where juveniles are involved. Although important and necessary, the need for written consent does not facilitate evaluation efforts. Some of the further attrition was also attributable to the juveniles themselves, although sometimes due to events beyond their control. Juveniles who had been pretested on the attitude tests failed to appear for their visit to the prison (agencies were responsible for transportation of these kids as with any others). Pretested juveniles went to Rahway, but failed to appear for their posttest. Both pre- and posttesting was done in the agencies by Janet and myself. Kids in the control group—who had not been anywhere or done anything despite knowing they were in a study—failed to show up for the posttest. Their motivation was obviously less than that of the experimental kids. Some kids got locked up, or moved, or simply disappeared somewhere in the process. Consequently, although hundreds of kids were involved at some early point, the hoped-for fifty experimentals and fifty controls were not achieved.

A different set of problems was presented by the agencies in the sample—problems which resulted in yet more attrition and in the experimental design becoming a quasi-experimental design in which assignment to experimental and control groups was not purely random for all agencies.

After the assignments, despite instructions and admonitions to the contrary, two sponsors took both experimentals and controls to Rahway, thereby losing the controls. This reflects their failure to recognize the nature and importance of a control group. In one of these cases, a subsequent group designated for attendance was held back and used as a comparison group. Two other sponsors failed to take their experimentals to the project as scheduled. One agency sponsor twice failed to show up at Rahway after being given dates and waiting two months on the waiting list each time. He was called several times to remind him of the dates. Because he had no good reason for the no-shows, the Lifers refused to reschedule the visit. One other agency sponsor, with a large number of pretested juveniles, simply changed his mind and backed out. It was decided to use these pretested juveniles in the comparison group. Thus, for five agencies the assignment was purely random; for one agency the experimentals and controls were selected separately; for two agencies (the high school and the YMCA) there were no experimentals; and for one agency (a police department) there were no controls.

Although dictated by reasons of feasibility, the design was still considered to be sufficiently rigorous to protect against the effects of extraneous variables on the outcome measures. Each juvenile in the sample was designated by the referring agency for participation in JAP in accordance with the selection criteria employed by that agency. The problems that occurred in maintaining the experimental design did not reflect any uniform pattern which might seriously bias the sample. Also, the sponsors did not know which juveniles were designated as experimentals and which as controls. However, the experimentals and controls cannot be assumed to be comparable. Instead, this needs to be confirmed and the differences accounted for. A total of forty-six experimentals and thirty-five controls was finally included in the study.

Looking for More Money

With all the problems and delays, it became apparent in the spring and early summer of 1978 that the evaluation could not possibly be completed by the end of September. Therefore, as is all too often the fate of researchers, other options including additional funds and time had to be sought if the study was to be brought to a successful conclusion. Of particular concern was the need to have six months transpire after the juveniles' Rahway visit to see if any new offenses (recidivism) would occur. This period is commonly called a time-at-risk period. A meeting was held with representatives of the Department of Corrections to propose that Janet's position be absorbed into the department's regular budget after September. Unfortunately, the proposal was rejected. On April 14, 1978, I received a letter from an assistant commissioner of the department which said in part:

> I am extremely concerned over the news that you now feel that your evaluation of the Lifers' Group program will not be completed with the time constraints of the grant period. . . . I am aware that you encountered some difficulties in obtaining access to the juvenile court records. However, since the initial delay in obtaining permission to use court records was approximately three months, I question why a six month continuation is now requested.

> You have suggested that the costs of Ms. Janet Storti's position be assumed by the State in order to complete the evaluation. I must advise you that, because of present budgetary constraints, there are no State or SLEPA funds available for continuation of this project. I must also point out that the request is rather extraordinary in light of your first commitment to complete the project in 10 months and for $20,000.[5]

A research proposal for just under $6,000 was submitted to the National Institute of Mental Health small grants section in May. These funds would have supported some part of the field research after September. It too was rejected. Why? " . . . the Committee questioned whether a posttest only control group design with such a poorly assessed treatment will yield any treatment effect after a four-to-six-month lag, a lag that at the same time is probably too short in terms of dependent variable behavior."[6] This was not a post-test only design. Also, it had been hypothesized that there would be no treatment effect no matter how long the follow-up. However, the funds sought would have permitted the longer follow-up period suggested.

Three private foundations or individuals were contacted about supporting the continuation of the evaluation. Two turned it down because of limited funds and one failed to respond.

The Federal Juvenile Justice and Delinquency Prevention Administration was approached on July 1, 1978. Our proposal to them was also rejected, but not until January 17, 1979. Their reasons were that the paper was said to be weak on "adequacy of the research design and methodology" and on "scope of proposed research."[7] We also had gone back to SLEPA in July 1978, asking for a ten-month continuation for approximately $12,000. Their response was to extend the study period through January 31, 1979, but without additional funds.

Beginning on October 1, 1978, the evaluation had to proceed as a part-time endeavor with a mixed bag of limited support from SLEPA, the Department of Corrections, and the university. The detailing of this part of the history of the study is intended neither as an excuse nor as an effort to criticize the agencies mentioned, but simply as an attempt to inform would-be researchers and evaluators of some of the realities and pitfalls which confront those who work in this business. The discussion is to clarify some of the difficulties and the obstacles which must be overcome in attempting a program evaluation of this kind. Two of the major failures on my part were in not anticipating the drawn-out court permission process and thus planning accordingly, and in not adequately communicating the nature of the risks inherent in research to two organizations which are by and large not familiar with these risks.

Criticisms of the Study Methods

I think it is important to describe those criticisms of the study that were focused on considerations of how it was done before further discussing the results. These criticisms came largely from two sources which can be conveniently grouped first into what might be called the lay critics (those who are not research scientists and were thus reacting more on common sense or intuitive grounds to what was done). This group includes some persons who work in juvenile or criminal justice agencies. Next are the critics who are researchers and/or statisticians. These persons are generally well versed in research and evaluation methods.

The Lay Criticism

The lay critics include mainly the Lifers themselves, members of the Lifers' Group Advisory Committee, some referral agents to the JAP, and many just plain believers and supporters in general. Some examples of the criticisms from this group follow.

> The program does not need defending . . . What has to be done is that this research has to be questioned. Let's stop accepting research based on very limited data. They have come out with broad, broad conclusions based on a follow-up of only 81 juveniles out of a total of 13,600 who have gone through the program.[8]
>
> Judge George Nicola
> (quoted in *Sunday Trentonian*,
> April 29, 1979)

> We question the motives of dilettantes who compromise their intellectual integrity by thrusting themselves into the national limelight with meaningless statistics deceptively presented as the product of scientific study. Out of fourteen thousand youngsters who have visited Rahway, the Rutgers' scholars surveyed a mere eighty-one, of which thirty-five made up a "control" group. Should a serious reputable scholar take this inadequate study to the *New York Times* and pompously declare our program doesn't work, and, most incredible of all, that it may actually cause crime? No right thinking academician of any stature would condone such unprofessional conduct. We dismiss the Rutgers' study for what it is—Nonsense![9]
>
> Robert J. McAlesher
> Staff Advisor to the Executive Committee,
> Rahway Lifers' Group
> (Prepared statement for U.S. Congress House
> Subcommittee on Human Resources,
> May 29, 1979)

I don't like the way they did it. The control group did not match up. Some of the teenagers had no records . . . Finckenauer was here one time in three years. He had his mind made up before he started.[10]

Lieutenant Alan August
(quoted in *Rutgers Daily Targum*,
January 23, 1980)

This criticism also included assertions that Janet Storti was unqualified to work on the study; that I personally spent too little time on it; and, as shown above, that I visited the project only a few times in the course of my study. My response to these criticisms is that they are absolutely without merit.

Although these particular criticisms are not really substantive, some others are. For example, Lieutenant August's statement reflects a view that I had a negative bias against the project from the beginning, which slanted the evaluation. The proposal which SLEPA funded clearly stated the null hypothesis to be tested in the evaluation as follows:

> The basic or key hypothesis underlying this evaluation is that the Juvenile Awareness Project has no effect, either psychologically or behaviorally, on the juveniles attending. We hypothesize no significant differences on pre- and posttesting experimentals, nor between experimentals and controls on posttesting. We also hypothesize no significant differences in behavioral outcomes between experimentals and controls.[11]

The basis for this criticism perhaps rests partially in a lack of understanding about what a null hypothesis is, but it also seems to derive from an absence of trust in evaluators. There is some feeling that evaluators simply concoct data and statistics to support some preconceived notion. Unfortunately, there are instances in which this has occurred. In any event, it is certainly possible. Perhaps the best response to this lack-of-trust issue that I can make was contained in my prepared statement delivered before the House subcommittee that investigated Scared Straight.

> I assured both the New Jersey State Law Enforcement Planning Agency (the funding source) and the New Jersey Department of Corrections that I would conduct an evaluation which would be as thorough, complete, and fair as possible within the limitations of time and resources, and, most important, I would let the chips fall where they might in terms of findings. If the project worked, I was prepared to say so; if not, I was also prepared to say that. In my judgment, to have done otherwise would have been to foolishly jeopardize my credibility as a social scientist. There was no particular gain to me personally or professionally, say in terms of publishing articles or reports, which would have been enhanced by faking the study. How-

ever, the losses from such a fraud, if discovered, would have been professionally catastrophic.

Another point made repeatedly by the lay critics was that the sample studied was too small to provide a meaningful assessment of the project. This criticism was echoed by the New Jersey Corrections Commissioner, who was quoted in the *New York Times* as saying he was not completely satisfied with my report because only eighty-one juveniles were studied.

Sample size is usually a function of the time and resources available to do a particular study. The issues of time and resources have previously been discussed in considerable detail. There are numerous research examples of the use of relatively small samples to generalize about considerably larger populations, for example, the Gallup, Harris, and Roper opinion polls. The secret, of course, rests in the science of sampling and the extent to which a sample is representative of the population that one wishes to describe.

It is also a fact of research methodology that small samples increase the difficulty of finding statistically significant differences between groups. This should be kept in mind when reading the findings in chapters 5 and 6. It is apparent from these chapters that my interpretations of the data were deliberately conservative so as to account for the relatively small sample size. Some more will be said about sample size specifically in the next section. None of the aforesaid should be interpreted as meaning that we would not have preferred a larger sample if that had been possible. All other things being equal, researchers almost always prefer larger samples to study.

Yet another criticism of the sample was that the group studied was not representative of the kinds of kids routinely attending the project. I think this issue has been adequately addressed in the earlier discussion of how the sample was chosen. The attrition of agencies and juveniles did not reflect any uniform pattern which should bias the sample. On the other hand, it is possible that the lack of cooperation on the part of some agencies could be interpreted as possibly limiting the more likely failures among both experimentals and controls. That is, agencies less than confident in how their outcomes would look might have been less inclined to participate in the evaluation. If this were so, the effect would be to inflate the results in a positive direction. This we should bear in mind when the findings are reviewed.

Last, there was the criticism that the experimental and control groups were not comparable, and thus my comparisons were unfairly prejudiced against the experimental group. This important point has been raised as well by the critical professionals. Since their challenge is a much more sophisticated one, it will be discussed in the next section and again in chapters 5 and 6.

The Professional Criticism

A number of critical responses to my research from fellow researchers have been chosen as representative of the types of criticisms that were made. These particular comments proved to be helpful because they stimulated new and additional data analyses in an effort to respond to the questions which were raised. First is a letter from a psychologist that was written to Corrections Commissioner William Fauver:

> As a social science researcher and methodologist, and as a strong supporter of New Jersey's efforts on the part of juveniles, I want to alert you to a very serious methodological flaw in Dr. Finckenauer's evaluation of the Juvenile Awareness Program. Unfortunately, *this* flaw is serious enough to render the evaluation uninterpretable and obvious enough to discredit it in the scientific/academic community.

> In order to insure the unbiased evaluation of any treatment, that is, to insure that treatment-control group differences are due to the treatment alone and not to extraneous factors, it is necessary that research participants be randomly assigned to treatment and control groups. Random assignment is the only procedure available to scientists that assures treatment and control group equivalence and comparability. So central is this procedure to experimental evaluation methodology that evaluations which do not use it cannot appropriately be called "experiments."

> . . . it is clear . . . that the 81 juveniles he studied were not randomly assigned to conditions. And despite Dr. Finckenauer's claims that the two groups were similar prior to treatment, there is ample evidence already available which suggests that the two groups *did* differ prior to treatment, and that they differed along at least one critical dimension. The *Times* reports, "Of the experimental group, twenty-seven had arrest records, nineteen did not. In the control group, fourteen had arrest records, twenty-one did not." These figures strongly suggest that the treatment or experimental group contained more delinquents, proportionately, than did the control group. As social scientists (and people in every walk of life) have long known, the best predictor of future behavior is past behavior. It is much more likely that the treatment group members . . . were arrested more frequently after the treatment than the control group members . . . because they were from a different, more delinquent population to begin with than that the Juvenile Awareness Program somehow "caused" them to commit crimes. Unfortunately, the cause of the treatment-control group differences found by Dr. Finckenauer are unknowable. Be-

cause we know that the groups were different to begin with—and may have differed on a countless number of other important character-istics as well as the one noted, it is actually not *possible* to make *any conclusions* about the effectiveness of the Juvenile Awareness Pro-gram on this study.[12]

This letter raises the comparability-of-groups issue and asserts that the absence of random assignment to experimental/control groups discredits the results. The problem of lack of randomness has already been discussed—the methods used to compensate for this problem will be described in the chapters on findings.

A letter to the editors of *Psychology Today* following that maga-zine's publication of my August, 1979, article entitled "Scared Crooked," made some of these same points, but further elaborated upon them. This letter, coauthored by the chairman of the Panel on Research on Rehabilitation of Criminal Offenders of the National Academy of Sci-ences, said in part:

> In reporting his own research on the effects on delinquents of the Ju-venile Awareness Program ("Scared Crooked," August), James O. Finckenauer asserts that his so-called experimental and control sub-jects were comparable in age, sex, race, delinquency potential, and prior criminal history. By "comparable," Finckenauer apparently means that the groups did not differ in statistically significant ways. But prior to treatment, 59 percent of the experimental group had a history of delinquency, whereas only 40 percent of the control group did. The experimental group had a higher delinquency "seriousness" score, more boys, and more minority youngsters than did the control group. All these differences, though not large, are in the direction of predicting higher risk of posttreatment delinquent behavior in the group exposed to treatment—exactly the result that was found. If the outcomes were tested against the existing data for each group before treatment, the change in delinquency would not have been signifi-cant, either.
>
> We believe it entirely possible that kids with greater tendencies to-ward delinquent behavior, whether it was manifested in a prior record or not, were more likely to be sent to Rahway for treatment. The reason for demanding randomization is that there are so many ways in which subtle biases can enter into group-assignment deci-sions made on any other basis. Randomization is the cornerstone on which experimentation rests, and is essential to the drawing of unequivocal inferences of cause. Finckenauer states that individuals were assigned randomly to the treatment or control groups. Howev-er, we received early reports on this research from Finckenauer's of-fice that indicated that efforts at randomization were not wholly successful, and that frankly label the study design as quasi-experi-

mental. How it became a randomized design, meriting the interpretations it has, deserves explanation.

> We do not believe that Finckenauer's study provides a basis for any conclusion about the effectiveness of the Juvenile Awareness Program other than that it will not be easy to find out how effective the program may be.[13]

In addition to the issues of comparability and random assignment, the letter implies that agencies were exercising some kind of selection bias in determining which kids went to Rahway. As explained earlier, that was clearly not the case. The agencies themselves had no say over which kids were experimentals and which were controls.

Next is part of an appraisal of my work by the director of research for an Arizona juvenile court center. This writer also proposes wrongly that the agencies controlled the selection process.

> First of all, there is the matter of attrition. Forty-six instead of fifty are in the experimental group and thirty-five instead of fifty are in the control group. The loss of four candidates in the experimental group could easily have happened by chance. Perhaps one or two moved; another may have refused to participate, etc. But it is highly unlikely that chance factors would cause the attrition of fifteen subjects from the control group.[14]

This same evaluator said the following about the issue of sample size:

> The original intent of the study was to have fifty experimentals and fifty controls. For reasons which I have not yet been able to determine, only thirty-five juveniles appear in the control group and forty-six in the experimental group. Dr. Finckenauer argues that statistically samples larger than thirty are adequate for estimating population averages and differences between groups, and he is quite correct in that increasing a sample from thirty cases to an infinite number of cases reduces the sampling error by only 4 percent. But the practical difficulties of doing a study like this argue strongly for a larger sample.[15]

This writer did concur that the general finding of my study, " . . . that the program has no effect, is valid."

Finally, the staff director of the U.S. House Subcommittee on Human Resources submitted my reports, along with the Department of Corrections' 1977 study and Golden West Television's informal survey, to the Congressional Research Service of The Library of Congress. The three questions asked and the responses pertinent to my research were as follows:

Question 1. Was Dr. Finckenauer's sample size large enough to be representative of young people who had been through the JAP at the time of the study?

There are two aspects of this question to consider. In order to draw reliable conclusions about the eight thousand young people who had participated in the Juvenile Awareness Program, the sample must be large enough, and it must be chosen so that it is representative of the group.

In the case of the Finckenauer study, the sample was large enough to determine if the Juvenile Awareness Program had a large impact on the recidivism of the young people, but not large enough to determine effects of lesser magnitude. For example, if the program improved the recidivism rate of the participants by 30 or 40 percent, the sample size used by Finckenauer would show that the program had a significant effect. However, if the program actually improved the recidivism rate by about 10 percent, a sample of this size would probably show the program's effects to be insignificant.

For purposes of evaluating the JAP, the sample size used in the Finckenauer study was adequate to test the claims of those who viewed the JAP as a phenomenal success, but was probably inadequate to test the more moderate claims that the program is a good addition to an overall effort against juvenile delinquency. . . .

There are serious questions about the representativeness of the sample used in the Finckenauer report. There are two primary areas of concern. First, although care was taken to insure that the sample would be drawn from a representative group of the agencies which participate in the JAP, the actual sample was drawn from less than half of this group of agencies. Second, out of the one hundred youths chosen for the study, only eighty-one actually participated. No tests were performed to determine if there were any significant differences between those who did and did not participate in the study.

For these reasons it is not possible to have confidence that the Finckenauer sample was representative of the eight thousand youths who participated in the JAP. It should also be noted, however, that it is not possible to say for certain that the sample was not representative. The problem is simply that one cannot be confident that the sample was representative.

Question 2. Is the methodology used sufficient to support the conclusion that "the juveniles in the group which attended the Juvenile Awareness Project were somewhat more delinquent than the comparison juveniles, but not significantly so"?

The particular method used to test for real differences between the two groups was appropriate and consistent with standard statistical procedures. . . .

Question 3. Compare the reliability of the Finckenauer studies and the information found in The New Jersey State Department of Correction's "An Evaluation of the Lifers' Group Juvenile Awareness Program," and in Golden West Television's "An Informal Follow-up Survey."

. . . The Finckenauer reports claim to be rigorous statistical analyses and can be evaluated as such. . . .

. . . With respect to the success or failure of the JAP on the recidivism rate of the youths who went through the program, the Finckenauer reports are considerably more statistically reliable than either of the other reports. However, as noted above, the Finckenauer reports themselves are not without their problems.[16]

This appraisal points out that there are certain methodological flaws in my research, and these will be addressed in succeeding chapters. At the same time, the critique seems generally positive in its overall appraisal.

This interchange and discourse on the pros and cons of evaluation research was basically as it should be, healthy and informative. There have been those on occasion who seemed to hit below the belt and/or, in my judgment, assumed a condescending and even sarcastic posture; but by and large the dialogue was very professional and enlightening. The latter, I think, represents the search for knowledge at its best. We will next explore the findings which have been alluded to in these various discussions.

Notes

[1] Letter from Gordon A. MacInnes, Jr., Director, The Fund for New Jersey, August 2, 1977.

[2] Letter from The Supreme Court of New Jersey, January 25, 1978.

[3] Ibid.

[4] Letter from The Supreme Court of New Jersey, March 21, 1978.

[5] Letter from The State of New Jersey, Department of Corrections, April 14, 1978.

[6] Letter from The National Institute of Mental Health, n.d.

[7] Letter from The United States Department of Justice: Office of Juvenile Justice and Delinquency Prevention, January 11, 1979.

[8] Ken Carolan, "Is 'Scared' Straight?" *Sunday Trentonian*, 29 April 1979.

[9] Statement to U.S. Congress, House Subcommittee on Human Resources of the Committee on Education and Labor, *Hearings, Oversight on Scared Straight*, 96th Cong., 1st Sess., June 4, 1979, p. 148.

[10] Frank Argote Freyre, "Reality of Prison Life Detailed by 'Lifers.'" *Rutgers Daily Targum* (23 January 1980).

[11] Proposal to evaluate Juvenile Awareness Project Help.

[12] Letter to William H. Fauver, New Jersey Commissioner of Corrections, May 28, 1979.

[13] Lee Sechrest, Robin Redner, "Letter to the Editor," *Psychology Today* (November, 1979).

[14] Letter from Gene A. Fisher, Director of Research, Juvenile Court: Superior Court of the State of Arizona, May 21, 1979.

[15] Ibid.

[16] Memo to U.S. Congress, House Subcommittee on Human Resources of the Committee on Education and Labor, *Hearings, Oversight on Scared Straight,* 96th Cong., 1st Sess., June 4, 1979, p. 241.

chapter five

Changing Behavior

The Juvenile Awareness Project seemed to me to provide an excellent opportunity for testing the usefulness of fear and intimidation in deterring juvenile delinquency. The Lifers' Group and their supporters have emphasized this objective in so many words.

This part of my evaluation was grounded in deterrence theory, based upon the premise that it is deterrence that provides the project with its theoretical base. The project's guiding theme seems to be to deter juveniles from committing criminal offenses, whether or not they have previously committed them. All of this had to be only a premise on my part because there were no explicitly stated causal assumptions for the project. As is the case with most delinquency prevention efforts, no one seemed to have clearly thought through or presented the case in any definitive way showing why this particular approach should be expected to work.

As already indicated, a number of substantial differences exists between the available research on deterrence and this study of the Juvenile Awareness Project. However, if one mentally constructs a three-legged deterrence model based upon perceptions of swiftness, certainty, and severity, it seems reasonable to assume that the Lifers' Group cannot influence perceptions of swiftness and certainty. These legs in the model are dependent upon the actual or perceived reactions of the juvenile justice system—the police, intake, the juvenile court, probation, and finally training schools and reformatories.

That leg of the deterrence model remaining is perceptions of severity, of harshness. How awful are the consequences? How bad can prison and punishment be? The Lifers' Group, and others who emulate the scaring technique, must deal with the constraint of being limited to this one leg, and must attempt to convince youths who are amenable to convincing that confinement in a maximum security prison is a reasonably likely consequence of their future involvement in delinquent behavior. (Not only did this seem to be a difficult if not impossible task, but its potential for success was limited by the results of considerable research evidence which showed that perceived severity has no particular deterrent effect.) It doesn't matter how bad it is; if the targets, whether juveniles or adults, are not convinced that there is a reasonable certainty—an unacceptable risk—of the punishment occurring, they are not likely to be scared straight.

The goals of the research reported in this chapter were to evaluate the subsequent behavior of juveniles exposed to the Lifers and the prison, and to compare this behavior with that of the control group.

The Methods for Assessing Behavior

Juvenile court records in the six New Jersey counties from which the eighty-one juveniles came were surveyed for a period of six months after the experimental group visited Rahway and after the control group was pretested. This was done to determine whether or not there was any recorded delinquent behavior for either experimentals or controls. It should be noted that these court records contain only information that has been officially reported to the juvenile court. The information may exist in the form of complaints, arrests, or adjudications (convictions). The records were similarly obtained for all cases using the same criteria.

Where records of delinquency were found, they were reviewed for type of delinquency (before and after visit or pretest) and number of delinquencies (before and after). Type of delinquency was weighted according to seriousness by classification as a juvenile in need of supervision (JINS) offense or a juvenile delinquency (JD or criminal) offense. The former classification consists of what are known as status offenses. These include such behaviors as running away, truancy, and incorrigibility, which are not crimes if committed by adults. They are unique to the juvenile status, thus the phrase status offenses. This weighting permitted a rough determination of not only whether one group committed more offenses than the other, but also whether these offenses were more or less serious. For comparative purposes, a mean seriousness of delinquency score for each juvenile was developed. Nondelinquency was weighted as zero, JINS offenses as one, and JD offenses were given a weight of two. The score resulted from multiplying each offense by its weight and then adding them for each youth. For those experimental juveniles having prior offenses, subsequent offenses could be considered an indicator of recidivism.

Initial Findings

Initial examination of juvenile court records revealed that nineteen of the forty-six youths in the experimental group (41 percent) had no record of prior offenses. This finding was a surprise because I, and presumably many others, had been led to believe that all referrals to the Juvenile Awareness Project were delinquents. Certainly the *Scared Straight!* documentary very strongly gave this impression. Among those who had visited the prison, the number of offenses for those with prior records ranged from one to as many as eleven. The seriousness of delinquency scores ranged from zero for those with no priors to twenty-two. The mean seriousness score was 4.26; excluding the nineteen nondelinquents, it was 7.26. Among the controls, twenty-one of the thirty-five juveniles (60 percent) had no prior record. But, keep in mind that all these youths (experimentals and controls) had been selected for referral to the project by their sponsoring agencies. The number of offenses for control kids ranged from none to nine; seriousness scores from zero to eighteen. The mean seriousness score was 2.51; excluding nondelinquents it was 6.29.

This background information on prior records raised some concern about the comparability of the two groups in terms of their criminal histories, and I decided that this should be tested. The results which are shown in table 5-1 indicate that the two groups did not differ, in a statistically significant way, on the mean seriousness score of their delinquency.

Table 5-1
Comparability of Experimental/Control Groups
by Prior Delinquency Records

	Priors	No Priors	Total
Experimentals	27 (58.7%)	19 (41.3%)	46 (56.8%)
Controls	14 (40.0%)	21 (60.0%)	35 (43.2%)
Total	41	40	81

$x^2 = 2.785$; 1 df; n.s.

It was decided to further test their comparability by using the mean seriousness of delinquency scores (including nondelinquents). A difference of means test again showed no statistically significant difference between the mean seriousness score of the experimental group and that of the control group (t = 1.43, df = 79).

These results lead to the conclusion that overall the two groups were comparable. When the nondelinquents were excluded from the analysis, the difference between the mean seriousness scores for experimentals and controls was even further from being significant (t = .37, df = 40). The juveniles in the group that attended the Juvenile Awareness Project were somewhat more delinquent than the comparison juveniles, but not significantly so. Others disagreed with this judgment, however, and this important point will be addressed shortly.

Outcomes: Success or Failure?

Each juvenile's court record was tracked for six months after the visit or after pretesting in the case of the controls. Using further recorded offense regardless of disposition as the definition of failure, the results are shown in table 5-2.

Table 5-2
Comparison of Experimentals/Controls by Outcome

	Success	Failure	Total
Experimentals	27 (58.7%)	19 (41.3%)	46 (56.8%)
Controls	31 (88.6%)	4 (11.4%)	35 (43.2%)
Total	58	23	81

$x^2 = 8.73$; 1 df; $p < .01$; C = .44 (corrected)

This table indicates that a significantly higher proportion of the juveniles who did not attend the project did better in terms of subsequent offenses than did the group that attended. The relationship between the variable of group and outcome was a moderately strong C = .44. This surprising and unexpected finding seemed to call for further examination and analysis of the data.

Among the experimental group, the success rate was twenty-seven out of forty-six (58.7 percent). This was certainly a far cry from the 80–90 percent success rates being claimed by the Lifers, by the supporters of the Juvenile Awareness Project, and being touted in the film. Among the twenty-seven youths with prior records, fourteen (51.8 percent) were successes; conversely, the failure or recidivism rate was 48.2 percent. This was not only not better than, but in some instances was worse than recidivism rates from other programs designed to prevent or treat juvenile delinquency.[1]

An interesting outcome with the experimental group was that six of the nineteen youths (31.6 percent) with no priors had subsequent records of delinquency. This result could be explained by several possibilities. First, there is something about the project that actually stimulates rather than prevents or deters delinquency. Or second, these kids were simply hidden, closet delinquents who happened to get caught after attending the project. The result could also be used to test the assumption that it is with this nondelinquent or hidden group that the Lifers can perhaps be most successful. A comparison of their outcomes with those for the nondelinquents in the control group lead to the results illustrated in table 5-3. (The nonattenders obviously did much better, but treating these data conservatively because of the very small numbers of cases led to a nonsignificant finding.)

Table 5-3
Comparison of Nondelinquent Experimentals/Controls by Outcome

	Success	Failure	Total
Nondelinquent Experimentals	13 (68.4%)	6 (31.6%)	19 (47.5%)
Nondelinquent Controls	20 (95.2%)	1 (4.8%)	21 (52.5%)
Total	33	7	40

$x^2 = 3.3$ (corrected for continuity); 1 df; n.s.

It seemed that more of the nondelinquent controls were successful than their counterparts in the experimental group, but not significantly so. The Lifers were more successful with nondelinquents alone than with their overall group (68.4 percent versus 58.7 percent) successes. However, this success rate was still considerably short of the claimed success rates. It was even less favorable when compared with the success rate of the nondelinquent controls (95.2 percent). As noted earlier, the Lifers have a rough typology of the juveniles referred to their project in which the youths are classified as the "good," that is those with no involvement in crime; the "bad," those with only minor infractions; and, the "ugly," those who have been incarcerated or are in serious danger of being locked up. Does the Juvenile Awareness Project scare the so-called "good" kids straight? The answer appeared to be no.

What about the "bad" and the "ugly" kids? A comparison of only those with prior records of delinquency is shown in table 5-4.

Table 5-4
Comparison of Delinquent Experimentals/Controls by Outcome

	Success	Failure	Total
Delinquent Experimentals	14 (51.8%)	13 (48.2%)	27 (65.8%)
Delinquent Controls	11 (78.6%)	3 (21.4%)	14 (34.2%)
Total	25	16	41

$x^2 = 2.76$; 1 df; n.s.

Again, more of the controls were successful than experimentals (78.6 percent versus 51.8 percent), but the difference was not significant. The conclusion seemed to be that the Lifers were relatively more successful with the "good" kids than with the "bad" or "ugly" kids, but that overall the project was not particularly successful with any of these youths when outcomes were compared to those of the control group.

Outcomes: Seriousness

The next step in the comparative analysis of the outcomes of the experimental and control groups was a difference of means test for the mean seriousness scores of the two groups. Whereas the first findings dealt with the proportions of successes and failures, these results would tell us something about the number and seriousness of subsequent offenses. The scores were for subsequent offenses committed within the six-month follow-up period. The results shown in table 5-5 compare mean seriousness of delinquency scores for all experimentals and controls and for the nondelinquents only (those with no priors). The latter comparison again tested the assumption that these youths were perhaps the best targets for the Lifers' efforts.

The results illustrated in table 5-5 reinforced the earlier finding that the experimental group did significantly worse than the control group in terms of outcomes. More experimentals than controls committed subsequent offenses and their mean seriousness of subsequent delinquency scores was significantly higher. As a subsample, the nondelinquent experimentals did worse than their nondelinquent counterparts in the control group. Once again, the project did not have better results in a comparative sense with those who seemed most likely to be deterred.

Table 5-5
Comparison of Experimentals/Controls by Seriousness of Outcomes

	Mean	t value	df	2-tail Probability
Experimentals (N = 46)	1.2			
		2.67	78.19	.009
Controls (N = 35)	0.3			
Nondelinquent Experimentals (N = 19)	0.8			
		1.84	19.42	.08
Nondelinquent Controls (N = 21)	0.09			

Criticisms, Subsequent Analyses, and Results

The negative findings previously discussed were in a report dropped off at the New Jersey Department of Corrections on a Friday in April, 1979. In less than a week, these results were in circulation and engendered an immediate outpouring of response that rolled across the state and country. At this point I want to discuss the major criticisms leveled at my research and the way in which it was done.

As stated in chapter 4, deficiencies were pointed out by persons who reviewed or read about the study and offered criticisms of it. Most of the criticism that was received questioned the results on the grounds that the methodology was flawed. In order to correct for any deficiencies and to be responsive to the questions that were raised, I undertook several additional analyses of the data just presented. One of the points raised earlier pertained to my failure to maintain pure random assignment of all the juveniles to either the experimental or the control group. This is a procedure, known as an experimental design, which I agree is critically important and should be sought whenever possible in evaluation research. However, because of events beyond our control, the randomization broke down in the case of three of the referral agencies. One police agency took all of their eleven juveniles to Rahway instead of just the six who were supposed to go. Two other agencies, with eight and three juveniles respectively, did not take their experimentals to the prison.

I subsequently removed these particular cases (twenty-two), and reanalyzed the data. The result was a failure rate of 31 percent among the experimentals and only 17 percent among the controls. This finding is not statistically significant, but the earlier conclusion that nonparticipants do as well or better than participants continued to hold when the cases which could be questioned were removed.

Another comment reported earlier referred to the loss of four juveniles from the experimental group and fifteen from the control group. The reasons for those losses were detailed in chapter 4. Here I decided to use what might be called a hypothetical "worst case example" to partially compensate for the attrition and to see what effect this might have on the findings. The way the example works is as follows: Suppose in the worst case (worst from the viewpoint of my conclusions) that all four of the lost experimentals had been successes and all fifteen of the lost controls had been failures. Although this may seem improbable and somewhat like a stacked deck, it was certainly not impossible. What would the results look like? There would have been thirty-one out of fifty successes in each group—an identical 62 percent success rate in both. Two conclusions would then have been warranted. First, 62 percent is still considerably short of the claimed 80–90 percent, particularly when one-half or more of the juveniles were nondelinquent to begin with. Second and more important, the absence of any difference in outcomes would lead to the conclusion that the project had no effect. Again, the basic conclusion would still stand.

Finally, a major reanalysis of these data was undertaken, using a more sophisticated statistical technique. This technique enabled me to statistically control and account for the effects upon subsequent delinquency of differences between the two groups on prior offense history, age, sex, race, and delinquency probability. There were significant differences in subsequent delinquency between the attenders and nonattenders once all these background characteristics were accounted for; *the experimental group still does worse than the control group.*

Specifically, I found that prior offenses, age, and sex are significantly correlated with subsequent offenses. This confirmed what some of the commentators had suspected. However, once the effects of all other variables, including these three, have been accounted for, the experimental-control group factor is still significantly correlated with subsequent offenses (see table 5-6). This means that any differences in the characteristics of the two groups are not causing the differences in outcomes between them. It simply reiterates the conclusion that those juveniles who visited Rahway and confronted the Lifers behaved considerably worse after their visit than did the juveniles who did not visit. A further finding (see table 5-7) is that sex accounts for the greatest amount of variation in subsequent offenses, that is, 6.3 percent. Group (experimental or control) accounts for the next largest proportion, 5.6 percent. Prior offenses and age then explain 5.3 percent and 5.1 percent respectively.

Prior seriousness of delinquency scores, age, and sex are also significantly correlated with subsequent seriousness of delinquency scores. However, the experimental or control group factor is still significantly correlated with this outcome when the other variables are controlled (table 5-8). Prior seriousness explains 15 percent of the variance in subsequent seriousness, and group explains 6.7 percent (table 5-9). These results also affirm the earlier conclusions.

The results from these reanalyses, particularly the last, effectively refute the criticism that the evaluation is seriously flawed, uninterpretable, and discreditable. There is certainly a basis for reaching conclusions about the effectiveness of the Juvenile Awareness Project.

Table 5-6
ANOVA* for Subsequent Offenses

Variable**	Degrees of Freedom	F	Significance
Sex	(7,73)	2.96	<.01
Race	"	0.94	n.s.
Low Risk	"	1.14	n.s.
High Risk	"	0.31	n.s.
Prior Offense	"	7.87	<.01
Age	"	7.40	<.01
Group	"	5.43	<.01

* The analysis of variance tests the correlation coefficient against a
  hypothesized correlation of zero.
** Variables were entered into the equation in a predetermined order.

Table 5-7
Regression Analysis of Subsequent Offenses

Variable*	Multiple Corr. Coefficient	R²	RSQ Change	Corr. Coeff.	Unstd. B	Std. (Beta)
Sex	.251	.063	.063	−.251	−.393	−.200
Race	.256	.065	.002	.162	−.195	−.122
Low Risk	.276	.076	.010	−.126	−.364	−.217
High Risk	.284	.080	.004	.061	−.203	−.113
Prior Offense	.365	.133	.053	.273	.967	.341
Age	.429	.184	.051	−.133	−.171	−.312
Group	.491	.241	.056	.217	.394	.250

*Variables were entered into the equation in a predetermined order.

Table 5-8
ANOVA* for Subsequent Seriousness of Delinquency Scores

Variable**	Degrees of Freedom	F	Significance
Sex	(7,73)	3.17	<.01
Race	"	2.33	n.s.
Low Risk	"	0.82	n.s.
High Risk	"	0.19	n.s.
Prior Delinquency seriousness score	"	17.58	<.01
Age	"	4.89	<.01
Group	"	7.06	<.01

* The analysis of variance tests the correlation coefficient against a hypothesized correlation of zero.
** Variables were entered into the equation in a predetermined order.

Table 5-9
Regression Analysis of Subsequent Seriousness of Delinquency Scores

Variable*	Multiple Corr. Coefficient	R^2	RSQ Change	Corr. Coeff.	Unstd. B	Std. (Beta)
Sex	.248	.062	.062	−.248	−.743	−.197
Race	.251	.063	.001	.148	−.560	−.183
Low Risk	.259	.067	.004	−.084	−.566	−.176
High Risk	.263	.069	.002	.035	−.292	−.085
Prior Delinquency seriousness score	.468	.219	.150	.415	.131	.483
Age	.493	.243	.024	−.006	−.255	−.241
Group	.557	.310	.067	.274	.823	.271

* Variables were entered into the equation in a predetermined order.

Predicting Delinquency

One of the potentially more important background variables we decided to include in the study was something we called *delinquency probability*. This factor permitted us to assess the chances of any juvenile in the study becoming a delinquent. The variable was created by using the well-known Gluecks' Social Prediction Table. Admittedly, I decided upon this particular aspect of the study with some concern and a little trepidation.

This trepidation arose in part from my awareness that prediction of criminal behavior is a rather risky business. People, it seems, are such ornery creatures that they don't want to behave in any predictable manner. Prediction of criminal and delinquent behavior has been notoriously unsuccessful. More than thirty years ago, in a paper entitled "Assessment and Prediction Methods in Crime and Delinquency," Don M. Gottfredson said: "Despite the painstaking studies, item analyses, and validation studies . . . all currently available prediction methods still have only relatively low predictive power."[2] That statement is as true today as it was then. It means that prediction methods do not predict very well. For example, Stephen E. Schlesinger tried to predict dangerousness in juveniles, using in part some thirty different factors (predictors) identified from nine different studies as being "statistically related to violent behavior in children."[3] He found no systematic relationship between the predictor variables and such criterion (predicted) behaviors as violent offenses, burglary, or larceny, running away, or being a so-called person in need of supervision (PINS). Schlesinger's conclusion was: "Predictors of violent behavior identified by previous researchers were not substantiated by this study. Future efforts to predict dangerousness will probably meet similar success,"[4] or, in this case, lack of success.

The ability to predict delinquency is grossly imperfect, irrespective of the particular technique or combination of techniques that might be employed. So why did I make the effort in this study? There were several arguments or reasons for doing so. The first is that we had learned a great deal about prediction, despite its shortcomings, and we could learn more only by continuing to experiment with various prediction methods. Thus, employing the Social Prediction Table would enable us to determine how well it predicted delinquency for this particular sample. Second, apart from its usefulness as a delinquency prediction tool, the Social Prediction Table would also permit us to classify our experimental and control groups according to their risks of future delinquency. The two groups could then be compared to see whether or not they differed in any significant way on this classification. Because of these potential benefits, we decided that this would be a worthwhile endeavor.

The second source of my concern was the Social Prediction Table itself. This table was developed by Sheldon and Eleanor Glueck from their famous *Unraveling Juvenile Delinquency* study completed in 1950. This work of the Gluecks is considered to be one of the pioneering efforts in the prediction field. The Harvard-based, husband and wife team attempted to identify potential delinquents at a very early age—to identify "delinquency-prone or delinquency-endangered children." The original scale was developed from a sample of 451 delinquent boys in correctional schools, and a matching sample of 439 nondelinquent boys. From a mass of social, psychological, medical, and anthropological data, the Gluecks selected five factors that sharply distinguished the two groups. These five factors were: discipline of boy by father, supervision of boy by mother, affection of father for boy, affection of mother for boy, and cohesiveness of family.[5] The Gluecks used the percentage of delinquents in each sub-category of the five factors as a weighted failure score.[6] These scores were then grouped and group failure rates were calculated.

The procedures used by the Gluecks and their conclusions have been both "strongly supported and severely criticized."[7] Most of the controversy has centered on their sampling methods, which resulted in samples that were not representative of the delinquent and nondelinquent populations. Nonetheless, there is evidence from a ten-year validation study conducted by the New York City Youth Board that the scale could be "a good differentiator between potential delinquents (serious and persisting) and nondelinquents."[8]

The particular version of the scale used here was adapted by Samuel A. Kramer in 1961.[9] Kramer's adaptation used the five family items developed by the Gluecks, but he had the subject juveniles rate themselves on each of the factors. The Gluecks, on the other hand, had evaluated family situations by means of appraisals made by home visitors trained in social work techniques of observation.

Kramer modified the wording of the Glueck items to make the statements clear to the boys in his study. His revisions were carefully reviewed by teachers and others to make certain there were no changes in meaning or concept.[10] This conversion of the scale into a self-administered instrument made its use feasible in my study. The scale used by Kramer (the one used in my study), including weighted failure scores, looks as follows:[11]

Five statements are given in the following section. For each one check the idea that seems the best way to describe most of your life at home.

	Weight
1. The discipline given to me by my father (or person acting for my father) was:	
( ) Very strict	71.8
( ) Strict, but usually fair	9.3
( ) Sometimes strict, sometimes easy	71.8
( ) Usually easy	59.8
( ) Very easy	59.8
2. My mother (or person acting for my mother) gave me supervision that was:	
( ) Very helpful, with close watch over me	9.9
( ) Usually helpful, although sometimes she failed	9.9
( ) Helpful only when I asked for help or advice	57.5
( ) Most likely to let me do anything I pleased	83.2
( ) Completely useless, because she did not care what I did	83.2
3. My father (or person acting for my father) usually showed that he:	
( ) Liked me a great deal	33.8
( ) Liked me about the same as he liked his friends	33.8
( ) Neither liked me nor disliked me	75.9
( ) Disliked me most of the time	75.9
( ) Did not want me around	75.9
4. My mother (or person acting for my mother) usually showed that she:	
( ) Liked me a great deal	43.1
( ) Liked me about the same as she liked her friends	43.1
( ) Neither liked me nor disliked me	86.2
( ) Disliked me most of the time	86.2
( ) Did not want me around	86.2
5. My family (parents, brothers, sisters) has made me think that we:	
( ) Stick pretty close together in everything	20.6
( ) Would help each other more than we would help friends	61.3
( ) Can be equally happy at home or away from home	61.3
( ) Would rather be with friends than with relatives	96.9
( ) Have almost nothing that we like to do together	96.9

Kramer found in his study that "the Glueck index, dealing with family situations as perceived by the boys, proved to be exceptionally powerful in its discriminating effect."[12] He concluded that, "the Glueck scale is a powerful differentiating tool . . . in determining delinquency proneness."[13] Kramer's results convinced me to use his version of the Glueck index in this study.

One other issue which arose surrounding the decision to use the Glueck scale was the fact that both the Gluecks and Kramer (as well as many others) had used the scale with boys only. My concern was whether it could be used with girls as well, since there would be girls in the Juvenile Awareness Project samples. Fortunately, I had found a report by Hermann Elmering which led him to conclude that, " . . . the table is applicable to girls, even though it was initially constructed on boys only."[14] Therefore, I felt it would be applicable for use with girls.

The weighted items that make up the scale enabled us to classify juvenile subjects into low (below 250 points), medium (250–299 points), and high (over 300 points) probability of delinquency categories. The results of this classification of the juveniles in my study are shown in table 5-10.

Table 5-10 indicates that the two groups did not differ significantly on their probability of being delinquent. Thus one of the reasons for using the Glueck scale to assess comparability was successfully accomplished. But beyond that conclusion, the large size of the low probability category raised serious implications for the outcome measures, that is, attitude and behavior changes. If the Glueck scale was a valid predictor of delinquency—and that remained to be seen—it indicated that a large portion (more than 70 percent) of the kids involved in the Juvenile Awareness Project were not likely to be or to become delinquents, whether or not they visited Rahway. If this were so, it raised several interesting issues: Why did these particular kids need to attend the project? Why were referring agencies not sending more high-risk juveniles who might be more in need of deterrence? Finally, if the low-risk-of-delinquency kids did not in fact become delinquents, could the Juvenile Awareness Project legitimately claim credit for this "success"?

Table 5-10
Probability of Delinquency by Group*

Glueck	Experimental	Control	Total
Low	31 (70.5%)	24 (75.0%)	55 (72.4%)
Medium	10 (22.7%)	5 (15.6%)	15 (19.7%)
High	3 (6.8%)	3 (9.4%)	6 (7.9%)
Total	44	32	76

$x^2 = 0.68$; 2df; n.s.
* Five juveniles did not complete the scale.

Because there was a total of only twenty-one cases falling into the medium and high risk categories combined, these two were lumped together to make a "higher" risk group which was compared to the "lower" risk group. The groups were compared first on the basis of whether or not they had a prior delinquency record, and these results are shown in table 5-11.

Tables 5-11 and 5-12 clearly indicate that the Glueck Social Prediction Table, as adapted and used in this research, was not a very good predictor of delinquency. This is true regardless of when that delinquency occurred. Also, the Glueck scale did not predict pre- or post-delinquent behavior any differently or more validly for the experimental group than it did for the control group. There may be many explanations for this result, including the fact that this was a revised form of the scale that was self-administered. In any case, whatever the reason, the scale was not a particularly useful predictor here.

Table 5-11
Prior Delinquency Record by Risk

	Prior Record	No Prior Record	Total
Lower Risk	25 (45.4%)	30 (54.5%)	55 (72.4%)
Higher Risk	13 (61.9%)	8 (38.1%)	21 (27.6%)
Total	38	38	76

$x^2 = 1.64$; 1 df; n.s.

Table 5-12
Subsequent Delinquency Record by Risk

	Subsequent Record	No Subsequent Record	Total
Lower Risk	12 (21.8%)	43 (78.2%)	55 (72.4%)
Higher Risk	5 (23.8%)	16 (76.2%)	21 (27.6%)
Total	17	59	76

$x^2 = .03$; 1 df; n.s.

Some Individual Reactions

As indicated in the discussion of my plan for the study, one objective was to question kids who had visited Rahway some four to six months after their visit about their impressions and reactions to the project. A total of fifteen of the kids in the experimental group were interviewed. Seventeen control group subjects were also interviewed.

Five of these experimental group juveniles were from Ridgefield Park High School, which furnished most of the juveniles for the *Scared Straight!* documentary. When asked who decided that they should visit the Lifers' project, all of them said it was Sergeant Charles Martini, who also had been instrumental in recruiting kids for the film. One of these kids, a sixteen-year-old girl, said she thought Martini had decided to send her because she ran away a lot and because she had problems with her parents. She said she wanted to visit Rahway because her sister had gone and she was curious about it. Asked what she thought of her visit, she said, "Everybody was kind of quiet and was talking about how they were scared." Asked whether she thought the visit was helpful to her, she said: "Running away ain't a crime. The Lifers' Group didn't say nothing about running away!" She repeated this same thought when asked whether she thought the visits were helpful to other kids. "I don't know—it's hard to say. I ain't committed a crime," she said. She seemed to be saying that the shoe didn't fit, and therefore she wasn't going to wear it.

A number of surveys over the years have arrived at the conclusion that the rate of undetected delinquency is high. Large amounts of misconduct and lawbreaking seem to remain hidden in terms of the identities of the offending juveniles. The offenders are simply in the right place at the right time and do not get caught, or if caught, they are released without any official record. In addition, the surveys clearly reveal that all adolescents seem to be delinquent to some degree—at least as far as minor offenses are concerned.[15]

After their visit, each of the young people was also asked about his or her own delinquent behavior. This particular method of collecting information about delinquency is known as a self-report study. Anonymous self-administered questionnaires or confidential interviews have been used to uncover hidden or undetected delinquency. In our interviews, we assured the juveniles of the confidentiality of any information given to us. The importance of answering fully and accurately was also stressed. Still it must be recognized that there is some possibility of reporting error and of inaccuracies with this method. Curiously, error may arise from the possibility that some kids deny offenses which they have committed, but others may claim credit, so to speak, for things that they have not in fact done. Despite these shortcomings, this method has a considerable history and, if used judiciously, has been found to be a valuable supplement to official records as a source of information about the extent and nature of delinquent behavior.

Each juvenile was asked questions about twenty different offenses, ranging from the very minor, that is, doing things their parents had told them not to do, to some that are very serious, that is, robbing someone by threatening them with a knife, or a razor or a gun.[16] The youths answered these questions after their participation in the Lifers' project. The aforementioned girl, who emphasized that running away is not a crime, admitted disobeying her parents or other authorities numerous times (five or more); running away once; skipping school twice; and buying or drinking liquor at least half a dozen times. These are not particularly serious. However, she also admitted three petty larcenies (under $2), using dope (probably marijuana) numerous times, and selling dope at least three times. The latter offenses are obviously more serious and do constitute juvenile delinquency. She apparently was not deterred by her visit to the prison.

A second Ridgefield Park girl, this one seventeen years old, said she also was curious about the Lifers' Project and wanted to go. She said she was scared, but she hadn't been in trouble so she knew she wasn't like the others. This is a similar reaction to the first girl's. She said if she had been in trouble, she would have stopped after visiting the prison. On the self-report survey, she too admitted to skipping school, buying and drinking liquor, and using dope after her trip.

A third girl from Ridgefield Park, also seventeen, spoke about the corrections officers involved with the project. She said: "The guards were pushing and shoving—they yelled at me three times for smiling. I knew they weren't gonna hurt me." She also said, "I think it would be better if we [girls] went to women's prisons." This girl referred to getting mixed signals from her visit: "They yelled at you, then shook your hand. It was weird!" Asked whether the visit might be helpful to other kids, she said: "It works for people who want it to work—for those who let it sink in. Some kids got put in there for light stuff." This girl admitted disobedience, driving without a license, skipping school, and using and selling dope after her visit.

The fourth Ridgefield Park case was the only boy interviewed from that particular town. This seventeen-year-old said he too was curious about going but didn't really know why Sergeant Martini had referred him. He said the guards were more scary than the inmates. Asked if the visit had been helpful, he said if a radio was sitting in a car, he wouldn't think twice before taking it. However, he would think twice if somebody asked him to rob a bank. He too reported disobedience, numerous instances of driving without a license, and buying and drinking liquor. Also admitted were three larcenies ($2–$50 in two cases and over $50 in one case). He admitted destruction of property on three occasions, and numerous instances of using and selling dope. Obviously he was not scared straight by his experience!

The final Ridgefield Park juvenile, another seventeen-year-old girl, said she wanted to go to Rahway because she too was curious, but also because she could get out of school for the day. Her generally negative comments were: "After it was over, I thought it was a crock. After screaming at us for an hour, then they wanted to talk nice to us . . . The guards were more obnoxious than the inmates. I doubt if I were in trouble that I would be affected—it seemed like such a put-on. There should be more explanation of what's going on." Despite this reaction, this girl reported only driving without a license, skipping school, and drinking after her visit.

The next group of interviewees were all from an urban setting (Passaic, New Jersey); three African-American boys—two fifteen-year-olds and one thirteen-year-old. The thirteen-year-old, a seventh grader, said he thought he had been referred to the Lifers' Project because he had been caught in two B & Es (breaking and entering). He wanted to go, but said he didn't like the guards and didn't like "how the prisoners and guards treat other people." Asked if he thought the visit was helpful to him, he said, "Yea, I do not want to go to prison. I'm OK being on probation." He said the visit "may be" helpful to other kids. "If you want to go to prison, they can't help you," he said. "If you don't—they can!" What about his own reported behavior after his visit? He chalked up three petty larcenies (one of value, $2–$50); one destruction of property, three times using dope, and one fist fight. Curiously, he said he was doing "OK on probation!"

The first fifteen-year-old said he had been referred because of fighting and two B & Es. He said he "wasn't scared until the doors closed. The guy doing double life scared me the most." He also said the visit was helpful because "I haven't been in trouble—don't know no one who went that has." His self-report almost bears this out. He reported only some disobedience and using dope on three occasions. Not too bad!

The other fifteen-year-old was a seventh grader living with his mother, who was on welfare. He said he went to Rahway because everybody in his group went. He admitted he had been stealing, but said no one knew about it. He felt he would stop stealing because it "ain't worth getting into trouble for." He said, "Nobody wants to go to Rahway." He seemed to take his own words to heart, reporting only some disobedience of his mother after his visit. He seems a success, if his own report is accurate.

The final seven kids from the experimental group who were interviewed were some of the toughest and most delinquent juveniles in my sample. They all come from the city of Trenton, New Jersey, or its environs. These particular kids fully met the Lifers' characterization of being the "ugly" delinquents. Because of their "hardcore" delinquent histories, they provide a real test of the effectiveness of the Juvenile Awareness Project.

The first of this group was a sixteen-year-old boy. He was referred to the Lifers' Project by the Juvenile Aid Bureau of the Trenton Police Department because, he said, "they said I was bad—I was shooting dice and smoking reefer." He did not want to go to Rahway because he "didn't think I was that bad. I wasn't bad enough." He also said he wasn't scared because "I didn't think they were going to hurt me." Asked what he thought of his visit, he said: "It was alright . . . I didn't like the place. I was cool and waited to see what would happen. They didn't bother [hurt] me!" He said he was going to be more careful in the future as a result of his visit. He also felt the visits would be helpful to other kids because "It'll straighten 'em out a little!" However, this boy reported a number of offenses and violations following his visit. These included twice driving without a license, a half-dozen times buying and/or drinking liquor, a petty larceny (under $2 value), using and selling dope (at least three times for each), and beating up an innocent person. Depending upon the facts and circumstances, the latter may have been a felonious assault and battery. He does not seem to have been deterred by the project.

The second case was a seventeen-year-old white boy who had quit school and was working full-time. He was referred because he was on probation. He thought his visit was helpful to him, saying, "Yea, I ain't stole nothing since!" He also recommended the trip for others because "Them people scare you to death!" His self-report reflected that he had not stolen anything, as he said. However, he had numerous liquor law violations, and, more serious, he reported destroying property and having many fist fights and beating up innocent people. Perhaps the drinking and the fighting were related, but in any event, there appears to be a continuing problem.

The next boy, sixteen years old and African American, had been in the county youth house for several months at the time he was interviewed. He too had been referred by the Trenton Police Department. He offered some very interesting observations about his visit. Did he want to go? "I didn't mind. I had been there before and I was OK for awhile—then I got into some trouble again with this cop. So I thought going again would be good—I would be good longer." What did he think of the visit? "It's OK, It's not too scary. It stinks in there. I thought they might have remembered me—they didn't. I think some guys got picked on bad." Was the visit helpful? "Yea. You stay straight for awhile—but I ain't bad enough to go there. When I can go there, I'll just cut this out." What about other kids? "If they scared they ain't gonna get into trouble—if not they will." He seems to be a believer in the deterrent effects of fear, but what about its effects upon his own behavior? Subsequent to his visit he reported the following list of offenses:

1. Disobeying—5 or more times.
2. Driving w/o license—Once.
3. Skipping school—3 times.
4. Drinking liquor—3 times.
5. Stealing something worth $2–$50—5 or more times.
6. Stealing something worth over $50—5 or more times.
7. Destroying property—3 times.
8. Stealing a car—Once.
9. Breaking and entering—5 or more times.
10. Using dope—3 times.
11. Selling dope—3 times.

This boy obviously was not scared straight, even following two visits.

The fourth boy was also sixteen years old, African American, and in the county youth house. He was referred by his probation officer for stealing and for a breaking and entering. He was interested in visiting Rahway because he had heard about it from some other kids, and he wanted to see what it was like. His impressions were that the place was noisy. He said, "I thought they might kill me—some of the things they said scared me." He thought the visit helped him to stay straight for a while, but when asked why he got into trouble again, he said, "Some things just happen!" He was noncommittal about whether the project might help other kids. He too reported a string of postvisit offenses: disobedience, drinking, stealing, using and selling dope, and fighting.

The next boy had previously been at the Highfields Residential Group Center, indicating he had been a failure on probation. He too was sixteen and African American, and had been referred by his probation officer. What did he think of his visit? "We were pushed and shoved. The guards were real nasty. They snatched our lunches away and we couldn't eat until we got on the bus." He thought the experience was "kind of helpful." He said the "guards were rough, but pretty fair. It might help unless you're really bad." Did it help him? On most offenses he was clean, but unfortunately he reported three breaking and enterings since his visit.

Another youth house resident was the sixth interviewee. It should be emphasized that none of the youth house kids were in the youth house immediately before their Rahway visit. A fourteen-year-old boy, who was also African American, had been referred by the police department's juvenile aid bureau. He said he was "not scared—but kept cool." He "saw other boys shook up physically," but decided that he "was not going to get hurt." Asked if he thought the visit was helpful to him, he said: "No! It made me think, but fighting is different. They didn't talk about what happens when you get into fights, and I ain't killed nobody." He also did not believe the visits are helpful to other kids because "most of the kids weren't that bad." He reported disobedience, destroying property, using dope, and fighting following his visit.

The final interview was with a sixteen-year-old white boy, referred to the Juvenile Awareness Project by the Trenton Police Department. He said he didn't want to go to Rahway, but was told he had to go to "teach me a lesson." He said the visit did teach him a lesson "for a while." He thought the project was helpful because it showed him and others "what it's like" and "how it is." His self-reported behavior doesn't seem to indicate he learned the lesson the Lifers were trying to teach. He reported disobedience, driving without a license, running away, skipping school, buying and drinking liquor, property destruction, and using dope after going to Rahway.

By and large, these results are pretty dismal. There were certainly not any glowing successes to report. On the contrary, in almost every one of the fifteen cases described there were subsequent delinquencies, some more serious than others. The "ugly" delinquents seemed particularly impervious to any deterrent effects from their confrontations with the inmates and the prison environment at Rahway.

Given the past findings of others, my expectations were that self-reported offenses would exceed officially recorded offenses over the same period and that more juveniles in both the experimental and control groups would report being delinquent than had been disclosed in the juvenile court records. Let us look first at the court records of the fifteen juveniles who reported the delinquencies just presented.

- Of the five young people from Ridgefield Park High School, only one had any record of a subsequent offense. The one sixteen-year-old girl was charged with incorrigibility, a noncriminal or status offense. Because this occurred more than six months after her prison visit, it was not included in our outcome data reported earlier. Officially, these five juveniles were all successes. However, unofficially at least three of them could be considered serious delinquents based upon their own reports.

- Of the three Passaic boys—two age fifteen and one age thirteen —only the youngest reported any serious criminal behavior, and he was the only one who had a court record. This boy's record showed three JINS (incorrigibility) offenses, but no criminal offenses during the six-month follow-up period. The juvenile justice system seemed to have the right boy in this case, but for the wrong things. The self-reported and officially recorded behavior seem pretty consistent in these three cases.

- The seven boys from the Trenton area all reported a string of minor and serious offenses during their postvisit period. All of them also had official records during the six-month follow-up, although the number of official offenses was far less than the number of self-reported offenses. Two boys recorded one arrest each; four boys had two arrests each; and one boy was arrested three times in the following six months.

Seventeen juveniles in the control group were similarly questioned about their delinquent behavior during the preceding six months (the same follow-up with the experimentals and with the official records check).

The results both confirmed my expectations and also substantiated previous findings from self-report surveys. With only one exception (a boy in the control group who had a known arrest for possession of stolen property but did not report anything more) all the juveniles reported engaging in more misconduct and actual lawbreaking than was officially known. Offenses in the control group ranged from skipping school, to drinking and smoking marijuana, to petty larceny. Only three of the thirty-two juveniles interviewed—including the boy mentioned above—denied any misconduct. Thus, just over 90 percent admitted to being at least minor delinquents. Many more juveniles in both groups reported delinquent behavior than had records for such behavior. This rate of hidden delinquency is high, as other surveys have found, but similarly it involves minor offenses more than serious ones.

Our original intent was to interview all eighty-one juveniles in the sample; however, money and time ran out. Because only partial samples could be interviewed, experimental/control group comparisons would not be valid. However, these results leave the impression that the experimentals were more seriously delinquent than the controls. This impression fits with the previous conclusions.

Notes

1 See, for example, the work of: Robert Martinson, "What Works?—Questions and Answers About Prison Reform," *The Public Interest* (1974): 22–50; David F. Greenberg, "The Correctional Effects of Corrections: A Survey of Evaluations," in *Corrections and Punishment* (California: Sage Publications, 1977); and Michael C. Dixon and William E. Wright, *Juvenile Delinquency Prevention Programs: Report on the Findings of an Evaluation of the Literature* (National Science Foundation, October, 1974).

2 Don M. Gottfredson, "Assessment and Prediction Methods in Crime and Delinquency," President's Commission on Law Enforcement and Administration of Justice, *Task Force Report: Juvenile Delinquency and Youth Crime* (Washington, DC: U.S. Government Printing Office, 1967), p. 181.

3 Stephen E. Schlesinger, "The Prediction of Dangerousness in Juveniles," *Crime and Delinquency* (January 1978): 40–48.

4 Ibid., p. 48.

5 Sheldon and Eleanor Glueck, *Unraveling Juvenile Delinquency* (Cambridge, MA: Harvard University Press, 1951).

6 Sheldon and Eleanor Glueck (eds.), *Identification of Predelinquents* (New York: Intercontinental Medical Book Corporation, 1972), p. 4.

7 Gottfredson, *Juvenile Delinquency and Youth Crime*, p. 178.

8 Maude M. Craig and Selma J. Glick, "Ten Years Experience with the Glueck Social Prediction Table," *Crime and Delinquency*, 9 (July 1963): 249–61.

9 Samuel A. Kramer, "Identifying Juvenile Delinquents Among Negroes," in *Identification of Predelinquents*, Sheldon and Eleanor Glueck (eds.). (New York: Intercontinental Medical Book Corporation, 1972), pp. 22–35.

10 Ibid., p. 25.

11 Kramer reported a test-retest correlation of .92 on his modified Glueck items. This result indicated a high degree of reliability.

12 Kramer, *Identification of Predelinquents*, p. 26.

13 Ibid., p. 28.

14 Herman Elmering, "Retrospective Validations of Glueck Table to Identify Delinquents in Various Countries," in *Identification of Predelinquents*, Sheldon and Eleanor Glueck (eds.). (New York: Intercontinental Medical Book Corporation, 1972), p. 15.

15 See for example the work of: Austin Porterfield, "Delinquency and Its Outcome in Court and College," *American Journal of Sociology*, 49 (1943): 199–208; Martin Gold, "Undetected Delinquent Behavior," *Journal of Research in Crime and Delinquency* 3 (1966): 27–46; Martin Gold and David Reimer, "Changing Patterns of Delinquent Behavior Among Americans 13–16 years old: 1967–1972," *Crime and Delinquency Literature* 7 (1975): 453–517; and James Short and F. L. Nye, "Extent of Unrecorded Juvenile Delinquency: Tentative Conclusions," *Journal of Criminal Law, Criminology and Police Science*, 49 (1958): 296–302.

16 See Appendix B for interview schedule.

chapter six

Changing Attitudes

As indicated earlier, one of the goals of my research was to look also at the psychological reactions of kids participating in the Juvenile Awareness Project. In order to do this, we decided to try to measure any attitude changes that occurred as a result of visiting the prison and confronting the Lifers. We made no attempt to look at the effects of any follow-up treatment which the juveniles might have received from their referring agencies. Such follow-up was either minimal or nonexistent in the history of the project. Where it did occur, we assumed it was similar for both experimentals and controls. Our assumption was based upon the fact that with a couple of exceptions, the kids came from the same agencies and would thus be treated equally.

We did not assume that changes in attitudes are necessary and sufficient conditions for changes in behavior. However, we did assume that attitude changes might be an important intervening link to behavior changes. In other words, you don't have to have changes in attitudes in order to have changes in behavior, but frequently the two do go hand in hand. We further assumed that the absence of any attitude changes would diminish the likelihood of finding changes in behavior.

Findings from this phase of the study of the project need to be understood from two perspectives. The first concerns the importance of measuring attitude change as a means of determining whether or not the project "works." There were those who loudly concluded, and perhaps some who would still conclude, that the project was not about trying to change attitudes, but rather was about trying to prevent or deter delinquent behavior. Therefore, this thinking goes, measuring attitude change is nothing more than an academic exercise that bears little relationship to the real world. After all, they say, isn't behavior what it is all about? Isn't that what is really important? The answer to these questions is that behavior is indeed important, but there must be some way of getting from here to there. Behavior is the "proof of the pudding," so to speak. But, behavior is often a function of attitudes and of the immediate situations in which an individual finds himself or herself at different times. Attitudes affect behavior, as well as perception, learning, etc. Since people who work with juvenile delinquents are generally not in a position to alter the environments in which delinquents or potential delinquents live, they usually concentrate upon the attitude part of the equation in attempting to prevent juvenile delinquency. We usually try to change behavior by changing delinquent attitudes. This is in fact the approach that was being followed by the Lifers' project. Therefore, evaluating its effectiveness seemed to us not only appropriate, but necessary.

The conceptual foundation for JAP rests in deterrence theory, whether or not this was intended. I previously indicated that research on deterrence points to the importance of the perceptual properties of punishments and other sanctions. The argument is that potential offenders are deterred by what they perceive to be the certainty, swiftness, and severity of punishment, whether or not that perception is accurate. The goal of the Lifers' project, which was to heighten the awareness or perception of the attending juveniles, is linked to that idea.

One can see, therefore, a complex series of interrelationships among attitudes, perceptions, deterrence, and behavior. Attitudes can influence behavior; attitudes can influence perceptions; perceptions can influence deterrence; deterrence can influence behavior, and so on. I therefore considered it critically important that we measure attitude change as an initial catalyst in this entire process.

Operating on this premise, the second perspective on the evaluation findings needed to focus on the question of whether or not the Juvenile Awareness Project in fact changes attitudes. This perspective will constitute the heart of the discussion in the remainder of this chapter.

The preceding thoughts on attitudes and behavior were commented upon by a reviewer for one of the criminal justice journals. This reviewer said: "He [meaning me] . . . argues, but not too effectively, that the mechanism of change is through alteration of attitudes. Indeed . . . we find a long (and erroneous) harangue on why attitude change is necessary prior to behavior change." The reviewer referred me to the literature on operant conditioning in psychology as "an antidote to [my] overstated position."

I hope that the preceding discourse clears up any confusion or misinterpretation of my intent. I did not and do not now claim that attitude change is necessary prior to behavior change, but rather that it may simply be an intervening link. That changes in behavior can occur without changes in attitudes is neither denied nor ruled out. Behavior modification is a prime example of that. Also, the so-called harangue was merely an attempt on my part to illustrate the complexity of the connections among attitudes, perceptions, deterrence, and behavior. I hope this position is not seen as overstated.

Group Comparisons

We were unable to adhere strictly to our intended experimental design with pure random assignment as I have already indicated. As a result, I considered it necessary to look at the similarity of the experimental and control groups. Such comparisons are generally recommended, even in cases where random assignment has been successfully accomplished. One way of looking at comparability is to test for statistically significant differences between the groups being studied on any relevant background factors. The two groups were compared on such factors as sex, race, age, and time lapse between pre- and posttesting. The purpose here was to make sure that there were no big differences between the groups which would have an effect similar to comparing apples with oranges.[1]

In the experimental group, there were thirty-eight boys and eight girls; in the control group, twenty-seven boys and eight girls. There were twenty-seven African Americans, seventeen whites, one Hispanic, and one other in the experimental group; there were fifteen African Americans, sixteen whites, two Hispanics, and two others in the control group. The average age of the experimental group was 15.4 years, ranging from twelve years old to eighteen years old. The average age of the control group was 14.6 years, ranging from eleven to eighteen years old.

Pretesting of the kids began in February, 1978, and was completed in October, 1978. Posttesting began in May and was not completed until November, 1978. The time lapse between the before and after testing ranged from one day for some juveniles to almost nine months for others. The reasons for this wide variation can be traced to some of the problems, administrative and others, already mentioned. Sponsoring agencies that had regularly scheduled tour days could visit the prison, and their subjects could be tested fairly quickly. Other agencies, on the other hand, were put on a two-month waiting list by the Lifers before they could visit. This resulted in different time gaps between pre- and posttesting. The longest lapses were for the two previously mentioned agencies that did not take their young people to the prison as scheduled.

For example, the nine-month gap was the result of one agency sponsor who was twice placed on the Lifers' two-month waiting list. He failed both times to transport his charges to Rahway on the scheduled day. After I decided, with his agreement, that his kids should be used as controls, we were still unable to arrange a posttesting visit for several more months. It wasn't that he was hostile or uncooperative, he simply couldn't seem to get his kids organized for this purpose. In other cases, the gaps resulted from delays in trying to catch up with the juveniles to posttest them. Some were school kids who were first tested in the spring. Because of the school summer recess, which intervened, we were not able to test them again until the fall.

Because of this variation, I decided that time lapse should be treated as an independent factor possibly affecting outcomes. This meant that this factor would be analyzed to see if were any decaying effects upon whatever attitude changes occurred. In order to do this, I broke down time lapse into three categories: less than one week, one to ten weeks, and eleven weeks or more. Most of the experimental group (54.3 percent) had a time lapse of one to ten weeks; but most of the control group (48.6 percent) had a time lapse of less than one week.

The Tests Used

Three different types of tests or scales were used to measure attitude changes. The first of these is something called the Attitude Toward Punishment of Criminals. This thirty-four-item scale was originally developed by two researchers named Wang and Thurstone in 1931. The statements making up the scale are focused upon the purpose and appropriate use of punishment and upon whether or not to punish criminals at all. These purposes were deemed suitable to evaluate a program whose ostensible intent is to heighten awareness of punishment, as exemplified by a maximum security prison. In addition, there were other arguments in favor of using this particular instrument. First, of particular importance to researchers, the scale was deemed to be satisfactory with regard to both reliability and validity.[2] Second, the scale has a simplified children's or high-school form which makes it appropriate for lower reading levels (but in fact, this simplified form was too difficult for some juveniles in the sample, and each item had to be read to them individually). Finally, the Attitude Toward Punishment of Criminals scale was used by Brodsky in his study of the Prison Profiles program at the Illinois State Penitentiary;[3] thus, there would be a basis for comparing results.

The second set of measures is called Semantic Differential (SD) scales. "The semantic differential is a method of observing and measuring the psychological meaning of things, usually concepts."[4] It was invented by psychologist Charles Osgood.[5] The actual SD is made up of a number of scales, each consisting of a bipolar or opposite adjective pair such as fast-slow, sharp-dull, large-small, etc. These pairs of adjectives are used together with certain concepts that are considered to be relevant to what is to be measured, in this case attitudes about crime and punishment. Among the more than five-hundred concepts identified by Osgood and his colleagues are the following: crime, justice, law, policeman, prison, punishment, and I (myself). Given the content of the Lifers' sessions with the juveniles, which contain discussions, or actually presentations, on crime, on law enforcement, on the criminal justice system, on what it is like to be in prison and to be punished, and on the kids themselves, these particular concepts were considered relevant and appropriate.

In choosing scales or adjective pairs, one is supposed to consider the extent to which they are evaluative, indicating suitability for use as attitude measures; their relation to the concepts being tested; and their likelihood of being understood by the kids. This latter point is particularly important for use in a self-administered measure with subjects who may not read very well. The ten pairs of bipolar adjectives selected were: good-bad, beautiful-ugly, clean-dirty, kind-cruel, pleasant-unpleasant, happy-sad, nice-awful, honest-dishonest, fair-unfair, and valuable-worthless. These pairs have all been found useful in measuring attitudes. Each set of adjectives was used with each concept. The scales themselves can be found in Appendix A.

Semantic differential scales were chosen because they are sufficiently reliable and valid for many research purposes.[6] They are also flexible and adaptable, as well as quick and economical to administer and score. The latter was an important consideration.

The final measure is the Attitude Toward Obeying the Law test. This scale comes from a study published by H. Ashley Weeks, entitled *Youthful Offenders at Highfields: An Evaluation of the Effects of the Short-Term Treatment of Delinquent Boys*. Weeks was interested in learning whether delinquents participating in a residential treatment project called Highfields changed their attitudes toward, among other things, breaking the law.[7] The ATOL was one of eight scales constructed for that purpose. It was adopted for use here because of its simplicity (it contains only four items stated in the words of the boys in Weeks' study); its results can be compared to those found by Weeks; and the nature of the items relate to the intended deterrent effect of the JAP. I considered it to be important and relevant to determine whether kids would express views more or less favorable to obeying the law after their participation in the program.

The entire test package of nine attitude measures and the Social Prediction Table (Appendix A) was pilot tested on a group of juveniles from Independence High School (an alternative school) in Newark, New Jersey. The results affirmed the feasibility and suitability of the measures with a comparable group of young people.

Did the Kids' Attitudes Change?

Each of the nine measures is presented separately, beginning with the Attitude Toward Punishment of Criminals. In each case, it is the difference score between the before and after testing that is being compared.[8] When time lapse between the pre- and posttesting was introduced as a possible source of variation, it had no significant effect on any of the outcomes.

Attitude toward Punishment of Criminals

The results from this test indicated that the juveniles in the experimental group who attended the project did not change their attitudes, at least as measured by this scale, *more* than did a comparable control group of juveniles who did not attend the project. There was a very slight but insignificant shift toward less punitive attitudes after the kids visited the Lifers' Project. This suggests that the visit stimulated some feelings of sympathy for the Lifers, who had to endure the pains of the punishment that they described to the juveniles. The mean change for the visiting group was –0.67. This compares with Stanley Brodsky's finding of changes of –0.66 for forestry camp boys and –0.29 for high school predelinquents. The results are obviously very similar. The mean change for the control group was 0.28, a very small shift toward more punitive attitudes in the posttest. The kids who didn't go to Rahway obviously didn't become sympathetic to the plight of prison inmates.

Crime

There was a significant difference between experimentals and controls in their shifts in attitude toward crime. The juveniles visiting Rahway became significantly more negative in their outlook on crime than did the comparison group. The mean change for the experimental group was –4.21. In contrast, the control group mean change was in the opposite direction, increasing 1.83. This change is clearly of the kind hoped for by the sponsors and supporters of the Juvenile Awareness Project. It indicates that the Lifers' Group did change the attitudes of these young people toward crime. The kids had a greater tendency to see crime as being bad after their visit to the prison.

Furthermore, the significant difference between the visiting and nonvisiting groups remained when time lapse was introduced as a possible source of variation. This result added to the confidence in the conclusion about the effect of the project on this attitude. The fact that time lapse did not have a significant effect is important because it suggested that this attitude change may not be subject to decay, at least over the period of time studied.

Law

There was no difference in the change between the groups on their attitude toward law. Both groups became more negative the second time they were tested. The mean change for experimental kids was –2.70; for controls it was –2.52. Law was perhaps a more esoteric and complex concept in the minds of the young people in this sample. As such, it was perhaps less likely than some of the other concepts to be subject to change through exposure to the Lifers' program. Because a negative shift occurred in both groups, it cannot be considered meaningful.

Justice

The result was no difference in the change between groups on their attitude toward justice. Both groups shifted in the negative direction, but the change was more pronounced for the controls (mean = –2.03) than for the experimentals (mean = –0.67). Justice is also a complex and multifaceted concept, probably not subject to simple manipulation. The fact that no significant changes occurred in attitudes toward law and justice is not surprising, given the nature of these concepts. They are relevant, but simply may have been beyond the scope of the project's possible effects.

I (Myself)

One of the purposes of the evaluation was to determine whether or not the JAP had any effects upon the kids' self-perceptions. The concept I (Myself) was used in the Semantic Differential scales as a way to measure any such effects. The result indicated no difference between experimentals and controls on this factor. Mean change for the experimentals was only –0.04; for controls it was 1.63. The project seems to have had no effect upon this measure of self-perception. Changing self-image, another complex notion, also may have been beyond the scope of the project.

Police Officer

There was no difference in the changes between the groups on their attitude toward the concept police officer. Although a less esoteric concept than law and justice, the ideas, which are conjured up by the term police officer, were somewhat removed from the direct influence of the Juvenile Awareness Project. Because of its symbolic meaning it was not an irrelevant concept, but the results indicated that the existing attitude was not subject to change by the Lifers.

Prison

One of the major purposes of the Juvenile Awareness Project was to influence attitudes about prison. Although there was a shift among the attending juveniles in the direction of becoming more negative about prison, this shift was not significantly different from that of nonattenders. This result was complementary to that from the Attitude Toward Punishment of Criminals scale discussed earlier. The mean change for the juveniles visiting Rahway was –1.46. For the control group it was 1.83. This change also was in the direction desired by the sponsors and supporters, but it didn't reach statistical significance. Whether or not it was socially or behaviorally important is a separate issue that was left to others to decide. Learning that prisons are bad may generate a group of prison reformers, but whether they will also be crime-free is another matter.

Punishment

Again, no significant changes appeared between the groups in their attitude toward punishment. Surprisingly, the overall change was in the direction of becoming slightly more positive toward punishment on the posttests. The mean change for the experimental group was an almost imperceptible 0.04; for the control group it was 1.20.

Attitudes toward Obeying the Law

As mentioned previously, the ATOL measure is a four-item scale employed to test directly the deterrent effects on perceptions resulting from participation in the project. Each of the scale items was scored one to four, resulting in a range of possible scores for the entire scale of from one to sixteen. Low scores indicate more favorable attitudes toward obeying the law, and high scores indicate less favorable attitudes. The attending juveniles shifted very slightly (mean change = –0.06) toward more favorable attitudes after participation in the project. The control group change was in a similar direction, but of somewhat greater magnitude (mean change = –0.43). There was, however, no significant difference between the experimental group and the control or comparison group on this measure.

When this scale was used in the *Youthful Offenders at Highfields* study, posttest results classified into those for Highfields African Americans and whites and Annandale (the reformatory) African Americans and whites indicated "a slight tendency for all but the Highfields Negroes [*sic*] to show a more favorable attitude toward obeying the law by the time the boys take their posttests, but the differences are very small. Examination of the internal shifts indicate that two-fifths or more of the boys change, and that relatively about as many boys change favorably as unfavorably."[9] Three of the four groups, Highfields whites being the exception, showed no significant change from the pretest to the posttest. The results from my administration of this test were not terribly dissimilar to these, that is, a slight tendency to be more inclined to obey the law.

The preliminary conclusions from all this were that the results were mixed. We did not, however, find any overriding reasons to reject our hypothesis that the Juvenile Awareness Project has no effect on the attitudes of the juveniles attending.

That these results could be subject to a somewhat different interpretation was apparent from a letter to the editor of the *Los Angeles Times* prepared by the KTLA-TV publicity office. It should be recalled that KTLA first telecast *Scared Straight!* and is affiliated with the filmmakers. The letter read as follows:

> The results of the Rutgers University School of Criminal Justice evaluation of the Juvenile Awareness Program show a significant change in juvenile attitudes toward crime. The evaluation measured attitude changes of an experimental group who went through the program as compared to a control group who did not. Both groups were matched for age, sex, race and potential probability of becoming juvenile delinquents.

> The experimental groups showed a significant change in their attitude that crime was not desirable. This change did not occur in the control group. The obvious conclusion is that the Rahway Juvenile Awareness Program is successful in changing the attitudes of youngsters toward crime.

Moreover, the evaluation shows the program is not affected by race or sex. The program is just as effective for whites as blacks, for females as males. Age did prove to be a variable factor: younger children were more affected by the program than older children. The age range of the children tested was 11 to 18.

None of the children suffered adverse emotional [e]ffects as a result of going through the program.

"One of the key results of the evaluation indicates sponsors should take more care in selecting high-risk, potential delinquents to go through the program," says Assistant Professor James Finckenauer, Rutgers School of Criminal Justice. There are available to any sponsor simple testing and scoring methods that give highly accurate juvenile delinquency potential measurements.

The consensus is that a carefully structured and controlled Juvenile Awareness Program where sponsors carefully screen participating children is an inexpensive, effective deterrent to juvenile delinquency.

After these findings were reported to the New Jersey Department of Corrections and our first report became generally available, some who reviewed it criticized the data analysis and the results. A second analysis was therefore undertaken using the same technique employed with the behavior outcomes (multiple regression analysis). This technique permits a researcher to analyze the relationship between a dependent variable (in this case, attitude change) and a set of independent variables (in this case delinquency probability, race, sex, age, time lapse, and experimental or control group). The characteristic making it most useful here is that it allows you to control for other confounding factors in order to look at the specific contribution of any one factor to the outcome. Among the few noteworthy results from that reanalysis was that delinquency probability, as predicted by the Glueck Table, was significantly correlated with changes in Attitudes Toward Punishment of Criminals. Experimental and control group differences in attitude toward crime were still significant, that is, didn't wash out, when the other five factors were controlled. In addition, age was significantly correlated with differences in attitude toward justice, toward prison, and toward punishment. These results did not provide any reason to alter the main conclusion about the general absence of project effects upon attitudes.

A Truncated Additional Sample

One of the original objectives of the study plan was to select and interview a random sample of approximately fifty juveniles who had participated in the project since its inception in September, 1976. Because our money was exhausted, these planned interviews had to be scrapped. However, I decided that at the least a records check of a random sample of previous attenders would provide informative before-and-after data on the effect of the Lifers' intervention. Since the original sample was smaller than expected (eighty-one out of one hundred), and since checking court records is not terribly time nor resource consuming, I decided to increase the size of the projected random sample from fifty to one hundred twenty.

This sample for before/after analysis of a new group of juveniles was obtained from the prison's roster of all juveniles who had attended the Juvenile Awareness Project. A random sample of sixty juveniles who attended the project during the first six months of 1977, and another sixty who attended during the first six months of 1979 was chosen. The 1977 sample was planned to represent the first six months of daily operation of the project and would allow for a follow-up period of up to three years since their attendance. The 1979 sample would follow the considerable publicity which the project had received, the *Scared Straight!* documentary, and two evaluation reports, including my own, which was completed the previous December. There would be a six-month to one-year follow-up period for these latter juveniles. The one hundred twenty juveniles came from seventeen of the twenty-one counties in New Jersey.

However, a funny thing happened on the way to data collection! In November, 1979, I sent a letter to the juvenile court judges in the seventeen counties requesting access to any juvenile court records that existed on the sampled juveniles from their respective jurisdictions. I enclosed a copy of the permission letter which I had received from the New Jersey Administrative Office of the Courts in March, 1978. I did this in the belief that this sample was already included in the previously approved study plan since it was part of the original proposal as approved. However, on December 7, 1979, I received a letter from the AOC saying in part:

> My concern is that the one hundred twenty juveniles whose juvenile records you now wish to access represent a new and additional sample. If this is so, then you would need Supreme Court approval to access the records of this new sample.
>
> I would very much appreciate your advising me by letter as to whether or not my analysis of this situation is correct. Meanwhile, by copy of this letter I am recommending to the presiding judges that they hold off assisting your efforts until this matter is resolved.

Needless to say, I was not pleased with this new development. However, recognizing that you cannot successfully fight city hall, I engaged in a series of communiques—letters and telephone calls—with the AOC over the next six months. Finally, on May 13, 1980, I received the following letter from them:

> In recent letters to the AOC you requested permission to access certain juvenile court records with respect to your study of the Juvenile Awareness Project Help Program. Please be advised that the Administrative Director has determined that the potential benefits of your further research at this time do not justify further access to juvenile court records. We appreciate your recent efforts on this issue and anticipate continued mutual cooperation in the future.

I appealed this decision to the administrative director, but without success. *C'est la vie!*

Before the December 7 shutdown occurred, the judges in four counties had individually approved my access to their court records. I was thus able to check out thirty-four of the one hundred twenty juveniles in the random sample. These thirty-four juveniles did provide some interesting findings. First, 71 percent of them had no records of delinquency prior to attending the Lifers' project. This rate of nondelinquency is even higher than that for the earlier sample. Their success rate (79 percent) was also higher than that of the control group. This figure has both a plus and a minus feature. The plus is that some of the thirty-four had a follow-up (exposure to risk) period of approximately two and one-half years. The minus is that most of them were not delinquent at the outset. Once again it is a situation in which nondelinquents remained nondelinquent.

Only twelve of these young people had any records, either before or after their visit. The offenses for these twelve are broken down by when they occurred as follows:

Before and After	5
Before Only	5
After Only	2

The recidivism rate (repeat offenders) was 50 percent. The failure rate (all subsequent offenders) among the delinquents was 58 percent. Neither of these is at all impressive, but the numbers are obviously very small.

Finally, in yet one more way to assess recidivism, I used what has been called suppression effect.[10] This simply means that if a treatment or other intervention is effective, delinquent behavior may not vanish, but it will occur to a lesser degree than was the case before intervention.

In a rough approximation of this notion, I looked at the delinquency seriousness scores, both before and after, for the twelve juveniles in this sample who had records. The mean seriousness score for prior offenses was 5.7, for subsequent offenses 2.8, an average difference (decline) of 2.9. Admittedly the exposure-to-risk period in which offenses could have been committed was shorter after the visit than it was before. Despite this, the suppression effect from before to after is not significant ($t = 1.035$; $df = 11$). The conclusion is that the Juvenile Awareness Project did not seem to have had any notable effect upon these juveniles.

This truncated sample partially confirms the earlier results. It was an unfortunate blow to the search for knowledge about youth aversion programs that the New Jersey Administrative Office of the Courts determined that there were no "potential benefits" from "further research." Utilization of the suppression effect criterion with a considerably larger sample could have been extremely productive and informative.

Conclusions

As a result of these research findings, particularly the earlier ones, a number of observations have been made about the Juvenile Awareness Project. It seems to me that the success rate from the project fell considerably short of the phenomenal 80–90 percent rate originally touted by its supporters and stressed in the *Scared Straight!* documentary. After the release of my findings, the Lifers' Group and others vigorously attacked the study. Among other things, the Lifers said that they had never claimed any particular success rate for their project. They said that any figures were collected and reported by others—presumably Judge George Nicola. However, I uncovered a letter to the "Helen help us!" column in the *Newark Star-Ledger* for August 28, 1978. This was before the release of either of my reports and before *Scared Straight!* The letter from the then secretary of the Lifers' Group said in part: "The Lifers' Group has been in existence since 1975. Our Juvenile Awareness Project was started in 1976. During this period, some eight thousand young people have participated—and we have been able to reduce their recidivism rate from 86.2 percent to 10.2 percent."

With a little arithmetic, the flipside of a 10.2 percent recidivism rate is an 89.8 percent success rate. It would seem that at least some Lifers did make the questionable claim. The Lifers and others backed off from these figures following the initial release of my results. However, they replaced them at various times with new claims: 59 percent success in the visiting group cannot be considered a failure; and further, if even one young person is helped, that is sufficient reason to justify the project.

My response to these was to reiterate the substantially better performance, in all respects, of the nonattending control group, and the fact that a large number of the juveniles were already nondelinquents and thus already "successes." As to the helping only one young person rationale, one can decide for oneself whether it would all be worth it, and whether there would have been all the hoopla and panacea phenomenon effect if that had in fact been the case and was stated as such. I personally think not!

Zealous project supporters and "media hype" specialists seemed to fail to take account of the complex nature of juvenile delinquency and of the overwhelming absence of success with most previous prevention and treatment efforts. Consequently, they raised unrealistic expectations and goals for the project by selling it as a cheap, easy, simple and effective cure-all.

I also observed that the nature of the Lifers' project was atypical when compared to other prevention and treatment programs. It was strictly a "one shot" effort for the most part, and did not engage its clients over any period of time. This characteristic both militated against its success and made comparisons to other programs somewhat untenable.

The controversial *possibility* also exists that the project actually set in motion a "delinquency fulfilling prophecy" in which it increased rather than decreased the chances of juvenile delinquency. This possibility cannot be dismissed in light of the finding (substantiated by the subsequent reanalysis of the data) that experimental group juveniles, including the nondelinquents, did much worse than the control group juveniles in their follow-up behavior. There are several possible ways in which this could have occurred—and these needed to be examined by further research on this project and others patterned after it. The project may have romanticized the Lifers—and by extension other prison inmates—in young, impressionable minds. Or, the belittling, demeaning, intimidating, and scaring of particular youths may have been seen as a challenge—a challenge to go out and prove to themselves, their peers, and others, that they were not scared.

In sum, my research strongly suggested that the Lifers' project was not scaring kids straight. If nothing else, the findings challenged, and in my judgment, debunked any thoughts that this approach could be a panacea.

Notes

[1] The results of the significance tests were as follows: sex ($x^2 = .11$; $p = .74$); race ($x^2 = .32$; $p = .57$); age ($x = .42$; $p < .50$); and time lapse ($x^2 = 6.75$; $p = .03$).

[2] Marvin E. Shaw and Jack M. Wright (eds.), *Scales for the Measurement of Attitudes* (New York: McGraw-Hill, 1967), p. 163.

[3] Stanley L. Brodsky, "The Prisoner as Agent of Attitude Change: A Study of Prison Profiles' Effects," *The British Journal of Criminology*, 10 (July 1970): 280–85.

[4] Fred N. Kerlinger, *Foundations of Behavioral Research* (New York: Holt, Rinehart and Winston, 1965), p. 564.

[5] C. Osgood, G. Suci, and P. Tannenbaum, *The Measurement of Meaning* (Urbana: University of Illinois Press, 1957).

[6] Ibid., pp. 140–53, 192, 193.

[7] H. Ashley Weeks, *Youthful Offenders at Highfields* (Ann Arbor: The University of Michigan Press, 1963), pp. 80–81.

[8] The results of the analysis of variance for difference between means on the pre- and posttests were as follows: ATPC ($f = .068$; $p = .795$); Crime ($f = 5.806$; $p = .018$); Law ($f = .004$; $p = .95$); Justice ($f = .157$; $p = .693$); I (Myself) ($f = .233$; $p = .63$); Police Officer ($f = .162$; $p = .688$); Prison ($f = 1.421$; $p = .237$); Punishment ($f = .212$; $p = .646$); ATOL ($f = .383$; $p = .538$).

[9] Weeks, *Youthful Offenders at Highfields*, p. 81.

[10] Charles A. Murray and Louis A. Cox, Jr., *Beyond Probation: Juvenile Corrections and the Chronic Delinquent* (Beverly Hills: Sage Publications, 1979).

chapter seven

Scared Straight and with a Twist

The preceding discussion raises a number of questions. What has happened to Scared Straight? Has it survived? What about the Scared Straight idea? Has its worth been demonstrated? If Scared Straight-type programs have continued and perhaps even flourished, without demonstrable proof of their value, what accounts for that? Does this experience give credence to the idea that there are certain mythical beliefs about how to combat delinquency? To address these questions, we looked at the current JAP and other programs, both direct spin-offs of the original and some that embody the general idea, but with a twist. We have examined available studies and evaluations, talked to knowledgeable people, and looked at media coverage as well. Our purpose has been to understand the current state of Scared Straight and the nature of the environment in which it seems to endure.

It might be assumed in the wake of the original negative results and controversy that this idea would have fallen by the wayside. Some conclusions tend to support this, implying that prisons have abandoned confrontational programs, that they have "gotten out of the business of trying to scare kids straight."[1] That is not, however, exactly what has happened. Some programs did die, but others re-invented themselves or simply continued, and some were newly born. Those that didn't die or change persist in employing the Scared Straight method despite, or in ignorance of, the evidence. Even though it has become more muted, the debate about what are or are not scare tactics and whether they work persists as well.

Many may have forgotten that the catchy title *Scared Straight!* was not the Rahway Lifers' name for their program. It was the title of the award-winning television documentary. *Scared Straight!* was thus literally a product of Hollywood and, by extension, of the media in general. Today when there is media attention it is generally supportive. Their focus on limited positive results and individual cases gives the impression that this approach works. In addition, the media have also become an outlet for marketing the Scared Straight idea through music and videos. The message to "go straight or else" comes in a medium for every audience. How much of that message *feeds off* the underlying belief and how much it *feeds* that belief are unknowns.

The Lifers' Juvenile Awareness Project

We begin this update on Scared Straight by looking at the Juvenile Awareness Project (JAP) as it exists. An example of recent media attention is an article (*New York Times*, May 16, 1996) that told of a small group of youths, aged twelve to eighteen, visiting the East Jersey (formerly Rahway) State Prison Juvenile Awareness Program for the day. The youths are described as being both offenders and potential offenders. The newspaper report gives us a snapshot perspective on Scared Straight—the archetype—as it enters its third decade.

The article describes JAP as being at its height in popularity, hosting approximately ten groups a week. This means that over 12,500 youths may visit the Lifers in a year. Space and times are now so limited that advance reservations are required. The methods used by the Lifers, at least as they are outlined in the article, appear to be the same "in your face, here's my story, brutal yet honest" approach to getting kids on the right track. The program is said to be now geared toward more hardened or troubled youths who are believed to respond best. How good is that response? The article reports a success rate of 51 percent! The bases for this precise indicator are not stated.

The *Times'* report concludes that some of the youths visiting that day had undergone a change in attitude. The reporter believed the youths were just putting on their "tough guy imitation" when they said the experience was little more than a show. Why she believed this she does not say. That belief is clearly evident, and so is the media's bolstering of support for the program.

Our discussions with the prison's official liaison to the Lifers' Group brings a more sober perspective. He observed that the kids seen by the Lifers are becoming increasingly hard to reach. The youths are unimpressed with the stories and tales they are told. Many, he said, are "wannabes" who actually look up to the Lifers because on the street a prison sentence is worn like a badge of honor.[2] This is an example of some of the limitations of seeking deterrence through vicarious experience, especially in an environment in which the benefits of crime are seen to outweigh the costs.

According to the *New York Times* article, the Lifers say they now give youth "information and statistics" rather than "prison hell stories."[3] Ironically, however, the same article described a scenario in which photos depicting horrific images of prison hangings and stabbings were distributed to the youth. A Lifer gave a graphic description of prison rapes. After seeing the photos and stories, the youths were said to be impressed.[4] Prison hell stories thus still seem to be a major aspect of the program. There could be several explanations for this. One is the gut-level belief in the value of aversion and deterrence in influencing behavior; another is the simple fact that the Lifers have few other options that they can employ to try to prevent delinquency.

Just as they argued twenty years ago, the Lifers still say their main hook rests "in using ourselves as poor examples, we are explaining and showing that a life of crime really leads to nowhere." They believe that because they have experienced both crime and the results of crime, youths may be more inclined to heed their advice. Their voice is the voice of experience. The voices of others, such as parents or friends, may be ignored. The Lifers think that youths can relate to inmates' stories and thus draw lessons from those best situated to teach those lessons.[5] This is a clear illustration of the belief in deterrence through vicarious experience.

The current program is still geared toward three classifications of attendees—the good, the bad, and the ugly. These classifications refer to youths with no criminal history, ranging up to those having extensive juvenile records. The talk sessions are supposedly geared to the particular participants present. The Lifers request information from those sponsoring the youths who are to attend in order to decide about the nature of the individual sessions. The Juvenile Awareness Project in its original Scared Straight form (emphasis upon scaring) was and is said to be best directed toward the ugly. But with all groups, the Lifers try to dispel any preconceived notions about prison, crime, and their ramifications and to replace such notions with realities. They view it as combining education and real-life experience.

Effectiveness is said to be assessed in a variety of ways—but mostly by corresponding with youths who attend the sessions and later inform the Lifers of their success.[6] However, as for any actual follow-up data on the attendees, the same old problem exists: the Lifers indicate that the juveniles attending the programs are very difficult to track because of the special manner in which juvenile records are maintained and sealed. It appears that there is considerable reliance upon word of mouth with respect to how juvenile participants fare after their visit. Combined with the fact that the "good" kids, that is, those with no prior criminal history, make up some portion of the so-called successes, it is really impossible to know the accuracy of the success rate across the board.

The Lifers run two programs concurrent with the original Juvenile Awareness Project: a Parental Awareness Program and an Outreach Program. The first is directed toward parents and "concerned adult citizens" and serves as a forum in which the nature and content of the JAP is discussed. The Lifers use these sessions to get feedback regarding their efforts.

The outreach program is designed to acquaint youths attending the Juvenile Awareness Project with services and general help in a variety of areas, ranging from drugs to emotional problems. The Lifers act as a referral source and are currently seeking permission to operate a twenty-four-hour hotline to serve that same purpose. Additional outreach activities include college and high school forums developed to educate students about the critical difference between theories of crime and criminality, and the reality of prison.

Materials describing the JAP do not explicitly deal with the manner in which youths are addressed during the prison encounters. As we know, a harsh, confrontational manner had been the norm. An indication that this approach is still predominant is a statement in the parental consent form in which parents and guardians are warned of the generally harsh manner in which the Lifers deliver their messages of prison violence, homosexuality, and despair. The same form assures parents that, while harsh, "the effectiveness of the program has shown positive results."[7]

In his book, *Lifers: Learn the Truth at the Expense of Our Sorrow*, Richard Wormser offers a very sympathetic account of the experiences of the Lifers with respect to the Juvenile Awareness Project. His message is directed mainly to youthful offenders and at-risk youth. Here the Lifers respond to the old criticism that the original intent of the JAP was to change young people "only with extreme scare tactics." They deny that their program was built on such tactics alone and claim that "the heart of the program was in fact one-on-one counseling that often continued by mail or telephone over an extended period of time."[8] This "aversive reaction" to aversion has, for the most part, become the norm wherever Scared Straight continues.

The Twists on Scared Straight

Scared Straight programs along the lines of the original are found in Georgia, South Carolina, Wisconsin, New York, Virginia, Alaska, Ohio, and Michigan. But today we do not have only the traditional model. The Scared Straight idea appears in many shapes and sizes in the 1990s. For example, the Los Angeles Police Department runs what they call the Juvenile Impact Program. Along with parenting sessions and counseling, there is a feature modeled after the original Scared Straight in which youthful offenders and would-be offenders visit the abandoned Los Angeles City Prison where former inmates "yell and scream" and paint a harsh picture of prison life. That picture includes sexual misconduct and deprivation.

The Louisiana State Penitentiary has prison tours for youths in which they meet prison inmates who tell them personal stories. The youths also view skits depicting prison life and participate in a question-and-answer session. Approximately one hundred youths a month visit the prison, and the program is booked six months in advance. Although the effectiveness of the program has not been assessed, there have been numerous supportive articles in the local newspaper, and a bill was introduced in the Louisiana Senate providing for all public high school students to visit a prison before graduation.

In Massachusetts, there is the Prison Voices Program for middle and high school students at the Bay State Correctional Center. The inmates there stress that they are not a Scared Straight program. They discuss with participating youths the behaviors that led them to prison, the choices they made, and how things may have been different if their choices had been different. Besides this program, Massachusetts also has Project Youth at its Norfolk State Prison.

Indications of the attractiveness and staying power of the Scared Straight idea are especially apparent in the way it has metamorphosed into multiple varieties. There are the inmates from the Cybulski Correctional Institution in Connecticut who have gone on the road with a play called "G-Money's World," in which they tell their stories and give audiences a view of prison life.[9] Authorities in Los Angeles bring youths to the city morgue to see the results of violence in an attempt to curb gang homicides.[10] Something called *The Inmate Talk Show*, in which prison inmates discuss prison life and the consequences of crime, has been proposed for local television cable channels in the Fort Worth, Texas, area.[11] HBO has what has been depicted as a Scared Straight series in which prison issues are addressed in a realistic manner.[12] Entering the world of cyberspace, there is a web site on the World Wide Web featuring lifers seeking penpals "on the wrong side of life and self-destruction, to help talk some sense into you and put it to you in a way where you can truly understand."[13] There are also Scared Straight videos, such as *Multiple Choice* and *Beyond Fear*, that attempt to deter youths with candid talk and footage of prison scenes.[14]

Further afield, but in the same genre, are programs that operate on the premise of Scared Straight. A school in Raleigh, North Carolina, offers a sex education curriculum that includes photos depicting the effects of sexually transmitted diseases.[15] *48 Hours* featured "Scared Sober, Part One" depicting a program in Pennsylvania which has youths attend a mock funeral to illustrate the effects of drinking and driving.[16] The Young Traffic Offenders Program in Kansas City, Missouri, requires day-long tours of hospitals, to reflect the perspective of a traffic accident victim in order to scare young drivers with the "grim and grisly" consequences of unsafe driving.[17] In Texas, delinquent youths are taken to the autopsies of violent crime victims in hopes that horrible real-life images will scare the youths out of crime.[18]

The underlying principle for all these efforts is the same: If young people are made aware of the terrible consequences of their actions, they will stop engaging in those actions. The logical extension of that principle is, of course, that the more horribly those consequences can be portrayed, the more likely that the youths will be deterred. This is seemingly the core belief stimulating all these efforts. It is obviously a belief with staying power, since each of these programs began or continued despite research evidence that simple deterrence delivered in the Scared Straight format does not work.

One of the more unusual examples of the staying power of Scared Straight is found in a 1994 report by the U.S. Office of Juvenile Justice and Delinquency Prevention. It is unusual because one expects special care—a detailed evaluation of the program—in choosing programs to be showcased at the national level. The report is entitled "What Works: Promising Interventions in Juvenile Justice" and is based upon nominations from practitioners for "programs that work." Nominated programs were screened to determine if they met the success criteria, and ostensibly those that did were then highlighted in the report.

An Ohio program called Convicts Against Prison Sentences (CAPS) is one of these highlighted programs. CAPS was started in 1985 as an attempt to keep juvenile delinquents from continuing their life of bad choices. The program is said to be fundamentally different from Scared Straight in that it does not use scare tactics in the inmate presentations.

The CAPS program literature recognizes that although various factors may contribute to delinquency, there is a cognitive element that affects behavior. CAPS tries to influence this process by providing the attending youth with stories and a short-lived experience of life on the inside. Juveniles participate in CAPS as a court-ordered condition of probation. Failure to attend may result in a warrant for the juvenile's arrest.

Inclusion in the OJJDP report is said to be premised upon critical program components, including evaluation results. This critical factor seems, however, to have been missing in the case of the CAPS program. No external evaluation of CAPS has been conducted. We were told that juvenile arrest records are tracked for those who have participated in the program, and that in 1991 a local newspaper publicized the program's success rate as being 80 percent for felons and 79 percent for misdemeanor offenders.[19] Surveys of attitudinal and behavioral changes have also been administered, but their current whereabouts are not known.[20] Despite this rather tenuous state of hard information, the success of CAPS in deterring juvenile offenders and helping them to make informed decisions has been hailed and promoted by no less than the national body on juvenile justice matters.

Praising the success of programs without the support of hard data seems to happen over and over again. Before considering why that is, let us examine the hard data that are available to proponents of the Scared Straight idea.

The Effects of Science on Scared Straight

Some concluded Scared Straight was a discredited idea—a conclusion we now know was premature. The spotlight moved off Scared Straight in the mid-1980s, as attention shifted elsewhere. Ironically, that shift may have actually contributed to the survival of programs of this type. It may also, however, have led to the absence of subsequent evaluations. While it might seem that any ongoing programs for juveniles would be subject to continuing evaluation, particularly under these circumstances of controversy and questionable effectiveness, the facts indicate otherwise. Further studies have been conducted only very sporadically, with most occurring shortly after the eruption of the original Scared Straight outcry. What follows is a brief look at what research is available.

We want to make clear at the outset that one problem in interpreting results is that there is no common agreement on what "effectiveness" means. Exactly what are the Scared Straight-type programs trying to achieve? Recidivism—do the attendees offend or re-offend—would seem to be the most obvious and significant indicator. In many cases however, recidivism data are unavailable, incomplete, or poorly reported. We are left, therefore, with alternative measures, some better than others. These include effectiveness in changing young people's attitudes about delinquency. There is a widely used but vague indicator called "education," generally defined as "learning the reality of prison life." Then there is the latent goal (latent because it makes no sense as the manifest goal of a delinquency prevention program) of any positive effects upon the participating prison inmates themselves.

The problems with tracking subsequent offending, and these are not unique to programs of this kind, often result in turning to criteria that are more achievable or more measurable or both. The threshold of success (What is the level for concluding something works?) is obviously made ambiguous when only anecdotal information is used, or when emotional arguments about the worth of saving even one child from a life in prison are put forth.

Methodological problems are very apparent in the program evaluations as well. Besides poor outcome indicators, the most common problems are absence of experimental research designs using random assignment, and inadequate follow-up periods. The absence of controls has been a stumbling block for many program evaluations. The lack of follow-up is usually a function of weak design and lack of time and money.

Most of the evaluation studies described below are published studies. Internal (unpublished) evaluations, when they exist at all, are not readily available. The latter could be attributed to the poor quality of the research or to their poor results, either of which might discourage their dissemination.

A Look at Other Programs

The SQUIRES Program

The San Quentin Utilization of Inmate Resources, Experience and Studies Program (SQUIRES), which originated in San Quentin prison in California, has been in operation since 1963. In fact, the inmate members of the SQUIRES Program state that their basic concept served as the foundation for the Lifers' Juvenile Awareness Program. Today, however, they are quick to separate themselves from Scared Straight. Their motto, "We Don't Scare Straight, We Communicate," reflects this desire not to be so classified. The inmates claim that the distinguishing factor is their success in delivering counseling to youthful offenders on matters such as drug use, AIDS, family relations, education, and violence, through open communication between inmates and youths—and *not* by the use of intimidation.

Youthful offenders are referred to the program by some fifty-eight agencies. These agencies include any that are responsible for youthful offenders or those youths at risk of becoming offenders. The sessions are conducted twice a month, with an ideal attendance of fifty youths at each session; but because of recent surges in referrals, the program has been running sessions with as many as seventy youths. A session consists of a tour, a rap session, and personal discussions with prisoners. According to their program description, "During the course of the tour, various members of SQUIRES will offer graphic descriptions of life and existence at San Quentin."[21]

The SQUIRES Program last underwent an in-depth evaluation in 1983, that because of the hoopla surrounding Scared Straight received considerable attention.[22] The Lewis study used a randomized experiment, with fifty-three experimental youth and fifty-five controls. Arrest was used as the measure of recidivism. A twelve-month follow-up showed no statistically significant differences in arrests between the two groups. A slightly longer time to arrest was noted for the experimental group, but Lewis concluded that this may have been the result of the experimental group being slightly older than the controls, and thus a difference in the maturity level of the two groups (a so-called "maturation effect") could have accounted for the result.

The SQUIRES evaluation did not rely upon recidivism alone as its measure of effectiveness. Changes in attitudes were also examined, on the assumption that attitudes are antecedents to behavior. The study found that in the experimental group there was a slight increase in positive attitudes towards the police and a less favorable orientation toward crime in general. Despite his findings, Lewis did not dismiss the value of the program. Perhaps in an effort to say something positive, he said that those youths who were deemed to be middle-of-the-road, or medium risk, *might* benefit most from such programs.

The absence of positive findings had no effect upon the program's continued operation. Today, the SQUIRES judge their own effectiveness by letters from participating youth (and others) describing how the program has influenced attendees. The program also encourages follow-up visits four to six months after the first visit. A third source of outcome information is contacts with referring agencies. The SQUIRES Program has not undergone another rigorous evaluation since Lewis' study.

See Our Side Program, Upper Marlboro, Maryland

The See Our Side Program is likewise claimed to be different from Scared Straight.[23] Again the difference is said to be its focus on education—a focus adopted because of the acknowledged ineffectiveness of scare tactics. The participating youths are referred by various agencies, including schools, churches, and Girl Scout troops. These youths range in age from twelve to eighteen and include both delinquents and nondelinquents. The basis for a referral is an agency's belief that a youth may benefit from the experience.

How is the education delivered? By means of a three-hour, four-phased program that operates as follows: Phase one, an orientation session, gives participants an opportunity to get comfortable in the prison environment and to get a general overview of some specific characteristics of the prison. Phase two is a tour of all areas of the facility. Phase three consists of interactive discussions with "carefully selected" inmates regarding prison life. In the fourth phase, attendees are asked to evaluate the program's effectiveness.

The participants' evaluations are cited as providing evidence that the program is effective in achieving its educational goal. On a scale of zero to one hundred, attendees have supposedly rated effectiveness at 78.2 percent! It should be noted that the attendees are completing these evaluations minutes after having been exposed to the inmate session. A study of subsequent delinquent behavior was reported to have found that the recidivism rate for those participating in the program decreased by more than half.[24]

The evaluators of this program also described a unique take on the question of cost-effectiveness.[25] Supporters argued that the program costs only 86 cents per youth, as compared to $44 a day for imprisoning that same youth; consequently, if only 6.36 jail days are prevented in a year, the program is worth it in monetary terms. Given the current concerns with respect to spending on criminal justice programs, many may find this argument compelling.

Stay Straight, Oahu, Hawaii

Hawaii's version of Scared Straight is one that was examined early on. Reacting to the controversy about scare tactics, it was described as nonconfrontational. Inmates did not scream and yell but used "factual storytelling and advice giving."[26] In their evaluation, Buckner and Chesney-Lind used a quasi-experimental design that post-matched three hundred male and female young offenders on seven variables.

They found that the experimental group actually did worse than the controls, but attributed this to the possibility of stigmatization or the negative influence of a particular subgroup within the experimental group, rather than to the intervention itself. While the Stay Straight Program is no longer in operation, there are no indications that its cessation was a direct result of the above evaluation.

SHAPE-UP, Colorado

Colorado's Showing How a Prison Experience Undermines People Program (SHAPE-UP) has been in operation since 1979. Again, program proponents stress that this is not a Scared Straight program. Their mission statement defines the focus of the program as *educating* "youths and their families about the negative consequences of prison life, and [providing] alternative strategies for dealing with destructive behavior and negative influences." Program literature describes this education as coming in the form of making youths and their parents aware of prison life and its precedents, focusing on "responsible decision making and constructive planning for the future."[27] It is described as being nonconfrontational, with no abusive scare tactics, but also no nonsense. The inmates operating the program are said to undergo extensive training before their involvement.

Almost 7,500 youth visited SHAPE-UP between 1987 and 1996. The majority were referred by either juvenile probation or diversion agencies. Tracking information on behavior and attitudinal changes is collected four months after program participation. In 1996, the program reported that approximately half of the attendees improved in school attitude, academic achievement, self-image, family relations, and peer relations. Recidivism rates, reported by the top two referring agencies, showed that after twenty-four months over 70 percent of attendees had had no new petition filed against them.

These findings are, however, quite different from those of an earlier study in which Berry used a quasi-experimental design and found no significant difference between experimental and control groups in their recidivism rates.[28] Additionally, no significant differences between the groups were found with respect to family influences. He found that diversion referrals were the least successful of all, and recommended that diversion's role in the program be terminated. Obviously that did not happen. Ineffectiveness was seemingly not a good enough reason to shut the program down. We can only speculate about the explanations for the stark discrepancies between the findings.

Project Aware, Mississippi

Cook and Spirrison conducted an evaluation of Mississippi's Project Aware, yet another nonconfrontational program with an educational format. This format was defined as having "no intentional scare tactics, intimidation or confrontation of juveniles."[29] In the study, juvenile offenders referred by the juvenile court were randomly assigned—ninety-seven youths participated in the five-hour program, and seventy-nine were controls. The result again was no difference in recidivism rates as measured by frequency of offending and severity of offense. There was however, a significant decrease in school drop-out rates for the experimental group. The researchers could offer no explanation for that result.

The Massachusetts Prevention Program

A program designed specifically for juvenile female probationers, this Massachusetts model entails youths spending four hours at a secure (locked) female institution. There they are supposed to learn about life in an institution. Following what are described as nonconfrontational talk sessions with inmates, it is hoped that participants are better able to make appropriate, informed choices and, once made, to accept responsibility for these choices. An underlying assumption is that with increased knowledge better-informed decisions will result. The program proponents also believe that the participating female inmates gain from their experience.

There is no evidence on how well this strategy works. There is, however, a male counterpart in Massachusetts. An initial internal evaluation of the effectiveness of that program ostensibly showed that of ninety-eight male juvenile probationers, 76 percent did not reoffend within one year of attending the program. Supporters of these programs conclude that further research must be conducted, particularly on the female version.[30]

Scared Straight in the U.K.

As mentioned in the first chapter, and as will be illustrated with a Norway case study, Scared Straight has not been practiced only in the United States. Other countries have established programs based on some of the same beliefs as those held here. Two examples of the U.K. experience, one in Great Britain and the other in Australia, are discussed in this section.

Great Britain came late to the Scared Straight phenomenon but has gone about it in a rather systematic fashion to determine how best and with whom best to use it. The British Home Office examined their experience and published the results in *To Scare Straight or Educate? The British Experience of Day Visits to Prison for Young People*.[31] What they call prison day programs were first established in 1991. After a somewhat rocky start, the British had twelve such programs operating in 1994, with plans for nine more.

The Home Office study looked at three programs that were ranged on a graduated scare factor continuum: "aggressive" (HMP Garth), "confrontational" (HMP Risley), and "nonconfrontational" (HMP Maidstone). The researchers did an extensive literature review, observed the programs, and interviewed persons involved in their various aspects.

HMP Garth uses the aggressive approach, modeling itself on the original Juvenile Awareness Project at East Jersey State Prison. Their motto is "Telling the Truth to Youth." Interactions between inmates and participating youths include frank talk of rape, drugs, and the monotony of the daily prison routine. There is a strong preference among those referring youths to these programs for this model. They view the aggressive approach as crucial to the program's success.

Although its initial approach was similar to HMP Garth, HMP Risley later became more specialized and changed its methods. It focuses on young motor vehicle offenders. The program is said to use a more educational approach. This education includes looking at pictures and films depicting the results of fatal automobile accidents, and increasing awareness about victims. Unlike HMP Garth, there is also a follow-up consisting of inmate visits to the youths at the place of referral, which is either a probation office or a social work agency.

HMP Maidstone took an entirely different tack. This program is also called educational—its objective being "to deter young people from crime by describing conditions in prison and by stressing how easy it is to end up in prison." This is supposedly achieved by delivering "an honest but hard-hitting description of life inside an adult prison."[32] The program also uses music, photos, and film.

The Home Office case studies concluded that there was potential for day visit programs that serve to inform youths about imprisonment and dispel popular media images. It was recommended that they should be primarily educational, that is, designed to inform youths about the realities of prison life. Although the same sorts of information would be conveyed, "education" should not include the tough, scare component.

The Australian experience with juvenile deterrence programs has been a turbulent one. First appearing on the scene in 1979, the programs underwent a decade of change and debate. Operations were suspended in 1991, as the result of assault accusations by a young attendee, but were then reinstated after insufficient evidence to support such allegations was found. After the reinstatement, an evaluation by O'Malley, Coventry and Walters was undertaken.[33]

Attitudinal and behavioral changes in participants were assessed through observation, interviews, and secondary data analysis. While a few participants were found to have short-term positive attitudinal changes following their experience, no overall improvement in attitudes was demonstrated. In some instances, participants actually exhibited significant negative results. An example is this description of one attendee, "offender expresses anger, fear and bitterness at the way in which he was treated . . . negating any positive aspects of the program."[34]

Preliminary findings regarding reoffending found that the program had little, if any, impact on delinquent behavior. It was further concluded that it was highly unlikely that such methods would have any long-term effect on participants' delinquent behavior. The belief in aversion and deterrence driving the program was unsupported. Recommendations following this study included discontinuing Scared Straight programs in favor of traditional educational and vocational programs. It was suggested that time and resources would be better utilized if directed toward the larger problems underlying delinquent behavior, instead of trying to scare this behavior out of youths.

With respect to our hypothesis about the continuation and promotion of programs in the face of overwhelming evidence contradicting their value, the Australian researchers said this: "Finally, there is evidence to support the view that implementation of the program reflected the impact of short-term political pressures rather than a sober consideration of the potential of the program for crime prevention."[35]

Conclusion

One of the factors in the endurance of Scared Straight appears to be the strong desire to do *something* about juvenile crime, and something that fits with getting tough. Our survey strongly shows that Scared Straight programs have had little success in deterring crime. In those cases where positive findings have been reported using tracking data (letters and other anecdotal follow-up information), there are a host of problems with the reliability of the information. These include what is called selection bias, that is, biased samples from which you cannot generalize. Second, there is an absence of comparisons with matched or control groups. There is therefore no answer to the question, "compared to what?" Third, claiming "success" for young people who were not delinquent to begin with is unfairly "stacking the deck."

One might conclude that we seem to be at the same point we were in 1982 following a review of the then-available information. Well—yes and no! Yes, because so far it looks like "same old, same old." But no, because a new and much more sophisticated means of comparing the relative effectiveness of programs is now available. That technique is called meta-analysis. We can delve much further into the Scared Straight approach with this powerful technique.

A Meta-Analysis of Scared Straight

Meta-analysis, a research technique used throughout the social sciences, is a relatively new research tool in criminal justice. Prior to looking at the results of what various meta-analyses tell us regarding the effectiveness of Scared Straight-type juvenile programs, let us briefly consider just what meta-analysis is and why it is important.

Meta-analysis differs from the more traditional methods of looking at a variety of studies using the kind of literature review we have just presented. This is because meta-analysis reexamines and combines the results of many individual studies addressing the same research issue. The units of meta-analysis become those individual studies. Its most frequent use in criminal justice has been in comparing treatment intervention for offenders.

While individual studies may provide rich, qualitative information on a particular treatment program, traditional summative literature reviews have been criticized for misleading conclusions. Lipsey, for example, accuses literature reviews of contributing to the unfounded "nothing works" conclusion regarding the effectiveness of juvenile corrections.[36] This is because an all-or-nothing determination about the effectiveness of a treatment approach is reached from a simple summary overview of all the results from all the studies. This is, in fact, very much what we have just done with the Scared Straight studies.

The primary problem with such a method is that not all studies are created equal. Those that may have used poor sampling techniques, inadequate sample sizes, or inappropriate study methods are given equal weight with those studies that have taken careful steps to make their findings more valid and reliable. Meta-analysis attempts to account for all these kinds of deficiencies and allows for the combined quantitative analysis of individual studies, thereby minimizing biases and random errors.[37]

Literature reviews, and the individual studies that comprise them, tell us whether the outcome data lead to a statistically significant conclusion. Meta-analysis goes beyond individual conclusions to integrate their statistical findings on a number of pertinent variables. In this aggregate analysis, a researcher might gather all the relevant studies regarding juvenile programs and identify variables, such as type of treatment, which are pertinent to what we are trying to find out. Many types of studies may be included in the analysis, from surveys to experimental and quasi-experimental designs.[38]

Meta-analysis is more apt to tease out effective results than are traditional research methods. Some may be skeptical of a yet more sophisticated method for judging program effectiveness—perhaps because they believe science has already been exploited in some nefarious way against their pet ideas. For them, let us hasten to add that besides our own, there have been a number of the more traditional literature reviews that included Scared Straight-type programs. Across the board, their consensus is that these programs are largely ineffective.[39]

Lipsey, in the most comprehensive meta-analysis to date on juvenile interventions, included eleven Scared Straight-type programs.[40] This is the largest sample of such programs to be subjected to meta-analysis. Not only did he find that the results did not support deterrence, but he also found that some programs may have had negative or opposite results.

What Lipsey called "deterrence" programs were the least effective of any of the programs included in his analysis, with the experimental groups consistently doing worse than their controls. The distinction did become blurred, however, when the target population of the deterrence program was high-risk offenders. This result is consistent with the findings of some other researchers.[41] Without knowing much more about the studies and the programs, and especially how "high-risk" was defined, it is impossible to say why this might be so. If these programs indeed work best with high-risk offenders, it would seem that would not support a current focus on developing less confrontational and more educational programs directed toward a general youth population.

Palmer pulled together the aggregate results of a number of meta-analyses. He showed that, consistent with the findings of individual evaluations, Scared Straight programs (labeled deterrence or confrontational) were repeatedly found to be unsuccessful. "No reviewer or analyst reported positive results for confrontation as a whole or even for several of its individual studies."[42] Again, this type of intervention was the least effective of all the types included in his study. Finally, Petrosino meta-analyzed five "juvenile prison tour" programs that had been evaluated using experimental studies. He found the youths attending the programs consistently did worse than those who did not.[43]

Speaking generally, Glaser tried to offer an optimistic view in the face of what seems to be overwhelming evidence about the ineffectiveness of correctional treatment. It is important to point out that he was talking about correctional programs in general, and not about Scared Straight-type programs specifically. He indicated that while studies may summarily conclude that certain programs do not work, or may even be harmful, at the same time those very same programs may actually be working for some youths in certain situations.[44] This seems to us to be akin to the reductionist argument described earlier that says if even one or a few youths are helped, that makes the effort worthwhile. There is also a slightly different take on this same rationalization. It says if nobody is harmed, and if it doesn't cost anything, what is the harm?

We agree that adopting a low threshold for success—a kind of drastic lowering of the bar—certainly makes "success" more achievable. But what is it that motivates lowering the bar? What is it about this idea that some go to extremes to try to justify it? And is it indeed the case that there is no harm being done?

The findings recited in this chapter are the best information we have. Their message is clear. But that message seems to have often gotten lost. We will try to further account for the survival of Scared Straight in the concluding chapter. But first, a visit to Norway.

Notes

[1] R. J. Lundman, *Prevention and Control of Juvenile Delinquency*, 2nd ed. (New York: Oxford University Press, 1993).

[2] Personal communication with Lt. Randy Sandkuhl.

[3] E. Nieves, "Tough Advice Gets Tougher to Get Across," *New York Times* 16 May 1996, B1.

[4] Ibid.

[5] Lifers' Group, Inc. East Jersey State Prison, Rahway, NJ 07065.

[6] R. Wormser, *Lifers Learn the Truth at the Expense of Our Sorrow* (Englewood Cliffs: Julian Messner, 1991).

[7] Lifers' Group, Inc.

[8] Wormser, *Lifers Learn the Truth*, p. 40.

[9] E. A. Cockfield, "For Inmates, Fictional Play Is Real Life Drama," *Hartford Courant*, 17 March 1996. WESTLAW: 1996 WL 4355893.

[10] George DeLama, "L.A. Hopes Dead Speak to Living," *Chicago Tribune*, 30 January 1993, 1.

11 R. Cadwallader, "Mansfield Council to Consider Proposal for Inmate Talk Show," *Fort Worth Star-Telegram*, 11 August 1997. WESTLAW: 1997 WL 11898799.

12 Drew Jubera, "Prison Drama a Grim Look at Life on Inside," *Atlanta Journal/ Atlanta Constitution*, 11 July 1997. WESTLAW: 1997 WL 3980301.

13 Penn-Pals: Prison Inmate Services Network, 1997. (Netscape Navigator 3.0): http://www.pennpals.org.

14 M. Weiss, "Video Hopes to Show Teens Results of Choice," *Atlanta Journal/ Atlanta Constitution*, 15 February 1996. WESTLAW: 1997 WL 8189495; S. Wong, "Prison Film Makes Its Point," *Hartford Courant*, 17 May 1997. WESTLAW: 1997 WL 10963743.

15 M. Kurtz, "Schools Sex-Lesson Materials Raise New Concerns," *News & Observer* (Raleigh, NC), 9 September 1997. WESTLAW: 1997 WL 7852210.

16 "Under The Influence" [Transcript], *48 Hours*. CBS, Inc., 11 January 1996. WESTLAW: 1996 WL 7819343.

17 A. Bavley, "ER Offers a Wake-Up to Drivers," *Kansas City Star*, 15 March 1997. WESTLAW: 1997 WL 3007563.

18 R. Tharp, "Probationers Sentenced to See Autopsies," *Fort Worth Star-Telegram*, 11 November 1997. WESTLAW: 1997 WL 11918463; S. Walker, "Texas Town Tries to Scare Kids Straight," *Christian Science Monitor*, 8 April 1997. WESTLAW: 1997 WL 2800363.

19 T. Prendergast, "Juvenile Offenders Get a Dose of Reality in CAPS Program," *Madison Press*, 12 June 1991.

20 Communication from Patrick Thomas, Probation Officer, Madison County (Ohio) Juvenile Court, July 30, 1997.

21 SQUIRES (program literature).

22 R. V. Lewis, "California Style: Evaluation of the San Quentin SQUIRES Program," *Criminal Justice and Behavior* 10, no. 2 (1983): 209–26.

23 J. J. Mitchell and S. A. Williams, "SOS: Reducing Juvenile Recidivism," *Corrections Today* 48, no. 3 (1986): 70–71.

24 Ibid.

25 Ibid.

26 J. C. Buckner and M. Chesney-Lind, "Dramatic Cures for Juvenile Crime: An Evaluation of a Prisoner-run Delinquency Program," *Criminal Justice and Behavior* 10, no. 2 (1983): 230.

27 SHAPE-UP (program literature).

28 R. L. Berry, "SHAPE-UP: The Effects of a Prison Aversion Program on Recidivism and Family Dynamics (Doctoral dissertation, University of Northern Colorado, 1985). *Dissertation Abstracts International*, 46–08A, 2449.

29 D. D. Cook and C. L. Spirrison, "Effects of a Prisoner-Operated Delinquency Deterrence Program: Mississippi's Project Aware." *Journal of Offender Rehabilitation* 17, no. 314 (1992): 91.

30 MA Prevention Program (program literature).

31 C. Lloyd, "To Scare Straight or Educate? The British Experience of Day Visits to Prison for Young People," *Home Office Research Study* 149 (1995).

32 Ibid., p. 37.

[33] P. O'Malley, G. Coventry and R. Walters, "Victoria's Day in Prison Program: An Evaluation and Critique," *Australian and New Zealand Journal of Criminology* 26 (1993): 171–83.

[34] Ibid., p. 181.

[35] Ibid., p. 182.

[36] M. W. Lipsey, "Juvenile Delinquency Treatment: A Meta-analytic Inquiry into the Viability of Effects," in *Meta-Analysis for Explanation: A Casebook*, edited by T. Cook, H. Cooper, D. S. Cordray, H. Hartmann, L. V. Hedges, R. J. Light, T. A. Louis, and F. Mosteller. (New York: Russell Sage Foundation, 1992).

[37] T. Palmer, *A Profile of Correctional Effectiveness and New Directions for Research* (Albany: State University of New York Press, 1994).

[38] T. Cook et al. (eds.), *Meta-Analysis for Explanation: A Casebook* (New York: Russell Sage foundation, 1992).

[39] Lundman, *Prevention and Control;* P. Gendreau and R. Ross, "Revivification of Rehabilitation: Evidence from the 1980s." *Justice Quarterly* 4, no. 3 (1987): 349–407; S. Lab and J. Whitehead, "An Analysis of Juvenile Correctional Treatment," *Crime and Delinquency* 34 (1988): 60–85.

[40] Lipsey, "Juvenile Delinquency Treatment."

[41] D. A. Andrews, et al., "Does Correctional Treatment Work?: A Clinically Relevant and Psychologically Informed Meta-Analysis." *Criminology* 28, no. 3 (1990): 369–404; Whitehead and Lab, "A Meta-Analysis of Juvenile Correctional Treatment."

[42] Palmer, *A Profile of Correctional Effectiveness*, p. 23.

[43] A. Petrosino, *What Works? Revisited Again: A Meta-Analysis of Randomized Field Experiments in Individual-Level Interventions* (Newark: Rutgers-The State University of New Jersey, 1997).

[44] D. Glaser, "What Works, and Why It Is Important: A Response to Logan and Gaes," *Justice Quarterly* 11, no. 4 (1994): 711–23.

chapter eight

Scared Straight Comes to Norway

It has become something of a mantra: the world is shrinking, every-thing and everyone is within reach, in more or less constant interaction, and influencing each other to an extent never seen before. Ideas and formulas go ocean hopping, those of the United States prob-ably more than most. "Americanization" has been a term of abuse in Europe and elsewhere for decades. Fearful for the future of their national or indigenous culture, numerous intellectuals have pointed to the United States as a source of shallow, prefabricated, and violent commercialism.

Others in the Old World see it differently, however, and look to the United States for solutions and inspiration. So be it that the United States is "crime-ridden," they say, it is also a country of bold solutions to its problems! One such solution in particular has caught the public's eye in Norway, namely the program known as "Scared Straight." Born in the United States and scathingly criticized there (after being evaluated and found lacking on most counts), this approach to crime prevention, nev-ertheless, survived at Rahway and elsewhere in the United States. It even spread beyond, into Canada and across the Atlantic to Britain, Den-mark, and Norway. In 1989, more than a decade after its near death in New Jersey, it was discovered by Norwegian prison officers, who studied on-site at Rahway. Scared Straight was exported, imported, and put to work in one of Norway's high security prisons in 1992.

Readers familiar with the original Juvenile Awareness Project (JAP) at Rahway and the history of its introduction to the U.S. public in 1979 will notice a number of striking similarities between the Ullersmo project and JAP, in content and ideology as well as in project history. The differences are, however, equally striking. Most importantly, the Uller-

143

smo project was shut down by the Ministry of Justice as a consequence of the evaluation that was published in January 1997. JAP still exists.

The four chapters dedicated to the Ullersmo project were written by Arild Hovland and Elisabet Storvoll and represent an extract from the evaluation. The first part of this chapter examines the historical background of the project, the dual aspect of the program, and prominent developments within the project. Next is a description of the controversy surrounding its going public. The latter part of the chapter explains the principles of the evaluation, these being somewhat different from the methods normally used to evaluate projects within this genre. Chapter 9 is dedicated to a detailed description of a confrontation (the primary application of the Ullersmo project), its actors, their actions, and the events preceding and following the confrontation. Chapter 10 provides insight into the actors' various—and variable—perspectives on what they were doing and what the project means to them. Chapter 11 then puts everything into context, focusing partly on processes, but also on theoretical and ethical issues. Central to the discussion is the question: Did the cancellation of the Ullersmo project *really* mean the end to Scared Straight in Norway?

Project History

Inception/Reception

Our focus here is on two aspects of the project's history: the actors and the institutional framework. The "real" start of the Ullersmo project possibly could be put at several points in time.

Chronologically the first of these possible starting points is in 1989 when Frank Nyborg, the prison officer who later founded and headed the Ullersmo project, took the initiative to bring a supposedly repentant, well-known drug criminal into contact with youths from various parts of the country. The expressed intention was drug prevention, through the recounting of this individual's fatally flawed life and criminal career. It was the same logic—that exposure to someone experiencing the consequences of committing crime would deter others from criminal behavior—that was later applied in the Ullersmo project.

Another possible starting point was also in 1989 when a film dedicated to The Lifers' Group project at Rahway was shown on one of the national TV channels in Norway. Nyborg, already occupied with drug and crime prevention but (then as now) looking for alternative avenues into the hearts and minds of young people, became greatly fascinated with the project at Rahway, so much so that he, on his own initiative and partly on his own funds, went to New Jersey late in 1989 to investigate the project at Rahway. There he was immersed in the exercise of prisoner-youth confrontations and talked with prisoners, officers, and youths. To him the project at Rahway seemed to be well founded and producing good results. He brought his ideas and experiences home, recounted them to the director at Ullersmo and his colleagues, and recruited a group of prisoners. Three years later the first juveniles entered Ullersmo for the Norwegian version of Scared Straight.

The prisoners were recruited first and foremost to participate in confrontations inside the prison. Some—the majority in fact—were also taken outside the prison to visit schools for low-key versions of their general presentation. They were both interested and supportive, though not without (obviously) self-interest motivations. They did what they believed in for the kids—and gained for themselves at the same time. Gains were both concrete and immediate: fellowship, a degree of freedom (visits outside); and seen in the long run: generally a larger degree of psychological/emotional stability, greater insights into their own and others' situations, and so on. On the flip side there were reactions from other prisoners, suspicion, and accusations. One prisoner was even moved to a separate ward after having been accused (probably rightly) of having squealed on fellow prisoners in a drug case. Did the prisoners contribute to the development of the project? Yes, and heavily so. They were presented a toned-down version of the Rahway arrangement, entered it, and immediately started shaping it according to their own preferences and personalities. Later, the officers stressed their own control over the prisoners; the prisoners, on the other hand, stressed their de facto control over the contents of the confrontations. Our conclusion was that the prisoners had more of a case than the officers. They defined more of the confrontations than the officers were able to admit, and more than should have been the case given the category of kids they were up against. In short, based on personal taste and convictions and on the momentum of any given situation during the confrontations, they crossed the line of permissibility on a number of occasions. But this is getting ahead of our story.

One might ask of these possible beginnings: Was it all a question of one man's frustration with the impotence of current methods in the prevention of juvenile delinquency? Was it a case of one man's profound experiences in the backrooms of society, and his coupling of these with a too-narrow understanding of the limitations of the Scared Straight approach? Should the responsibility for the project (including its failure) be cast on this man and his immediate superiors and colleagues? Or should it, instead, be placed at the feet of departmental authorities?

Could and should they have intervened? And if so, was their reasoning and rationality up to it, or were they too inadequately endowed with regard to both moral awareness and professional insights? Could the man responsible for the initiative, his colleagues, and the departments have investigated the outcomes at Rahway more thoroughly, and would this have led to another course of action? Despite the evaluations of ten to fifteen years ago, would they all have insisted on their common sense and gone ahead anyway? These questions soon became fundamental to the evaluation, in addition to the primary question asked by the ministries responsible for the evaluation: Was it likely that this approach would work? We return to this question toward the end of the chapter.

Into Schools and Prison

As already mentioned, the Ullersmo project found its actual and practical start in the cooperation between a drug criminal and a prison officer (two other prisoners were involved but were much less visible). Their *modus operandi* was visits to schools and various other arrangements throughout the country. This work, labelled variously "the school project" and "drug-free future," more or less constitutes the pilot project for the Ullersmo project. The drug-free label initially covered the Ullersmo project as well. A couple of years after the first "outing," Nyborg claimed to have received calls and letters from 123 schools asking for visits by prisoners. They visited approximately half of these and talked to 5,000 youngsters. According to him, he used approximately 2,000 hours of his free time on the project. Then this time, they started receiving young boys and girls for confrontations inside the prison, while visits to schools still continued.

The project was effectively dual—and thus succeeded in doing what the people at Rahway had wanted to do but never managed: to have youths coming in, but inmates going out as well. Ullersmo became a project in which prisoners partly confronted young people (defined as delinquent) inside the prison and partly were received as *raconteurs* at numerous schools and institutions in the eastern part of Norway. During the latter types of visits the prisoners faced officially nondelinquent children.

Bear in mind, however, that the people doing the job inside the prison were for the most part exactly the same people who did it outside. The ideology applied on the inside was the same as outside the prison, and the *community* that was involved in the Ullersmo project for several years was the source and definer of both parts. Let us have a closer look at this community, particularly since this is an aspect rarely stressed in the U.S. studies.

Social Developments within the Ullersmo Project

The Ullersmo project is an unusual phenomenon inside Norwegian prisons. Generally speaking, the relationship between officers and prisoners is one of mutual, though peaceful, and watchful antagonism. "Squealers" and other prisoners too closely associated with officers rapidly run into great problems with their fellow inmates. Ullersmo is, according to Norwegian standards, a very rough prison—and is known as such to the general public. Half of the prisoners are foreigners, most often sentenced because of drug-related offenses. Norwegian prisoners are there for the same reasons, but also for violent crimes, homicide and serious sexual offenses. Sentences are regularly long ones, ten years or more. The recidivism rate is high, around 80 percent. The use of drugs inside the prison is regularly portrayed in the media as a serious problem. The prison also has had its share of scandals or scandal-like headlines in national newspapers, related, among other things, to drug abuse, living conditions and high-profile escapes. This was the environment in which prison officers, first among them an officer responsible for the control of drug abuse, and prisoners, sentenced generally for homicide and/or drug-related crimes, created the Ullersmo project in 1991.

The Ullersmo project was founded on an express wish to "scare youngsters off a path of crime." This was Nyborg's own formula, stated in writing in 1994, and the one that the director of Ullersmo prison accepted.[1] There seems to have been no professional control in this founding period of the project. Nyborg and a colleague, Jan Korsvold (who were later estranged), went about it on their own, recruited prisoners, instructed them sparingly, and spread the word to relevant institutions. Newspapers of the period published articles which said that the project "presents brutal reality from the inside. Life's no dance on roses behind the walls of Ullersmo." The first couple of confrontations included the aforementioned well-known drug criminal. He left the project early on and later publicly criticized it.

The first confrontation between young boys and prisoners inside Ullersmo prison took place in February 1992. The boys came from a small town an hour's drive from the prison and were part of an effort by child welfare services and the police to rehabilitate young offenders. Contrary to the majority of the youngsters to go to Ullersmo, these boys were not institutionalized. They lived at home. All in all this seemingly successful program sent three groups to Ullersmo, seventeen boys in all. They were the reason the Norwegian minister of children and family affairs publicly endorsed the Ullersmo project.

Later, groups of boys and girls came mainly from one particular institution, a child welfare live-in collective that was closely identified and connected with the Ullersmo project. All together twelve institutions or agencies sent approximately 144 children to the Ullersmo project during its existence.

The project rapidly evolved into much more than an attempt to scare youngsters straight. Ideas emerged and hopes were expressed that this project, in addition to its supposed effects on the young visitors, should serve as a foundation for the rehabilitation of the prisoners themselves. The majority of the prisoners took to this hope, which was at least verbally supported by the founder of the project. For approximately three years, the prisoners occupied with the project were given reason to believe that the Ullersmo project would eventually have a separate section within the prison. This section was supposed to consolidate the community that the project's main actors had established early on and to use this community to rehabilitate both prisoners and youths. However, our experiences with the Ministry of Justice and the Prison Board, as well as with the realities of decision making in Norwegian prisons, seem to indicate that this was not a realistic plan, although, for a long period of time, it served as a main driving force behind the effort.

The years 1995 and 1996 were the period of evaluation for the Ullersmo project. It was also a period of slow internal disintegration within the project. What originally in 1994 had been a comparatively close-knit group of prisoners and officers withered over the next two years into a shadow of itself. In effect, when our report was published in January, 1997, the project had collapsed. Several developments contributed to the project's demise.

First, the evaluation took longer to do than those responsible for the project had counted on. The scrutiny and steady stream of questions both dampened the confrontations themselves and complicated the once "simple" answers and defenses of the participants. Second, and also connected with the evaluation, most user institutions stopped their participation, awaiting the results. Several of these institutions had been subjected to both internal and external criticism and were far from as dedicated to the ideas of the project as those who had established it. For example, the institution responsible for approximately two-thirds of the juveniles who had visited Ullersmo entered into a critical phase at the turn of 1995–96 that excluded the use of the project. Though dedicated to the ideas of the project, it had to concentrate on defending itself against severe and general attacks from the county authorities responsible for supervising child welfare institutions. The steady stream of "clients" dried up. Third, the social structure of the project crumbled. One long-participating prisoner was excluded because of drug charges; others moved to penal facilities outside Ullersmo. The remaining prisoners finally lost faith in the promises they had long believed in. One, a dedicated man and a driving force within the project, finally withdrew completely early in 1996, citing broken promises as the reason. Fourth, the two officers responsible (Nyborg and Korsvold) withdrew or became less effective within the project, partly for personal reasons, and partly because of the demands of other assignments. The coordination of an already loosely run project took on a character of chance and randomness, which of course became another source of frustration for those involved, the prisoners in particular.

The sum of these developments, and several other minor events, slowly dissolved the glue that had kept the project together socially. Without this glue, what was finally closed down in January 1997 was more of a concept than a project. There is, however, no doubt that the controversy surrounding the project could have been tempered and the project could well have been revived had the report concluded differently.[2]

A Controversial Project

The Ullersmo project caught national attention in Norway in August 1994 with the broadcast of a film showing a confrontation between prisoners and youth at Ullersmo prison outside the capital Oslo. Responsible for the broadcast was the dominant Norwegian National Broadcasting Corporation. As in the United States fourteen years before, the language was harsh, the images highly unusual, and the public as a result became partly shocked but also intrigued. The presentation was sensationalist and focused on the seemingly very controversial and unusual nature of the project. Close-up filming of prisoners and juveniles, of threatening and restless behavior, a soundtrack of inmates' shouting and the youths' subdued silence, together with shots of prison walls and steel doors, cells and barbed wire, constituted the footage and the main part of the film.

The film was immediately followed by a studio debate between the founder of the project; a central representative for the juvenile institutions that send youths to the prison; and a prominent official from the Norwegian office of "Children's Ombudsman," a subsidiary of the Ministry of Children and Family Affairs. The TV station clearly wanted to present the project in the harshest manner possible and attempted, according to the guests on the program, to initiate a heated argument between them, which did not occur. Doubts and beliefs were expressed in equal doses; the participants' profound concern for the youngsters who visited the prison was never questioned. The program ended with polite disagreement, though all agreed that there was a need for an evaluation of the project.

The day after the program aired, however, polite disagreement was replaced with fairly vehement disagreement as the issue exploded in national newspapers. The largest tabloids ran stories on the brutality of the confrontations, the threats issued by the prisoners, and the harshness of the prison. Conservative newspapers hailed the attempt as worthy of praise. The prisoners for their part shouldered the burden of defending the project, referring to their own destinies and claiming that had they undergone a similar experience at an earlier age, they might very well have been saved. Their statements were accompanied by pictures of them, taken either from the TV presentation or at the time of the interview. One of the papers did a follow-up on one youth who claimed that "the prisoners threatened to kill me."

This initial "storm" rapidly blew over, at first providing little more than a momentary frustration to the parties involved. What came soon after was more serious. Though the project was defended—on relatively thin bases—primarily by the minister in charge of the child welfare services, it was attacked both on professional and ethical grounds by several respected criminologists, psychologists, and social scientists.

Professor Nils Christie, a criminologist, worried about effects on both inmates and youths. Inmates may be pushed into extreme roles, he said, and the image of the prison was neither fair nor correct. The juveniles could easily come to regard the inmates as heroes and models, and themselves come to be regarded as such among their peers. Instead of being seen as poor, downtrodden beings whose fate is to be avoided, the image of the inmates might be one of heroic survivors of adversity. The project had no natural place in "our humane traditions," Christie claimed.[3] Others reiterated his views, interestingly enough relying primarily on the writings of Professor Lundman—whose text on this was based to a large extent on Finckenauer's evaluation of the JAP at Rahway.[4] This criticism was fundamentally negative though relatively balanced. Others went further, painting images of medieval chambers of torture, the Nazi regime, and the Gestapo. Their various phrasings aside, professionals' views were unanimously negative. They felt that the project was ethically inadmissible, had no natural place in Norwegian traditions, and had no or negative effects on the youths subjected to it.

The harshness and unidimensionality of the criticism, and the headlines it received in national newspapers, came as a great surprise to those responsible for implementing the program. They were prepared for criticism, but not for the strength of it. How could they be so surprised, given the relative brutality of the method and the unusual nature of it in Norway and given the evaluations referred to by the critics? Did the people in charge not know of these evaluations, even after visiting Rahway? Had not Alan August, the officer at Rahway when the founder of the Ullersmo project visited and who was prominent when JAP went national,[5] informed them of the evaluations and the controversy? To evaluators now familiar with both the Ullersmo project and JAP, the answer to this is both interesting and ironic.

Two departments or ministries were responsible for the project. The Ministry of Justice had allowed the project to run at Ullersmo but had given it very little attention. The Ministry of Children and Family Affairs seems not to have known of it. Upon being made aware of it, the minister in charge defended it, though her only reference was to one small visit to the Ullersmo project by some clients of a municipal rehabilitative effort. During the initial controversy and in the months after, the two ministries looked closer at the project and prepared a mandate for an evaluation of it. This started in April 1995, eight months after the broadcast. We will return to the evaluation project in the next section of this chapter.

Two characteristics seem to define much of the inner workings of the Ullersmo project: The first is a profound wish for publicity and support for the project; the second is a striking lack of knowledge on the part of those involved. The first characteristic is apparent in explicit comments as well as in the actions of officers and prisoners alike. They wanted attention, they told us, and knew this would happen once they got the project on national TV. The evaluation that came later was exactly what was sought. Through such an evaluation they hoped to gain support and to have their methods confirmed as valuable, necessary, and effective. All this they seem to have had in common with the people responsible for the JAP at Rahway, who sought publicity as a means to secure the survival of the project.[6] At Ullersmo the expected support remained absent and the project did not survive. Massive attention backfired in the form of critical newspaper stories, skepticism, and an evaluation that to the participants must have seemed to drag on longer than necessary. The complexity of the issues came as a surprise. Confronted with the world of academia, politics, and the media, prisoners and officers alike became insignificant, despite a stress in the final reports on their dedication and, with regard to the prisoners, their vulnerability.

The second characteristic, the lack of knowledge, proved fateful for the project;[7] the program's proponents had no knowledge of the long string of evaluations of Scared Straight-like projects. They had no knowledge of the Congressional hearing in 1979[8] nor of the profundity of the controversy that was more than a decade old in the United States. What they did have, and showed the evaluators, was a popularized and complimentary book on JAP published in 1991. The following statement made by an official at Rahway, and quoted in the book, is illustrative:

> Many teenagers are doing things . . . today [that] they might not have done were it not for the Juvenile Awareness Program. Some are in college; others have their own careers and businesses. They have married and are raising families, teaching others what they once learned in prison."[9]

Add the following statement, made by an official at Rahway and quoted in the book, and one might understand why this book clearly supported the use of the Scared Straight method: "We have evidence that it has worked for a large number of youths. The fact is that these men are very good at what they do."[10]

This book did not inspire critical reflections nor did it supply knowledge on the disputed history of JAP and similar projects. One might say, then, that the officers at Ullersmo and their prisoners acted in good faith—as did many in the United States if the evaluation reports of the 1980s are to be trusted. They simply did not know of the negative evaluations and the depth of criticism. Seen in this perspective, their use of the method was absolutely defensible. There is reason to believe, however, that they may well have acted the same—and even carried on with the project at present—even if they had known. A certain disdain for academics and a profound distrust toward "professionals" without practical insights permeate the thinking of many of those responsible for the Ullersmo project. This goes for prisoners, officers and institutional personnel alike—and is a point to which we will return.

Given the heated controversy, and the absence of knowledge of the history of this approach, it became clear that an in-depth evaluation was needed.

Evaluating the Ullersmo Project

The initial question posed to us at the start of our work was—as is always true when it comes to this kind of project—does it work or doesn't it? Does it produce the fruits promised by those who support it? Contrary to many of the critics, skilled as they are in the ways of psychology, sociology, and pedagogy, we approached the project from the point of *simply not knowing about previous evaluations*. We didn't know—didn't want to "know"—the results from previous projects. First, we were not sure whether the U.S. results would be applicable at all to this project, since they were produced in a country that is in many respects profoundly different from Norway. Second, we wanted to keep our minds as open as possible, and to talk objectively to the officers and prisoners and institutional representatives.

What exactly was this phenomenon with which we were faced? Was it the same as that referred to as Scared Straight in New Jersey, or something more or less different? Did the presentation on TV do justice to the activities that actually took place at Ullersmo? Was it "worse" or "better"? Would the images derived from the press and the broadcasts dissolve as soon as one took a closer look? These and many more questions represented our starting point.

It soon became clear to us that many of the conclusions presented in the media by proponents and opponents of the Ullersmo project had less to do with professional learning and concrete knowledge than with *ideology*. Because ideology was expressed as professionalism among criminologists, psychologists, and pedagogues, as well as among child welfare workers and prison officers, separating one from the other took some time.

Another important point refers to the concept of *context* and is related to ideology and professionalism. It seemed clear from the very beginning that any proper understanding of the Ullersmo project would have to come from seeing it as integrated within a number of contexts. The first of these is centered around the people involved—the administrators, the personnel at the institutions, the youths, and the prisoners. What were their connections? Could it be that this was some kind of small and fringe-like clique, not at all representative of the child welfare system in Norway? Or did they herald some significant development in these matters? Were they singular, or might others have done what they had done, given the opportunity? What about the ideas on which the Ullersmo project was built—surely they didn't just drop out of thin air? Were they the results of the frustrations of senior men oriented to the 1950s trying to cope with the changes taking place around them? Was it something personal, or did the project derive from some established ideology, perhaps some kind of professional, recognized thinking? Might it not be a good idea to focus on the genealogy of the project, the people and the acts, and the coincidences that culminated on TV in

August 1994? We thought so. Contextualization became, on the whole, our most important key to understanding the Ullersmo project.

As for effects, we decided early on to go about evaluating the project qualitatively, using processual analysis and cross-checks based on observations, interviews and literature. Our limitations were such that we could not replicate the U.S. studies, but we could utilize them as part of our total arsenal of methods, seeking the *highly probable* rather than the *proven*.

We were given a mandate for the evaluation by the Ministry of Children and Family Affairs and the Ministry of Justice. Let's take a brief look at this mandate.

The Mandate and Then . . .

The ministries focused on two issues in particular in the mandate. The first referred to the Ullersmo project and various questions in connection with it. The second was far larger and concerned the rehabilitation of particularly troublesome youths in general. Thus we were given the task not only of examining the Ullersmo project, but also of reflecting upon measures far outside the arsenal of the prisoners and officers inside Ullersmo.

Part of the mandate was similar to that of other evaluations of Scared Straight projects: Does the Ullersmo project prevent crime or doesn't it? But this is a narrow and secondary issue. Even if Ullersmo was successful, there would still be the larger question of whether this end justified the means. Thus, we approached the evaluation from a different perspective than did the evaluators of previous Scared Straight projects. Part of the reason for this was the issue of contextualization mentioned above. This combined with the professional background of the head of the evaluation—a social anthropologist—to produce a focus on the multiple meanings and understandings that could be attached to events, acts, ideas—and flux. The whole thing just would not sit still to be examined. You could not just speak of "the effects of the Ullersmo project" when that project constantly changed. You could not simply focus on the bottom line. Thus, our choice was for a processual analysis—interviews and participant observation coupled with literature reviews. We went for discovery, trying to follow the social, historical, and ideological loops of the project, and held on to our objectivity until the absolute end of our work, when conclusions had to be formulated. As the work progressed, our methods changed as well, adapting to information we received or to resistance we encountered. Thus, a *multiplicity of methods* together produced our total approach. The end result was a critical observation, but only the sum of results from a wide array of methods tipped the balance against the Ullersmo project.

Data

Our data were collected mainly from three areas: the prison system, the institutions sending youths to Ullersmo, and the youths who went to Ullersmo. Let us look at the prison system first.

In order to gain insight into the origins and workings of the Ullersmo project we interviewed one representative of the Norwegian Prison Board (part of the Ministry of Justice) and the director at Ullersmo prison. Both Nyborg and Korsvold were interviewed. Nine prisoners participated in the project at various times, for shorter or longer periods. Six of these inmates were interviewed. All in all, ten representatives of the prison system were interviewed. In addition to the formal interviews, we talked with most of these people on numerous other occasions.

In order to gain further insights into both the origins of the project and the understandings of the project among the officers, we travelled to the United States with the two officers running the project, where the four of us visited East Jersey (Rahway) State Prison. We also travelled to Tarrant County, Texas, where we were taken to see a boot camp, as well as given an introduction to the local system for handling juvenile delinquents. Rahway as well as the projects in Texas represented important influences in the Ullersmo project.

Back in Norway, participant observation was done both inside Ullersmo and during visits by prisoners and officers to schools. We were present at four confrontations inside Ullersmo and at two school visits. The latter were part of our effort to gain contextual understanding.

Twelve institutions sent youths to Ullersmo between 1992 and 1996. Representatives of all these institutions were interviewed. Fourteen representatives were interviewed altogether: two from each of the two institutions that had sent the most kids to Ullersmo and one from each of the remaining ten. All interviews of this kind were done at the institutions. One institution, responsible for more than half the youths who went to Ullersmo, received numerous visits by us. We were present at two confrontations in which the youths of this institution participated.

As best we can determine, 144 youths went to Ullersmo: 110 boys and 34 girls. These figures are slightly uncertain, because not all records were up-to-date at the institutions, and the officers at Ullersmo did not keep complete records of visiting institutions, numbers of youngsters, or their genders. Our mandate stressed the problems of sending girls to an all-male prison such as Ullersmo. Consequently, we tried to achieve a large proportion of girls for our sample. It was important also to have a representation of youths from all twelve institutions. All youths interviewed were selected randomly at the institutions. Thirty-eight youths from eleven institutions were interviewed. Most interviews took place between one and two years after the juveniles had been to Ullersmo. All interviews were taped and transcribed, and most lasted an hour and a half or two hours.

The Ullersmo project received extensive coverage in the news media, and there were some articles written by professionals in journals as well as for the newspapers. We collected as many of these as possible. There had been some correspondence between the Ullersmo project and various institutions, users and others, and between the project and the Ministry of Justice. All this information was collected together with documents from the Ministry of Justice and the Ministry of Family Affairs.

We tried as well to gather as much material as possible relevant to the U.S. debate on the Scared Straight approach. This material included professional papers, evaluation reports, and news material. Finally, we did a review of the literature on crime prevention and juvenile delinquency in general. This was our material. What image of the Ullersmo project emerged from it? Chapters 9 and 10 describe this.

Notes

[1] This statement of purpose was contained in a letter from Frank Nyborg to the director of Ullersmo prison, dated September 5, 1994.

[2] E. Keerdoja, "Prison Program Gets a New Boost," *Newsweek* 16 (1980); S. Langer, *The Rahway State Prison Lifers' Group: A Critical Analysis.* Unpublished doctoral dissertation, Kean College, Union, NJ: Department of Sociology; J. O. Finckenauer, *Scared Straight! and the Panacea Phenomenon* (Englewood Cliffs, NJ: Prentice-Hall, 1982).

[3] "Christie Opposed to Scaring Offenders," *Aftenposten,* 30 August 1994.

[4] Finckenauer, *Scared Straight!*; R. J. Lundman, *Prevention and Control of Juvenile Delinquency* (New York: Oxford University Press, 1993).

[5] Finckenauer, *Scared Straight!.*

[6] M. Israel, "The 'Scared Straight' Controversy," *New Jersey Monthly* 5, no. 1, (1980): 55–57, 91–106.

[7] Finckenauer, *Juvenile Awareness Project. Evaluation Report No. 2* (Newark, NJ: Rutgers University School of Criminal Justice, 1979); Finckenauer, *Scared Straight!*; Finckenauer and J. Storti, *Juvenile Awareness Project Help: Evaluation Report No. 1* (Newark, NJ: Rutgers University School of Criminal Justice, 1979); L. Gilman and R. K. Milin, *An Evaluation of the Lifers' Group Juvenile*

Awareness Program (Trenton: New Jersey Department of Corrections, 1977); Langer, *The Rahway State Prison Lifers' Group.*

[8] House Committee on Education and Labor, *Hearing before the Subcommittee on Human Resources,* 96th Cong., 1st sess., 1979.

[9] R. Wormser, *Lifers' Learn the Truth at the Expense of Our Sorrow* (Englewood Cliffs, NJ: Julian Messner, a division of Silver Burdett Press, Simon and Schuster, 1991), p. 200.

[10] Ibid.

chapter nine

Ullersmo in Action

Seen from the perspective of the founder of the Ullersmo project, it was never as severe as the JAP, even in the JAP's mildest form. Our review of the U.S. literature and a close analysis of the Ullersmo project seem to confirm this impression. The following figure illustrates this:

| Ullersmo '96 | Ullersmo pre '96 | JAP '92–6 | JAP pre '79 |

→ →

| Weakest form | Strongest form |

Ullersmo '96 represents the project during the evaluation. Ullersmo pre '96 represents the project at its height before and shortly after August 1994. JAP '92–6 represents that project as observed by the founder of the Ullersmo project during three consecutive visits. JAP pre '79 represents the project at Rahway prior to Finckenauer's two reports, and the near dismantling of it. It is interesting to note that the JAP of the 1990s, described as "a 'forum, discussion, seminar' type of approach" by Lundman,[1] is considered by the founder of the Ullersmo project to be more brutal than the Norwegian project in any of its phases.

The above figure does not represent the reality of these two particular projects. It is, rather, a representation of the understanding of the officers at Ullersmo of the two projects relative to each other. Furthermore, it is a representation of *form*, of the deeds done and the words uttered, not of ideological content. We find it necessary to comment on this since so many of the evaluations we have reviewed concentrate on form, neglecting the importance of underlying ideology. The Ullersmo project, as well as the JAP, represent an urgent need to communicate about the aversive consequences of deviant behavior. Throughout the varying history of the Scared Straight approach this communication has been expressed in a wide range of ways, some of which have been unequivocally condemned in Norway, whereas others have been considered substantially milder than the Ullersmo project.

Evaluators generally show a keen awareness of even relatively minor variations between confrontational projects.[2] Examples of the ways in which projects vary include: whether the youngsters' families are involved in some way or another; how thoroughly the youngsters are prepared for their visit; if follow-up occurs and how it is conducted; whether the confrontation is violent, abusive, or comparatively mild; if the confrontation is a once-in-a-lifetime experience or repeated; and so forth. Variations are considered as possibly relevant to the effects of the confrontational approach. They generally are not tested but are pointed to as pros and cons of this or that program. What authors rarely do in these evaluation reports, which are quite numerous though far fewer in number than actual projects, is reflect on the underlying ideology of the projects. Our contention has been and is: Give or take this or that, elaborate one aspect, remove another, do whatever to vary your particular program—your program still rests on the same reasoning as the others within this genre. The fundamental ideology is substantially the same, and we call its key component "a psychology of the major turning point." This refers to an intense belief that if the request is urgent enough, the event sufficiently frightening or realistic, those in charge of helping honest and strong-willed enough, and their power of persuasion great enough—it will surely work! This deep conviction, bordering sometimes on intransigence, has been the driving force behind the Ullersmo project.

We now turn to the actual confrontations, recounting one of these from a point twenty-four hours before the event to a point in the day after. This confrontation took place in 1995 and represents a toned-down version of the Ullersmo project. The referring institution (referred to as M) is the main user and for some years was closely associated with the project. Our presentation begins inside M, continues at the gates of Ullersmo prison, and ends with a description and discussion of the follow-up that evening and the day after.

Entering Ullersmo

Day 1: Preparations

We're in a live-in collective, located in the countryside an hour's drive from the capital, Oslo. The institution, M, has at any time approximately fifteen boys and girls living there. The vast majority of them are placed in M by local authorities, ostensibly as a last resort. They could not leave if they wanted to, and most stay for four to six months. M is known for its strict regimen and very close follow-up of its young clients. Most activities are regulated; any mistake or defined deviance from the rules is commented upon. Due to this, M has been for several years either lauded for its efficiency or severely criticized for its stringency.

The youths generally are considered problem cases with records of drug and alcohol abuse, theft, burglaries, and so on. Most are between fourteen and seventeen years of age. The personnel present them to us as fundamentally worse off than they look (which is quite nice and normal). Later, an inspection of documents on file at the institution reveals other histories. Somewhat contrary to the version given to us by the personnel, records indicate that these youngsters are often victims of parental abuse and neglect. This impression is confirmed when some of these youths and a number of their predecessors are interviewed. However, this aspect is rarely stressed, though the immaturity of these boys and girls is often mentioned. Generally they are presented to us as very disturbed young people. This fact is often referenced when those in favor of Ullersmo defend going there.

There's an evening gathering at M. Those present are arranged in a large circle in the living room. The theme of the hour is the visit to Ullersmo planned for the next day. We are told that five boys and girls will be going this time. Prior to this meeting, the researchers spent most of the day informally talking to the youngsters in groups or one-on-one. Agreement as to the effects of the visits to Ullersmo or the actual content of the experience was hard to find. The youngsters placed a value on fear itself, and there was sort of a competition among them: Who was most afraid? Talking of this, they referred to a boy who had several times asked to go to Ullersmo, but his request had been denied due to psychiatric problems. He was known to suffer psychotic breakthroughs due to a schizophrenic condition. This time he could go, they said. Otherwise he would "lose face" among his peers.

At the meeting the person in charge talks about the Ullersmo project:

> We leave at 5:00 P.M. When we get there we pass through the gate, cross an open square and go through a metal detector. From there on you won't see us [the personnel] for a while. You are taken to the dining hall of the prisoners where four prisoners will present themselves. This part takes approximately an hour. After that you're taken to a ward of security cells, used for confinement, to tie prisoners up and for controlled excretion. The latter is used to check for drugs with prisoners who have been out on leave. You are then taken one

by one or two by two into one of these security cells to talk with two prisoners. This will be calmer and quieter than in the dining hall and will take from half an hour to an hour. It varies. The whole visit takes between two and three hours.

A boy in the audience interrupts, telling how they are taken into the yard for some air after the visit to the security cells. After that they will talk to one of the officers. A girl who participated the last time M sent youngsters to Ullersmo recommends they leave their tobacco in the car outside the prison gate. "Otherwise the prisoners will take it from you," another boy explains. "It's going to be tough," says the person in charge. "The prisoners won't hurt you; it is not dangerous though not pleasant either." "Listen to the prisoners!" inserts a boy who has been to Ullersmo.

The youngsters are given the opportunity to ask questions. A girl asks if it is true that there are only violent prisoners at Ullersmo. The answer is that you will find "everything" at Ullersmo. The people there are serving a minimum sentence of six months; most have long sentences (the maximum in Norway is twenty-one years). A boy who has been talking several times before claims that all the prisoners they are going to meet are "killers." A girl protests, saying (correctly) this is not true. Another girl complains that this is enough, that they should stop talking now. Otherwise it will get too "tangled" for her. She is going to Ullersmo the next day. The personnel talk about the prison gate, how dreary it is. A girl confirms this and talks on about how stressed and agitated one becomes when the prisoners constantly walk and talk in front of and behind you.

The meeting ends at that. It has taken approximately fifteen minutes. This is the only arranged and concrete preparation these youngsters get. The institution has used the Ullersmo project at this point for almost three years, and the form of this meeting seems to be the typical one—fifteen minutes is the rule, not an exception. There are individual conversations about the confrontations as well, but these are left to chance and are not the usual pattern at this institution.

Day 2: Confrontation

This morning, during the routine gathering and after, there is hardly any mention of the Ullersmo project at all, save for the time of departure. At 4:30 PM. five juveniles (two girls and three boys), two personnel, and the two researchers leave in two cars.

The group arrives at 5:00 PM. The guards inside are notified via an intercom system at the gate. The main gate slides open (not, as is usual for the ordinary visitor, a door close by it) and the group enters an open courtyard lined with tall wire fences. A boy exclaims: "Oh, f...! This really isn't much like M. It's worse than the Berlin Wall!" Heads turning, the youngsters gawk at the wall, at the fences, and at the open tarred square. Through yet another gate the group finally reaches the main guardroom and the reception area. Inside, one of the two officers in charge of the project is waiting with two unfamiliar young officers, presumably recruited just for this occasion. The two are given the responsibility of processing the youngsters.

The researchers now part ways. One accompanies the personnel from the institution to a brief meeting with the prisoners who will "perform" that day. At this meeting, the institutional person in charge presents the general outlines of each of the juveniles' cases, their use of drugs or alcohol, and their criminal records. He uses no names, choosing instead to describe each youngster, thus facilitating recognition and use of the information during the confrontation. The person in charge singles out for special mention the boy mentioned above as having psychiatric problems. The prisoners should "go easy on him," he suggests. "He's here more or less to watch and must not be pushed." The young man in charge says these things with a slight grin on his face. He has been to Ullersmo before and knows the prisoners. They listen to what he has to say and accept it. One, however, remarks as we go toward the dining hall: "Maybe he shouldn't be here at all, then?!" "It's all right," remarks the one in charge.

The young visitors are not supposed to know that these briefing meetings occur; nevertheless, they often become aware of it as the confrontation progresses. Reflecting on this, one of the boys said that "they just went ahead, told me how I was, things that Ola, one of the personnel from the juvenile institution, had said." Shortly after his visit another boy wrote this for an assignment at school:

> The prisoner knew in advance what the boys had done. We noticed from the way they treated us differently based on what we had done. They kept walking around us, blowing smoke in our faces. They went easy on one of us who hadn't done any kind of crime.

The five juveniles have been taken to the dining hall where the confrontation is to take place. They are greeted by one of the officers running the project; his expression is sombre as they arrive. Unsmilingly he asks them if they have ever been to Ullersmo before. One of the boys tells him yes, that he's been to Ullersmo to visit a relative. Some of the others tell him that they have been to other prisons for visits. The officer gives them a short introduction to Ullersmo. He explains that only convicts with sentences of at least six months can come to Ullersmo and that more than 50 percent of the prisoners are foreigners, and so on. He stresses the fact that being in prison is far worse than life in an institution such as M. After the briefing, the officer leaves the room and the youngsters are left alone for the time being. Throughout, the boys and girls have been seated at a long table at one end of the hall. The rest of the furniture is stacked at the other end. Diagonally with respect to the five youngsters, behind a window slightly ajar, the personnel from M, the officer in charge, and the two researchers, stand watching. This is normally where officers spend their time as prisoners eat.

The prisoners arrive, with grave faces and in a row. There are four, and they place themselves in a line in front of the five youngsters. Three of the prisoners have done this many times before; one has his first appearance this day. The following quotation may serve to illustrate the feelings of the youngsters when they first face the inmates—it is taken from an interview with a young boy:

> And then these prisoners entered, all of them, suddenly closing the door behind them. I thought to myself, "Hell, aren't there supposed to be any officers here?" But it wasn't. I tried to smile the best I could, only one of them hit his fist in the table in front of me: "Wipe that grin off your face!" Then they started running 'round, mouthing and cursing for a while.

The inmates demand complete attention; the youngsters are immediately reprimanded if they are perceived as losing attention. This is done in a variety of ways. One boy recounts how "they banged the table and yelled at you if you didn't look them straight in the eyes." Others tell how the prisoners threw salt and pepper pots at the wall or wiped an ashtray off the table. One participant, familiar with previous visitors, remarks that they all knew that the salt and pepper throwing was supposed to happen. He considered it a well rehearsed trick. This is in fact true, a ritualized aspect of every confrontation. The accusations of lack of attention function primarily as an excuse to frighten.

Having obtained the attention of the youngsters, the prisoners take turns recounting why they have been incarcerated. They do this with apparent deep seriousness. The one who starts gives his number, as do the others when it is their turn. This depersonalization is a regular feature. The one talking first informs them that he has killed several times and that he has had grave drug and alcohol problems. He's been "in the system" since the late sixties. The next one has killed once, though he can't recall what happened since he was highly intoxicated when it happened. He also has been a drug dealer, and an addict for twenty years. The third one too has killed and has had very serious drug problems. He tells them how long he has been behind bars. All three—who have done such presentations many times before—bear visible marks from the lives they have led. The fourth, who has his first appearance, is locked up for drug dealing. Though not as visibly marked as the others, he is nevertheless a drug addict, which he tells the youngsters. Throughout the session the language is harsh and streetlike and frequently interspersed with curses.

While talking, the inmates wander the room as if restless. Sometimes they pass behind the seated youths, but mostly they are in front of them, though withdrawn relative to the one speaking at any moment. Their presence demands constant attention. The one who presented himself as a multiple killer has a habit of clicking his shoes, a fact that several youngsters pointed out in interviews as particularly distracting. After a while, several of the prisoners light cigarettes.

One of the girls is told to get up and introduce herself. She is asked to describe why she is at M and thus at Ullersmo this evening. Suddenly one of the inmates shouts at another one of the boys: "And you will keep your eyes on me!" The boy immediately looks straight at him. Another one of the inmates walks up in front of yet another of the boys, the one the personnel had earlier discussed as to whether he should come along. The boy gets up at once. "Have I told you to stand?" asks the prisoner. The boy says no. "Sit down!" The inmate addresses the boy next to the one who got up. He is told to take his hands out of his pockets and obeys instantly. One after the other the youngsters are told to rise and explain why they are at Ullersmo. One participant describes this part like this:

> We took turns. The thing started at the end of the table and I was in the middle. You were supposed to tell them your name and everything. If it wasn't perfect you had to repeat it many times. All got nervous, me too. One of us had to repeat it four or five times, getting quite anxious. You also had to tell them all that you'd done wrong.

The inmate presently dominating the confrontation wants to know whether any of the five has been to prison before. They all say no. He then directs attention toward another inmate who will tell them what it means to be incarcerated. He tells them that inside the walls of Ullersmo there are at present 140 people. They all have to get up at 7:00 A.M., after which the day is strictly laid out for them. They all have to work. He then tells them about the various assignments they are given. He enters into a seemingly very emotional description of the various and very numerous controlling measures prisoners are subjected to. Letters are censored, and there are raids at night in which seven or eight officers may come barging into anyone's cell accompanied by a dog looking for drugs. They will go searching for drugs with a vengeance, turning the cell upside-down to find them. "You'll have to undress and stick your ass in the air for them to search!" He tells them that one is never at ease, is always under surveillance, and may be subjected to thorough investigation. There are raids during the day as well, and there happen to be weapons inside the prison too. Then there are those incessantly annoying urine specimens they have to give. "Refuse it and you'll lose your possibility to go on leave. If it's positive they'll put you in isolation!" If an officer has any suspicion of drug use at all, they will force the prisoner in question to be placed under twenty-four-hour surveillance until he has emptied himself and it's recovered. As for visits from friends and relatives: "I have been here now for eight and a half years and haven't had a single visit!" And "there are 50 percent foreigners at Ullersmo," he tells them. "Imagine how nice you'd have it here. You would have been abused each and every day!" The reference to foreigners is an attempt to appeal to any feelings the youngsters may have against foreigners.

Another inmate now takes over addressing the girls. He talks about a facility for women closer to the capital. He knows some of the women there from his time on the street and at a rehabilitation center. The prison for women is no better than this one, he maintains; instead it is worse. Girls in jail are often rougher than the boys, more cynical. He tells them about a girl he knew. She was given a 120-day sentence. After two days in prison she was raped with a bottle, and it continued. It took her a long time to be accepted among the other girls. "So, you see, there's a lot to look forward to . . . this goes on at Ullersmo too!" he says to the boys.

"Anybody here have enough on them to go to jail?" he asks. One of the boys raises his hand and replies yes, though hastily adding that this is not what he wants. The prisoners then start discussing why he is living at M, stressing the point that his stay there is compulsory. You needed coercion to understand, they tell him. "You're lying!" one inmate suddenly interrupts the boy's response, adding that all the boy is doing is blabbing along, not taking them seriously. "That's what you've been doing constantly—till now! You have to think differently! You're just lying when you say you're gonna change your life!"

The four inmates move almost imperceptibly from one subject to the other and then to yet another one. Having observed this mode at other confrontations, as well as having interviewed the prisoners, the researchers recognize the event as partly improvised and partly very structured through long-standing practice. The inmates generally keep to a fairly fixed range of subjects, each inmate having established himself as responsible for one or two of these. One has a knack for speaking about alcohol and violence in combination. Another has spent time at a drug rehab center together with girls and women—which gives him the authority for talking to visiting girls about the consequences of crime and drug abuse for girls. He often focuses on the humiliation and degradation girls have to go through as part of being in a drug-infested urban environment or as prisoners. Yet another prisoner may concentrate on the fact that he comes from a fine and well-established family and that the rest of his family is well off. His downfall started with dyslexia and the experiences of failure and shortcomings in connection with that.

Subject follows subject, each being related to some personal experience. The prisoners' message may be summed up in three points: (1) Ullersmo is a hellhole in each and every way; (2) The prisoners themselves started at an early age and with minor crimes, but ended inside the walls of Ullersmo serving long sentences, having ruined their lives; (3) Their young visitors have barely begun. They may yet change but have to do so now. Otherwise it will very soon be too late. If they do not change they will surely end up at Ullersmo, where conditions are bad and they will be stepped on and ruined.

The prisoners try constantly to relate their own lives and experiences to those of the youngsters, making these relevant to them. It is done through recounting a steady stream of past events and themes and with sudden physical or verbal interruptions. "One day something goes wrong. Bang, you're stuck! I started out just like any of you kittens. It's a merry ride—all until you're behind bars in your cell. That's when your problems really begin!"

The five youngsters are completely quiet, speaking only when explicitly spoken to. One prisoner tells them that he did what they are doing now for many years. "It's only a matter of time before your hell starts," he maintains. "The day you can't pay your debts!" He describes to them the buying and selling of drugs, housebreaking, and the suffering his family has endured because of him. Once he almost killed a man who owed him some money with a shotgun. He shot the man in a parking lot in front of his family. "Your standards get skewed," he says. "Something happens inside your head and in your body. You start by pilfering, continue with car theft, pass over into violence and end perhaps with killing someone." He himself killed a man at a late-night party, "stabbing him thrice in the heart." He partied on. "What normal person does such a thing?"

Three-quarters of an hour has passed since the youngsters entered Ullersmo. Two of the other prisoners have told them how their careers started and brought them to Ullersmo. Suddenly and with a roar for attention one inmate sweeps some salt and pepper pots that were on the table in front of one of the girls to the floor! The girl looks petrified. She stares rigidly straight ahead, her face is flushed. Later, she says had anyone looked closely at her then, they would have seen her heart beating incessantly in her throat. The room falls very quiet.

The prisoners continue with their stories, their attention now on the girls, the message focusing on the degradation girls are subjected to in the drug environment. Their looks are spoiled, their self-respect goes down the drain, at last nobody wants them anymore. "Dames get worn-out like w . . .—and who wants a worn-out dame nagging for dope?" One of the girls is asked how she "wangles dope." There is an unspoken reference to prostitution hanging in the air. None of the inmates asks specifically about this, however. The girl replies that she does break-ins. The other girl says she gets money from her mother. One inmate asks how they imagine they are going to get drugs in the future. The two mention break-ins and the sale of stolen goods. The inmate then wants to know how they are going to go about it when there are no goods to sell and no money to spend. "Do you know what you're gonna do, honey? You'll sell your body!" "No!" she exclaims. Whereupon the inmate replies:

> And how many do you think have said so before you? You'll be offered drugs to sleep with someone. Think about it . . . you'll let him f . . . you. You bore him. It's only a matter of time, honey, till you end up on the street. And then you won't say no to some old geezer. An old pig in his sixties will come along—what happens? What happens to others facing the same in the same situation? You'll sell yourself!

The boy they have been asked to "go easy on" is asked to stand. He is asked a few questions about school but is allowed to sit within a minute. He is rarely addressed during this part of the confrontation.

Two inmates fetch a board measuring half a meter by a meter, to which a number of weapons are attached. Many of the weapons have been produced inside Ullersmo. The board is put on the table in front of the youngsters with a bang, and the inmates start recounting the brutality of Ullersmo. One of them tells them how, as a first-time convict inside Ullersmo, he was forced to carry drugs inside his body for several months—all for fear of reprisals. It ended only after he had beaten the man who forced him to do it. Only then was he let off the hook. "I was lucky."

Prisoners use other means to convey a sense of prison. Several youngsters have, for example, told us how they had to polish the shoes of the prisoners: "They wanted to show us how much power they would have over boys like us should we ever be put inside with them. They just commanded me to polish his shoes with some paper." And another time: "They threw salt and pepper pots around the room, forcing us to pick it all up. And when we got there to take it they kicked it on. They were supposed to show us who had the power, that Ullersmo was no place for us."

Among other methods used, the following were frequent: Some were forced to stand and hold an ashtray at arms length in front of them. One juvenile describes how an inmate "knocked the ashtray to the floor and told the boy to pick it up." Another boy, himself told to hold an ashtray this way, says: "I shook so violently that the ashes almost spilled. Then one of the prisoners told me that 'If you spill it, you lick it!'" Other kids describe how they too had to clean up the mess when salt and pepper pots were thrown to the floor or at some wall. There are descriptions as well of episodes in which kids have had to remove their shoes or some clothing, or of prisoners demanding and being given cigarettes from some of the youths. A few recount threats, either of violence or of sexual harassment, in case they end up at Ullersmo. "He kept smelling me, saying I smelled good. If ever you come here again you better watch out in the shower, and so on."

There are regular sequences in which inmates comment on the image of one or several kids. Some youths mention having to remove jewelry or other items signaling a certain image. For example, one boy says they weren't allowed to wear caps inside the dining hall, "Them prisoners tore it off, 'cause they didn't like it. They felt it represented some kind of uniform or membership in a gang or some such thing." Prisoners may also comment on the appearance of a youth. One youngster says: "I wasn't exactly pretty then, my hair half shaven, wisps sticking up here and there. The prisoners nagged and abused me for it all along." Another one mentions a girl being called "hooker and tart"—which was part of what the prisoners said to her initially as well.

Throughout the proceedings, the inmates consistently portray themselves as "trash" and failures, as examples absolutely not to be followed, as people with few chances left. Life inside Ullersmo is more than anything else lonely and precarious, an existence where you can trust no one. "It may seem as if the four of us are mates. We're not. We accept each other because of our sentences. What we have in common, and what is special about the four of us, is our desire to enlighten you who are young." "A straight life is boring, often terribly so, sometimes a drag; nothing happens. But no matter how boring it may be, it's a far cry better than being stuck here. A hell of a lot better than being shut up inside Ullersmo for eight years the way I am forced to be!" One of the other prisoners starts talking about the opportunity given to the youngsters as residents at M, saying that this is a chance they have to grab. "It's not only adults who don't get it, neither do you."

This institutional reference, and mentioning this in connection with possibilities never to return, seems to be standard. It represents the logical closure of the narrative that inmates and officers at Ullersmo try to construct for the youngsters. It is the final conclusion after all the premises have been laid out. The misery of the young is coupled with that of the prisoners, the experiences and tragedy of the latter being made valid for the young. Where the prisoners have long since destroyed their chances, the young boys and girls still have one left. The elements involved in the process of choosing the right path are: the institution where they live, the confrontation, a return to their senses, a change of course.

The assembly moves on, prisoners, officers, personnel, and researchers alike, through long and low corridors, out of the building and across the square that the youngsters have already crossed once. The next station is the security cells. The prisoner who has his first appearance this day converses with the boy who was subjected to the strongest verbal attacks inside the dining hall. They exchange a few words. The prisoner repeats and stresses what has just been said to the boy. None of the other prisoners talk to the youngsters but walk silently across the square.

Having reached the security cells, attention is first focused on a cell at the top of the corridor. This particular cell comes with a large, open window to facilitate inspection. There is a bed and a lavatory without an outlet. The cell carries the name of its single function: "Lavatory Cell." Any prisoner suspected of having drugs concealed inside his body is placed here under strict surveillance until he has emptied his bowels. This time the youngsters are taken inside the cell by two of the inmates, who explain its use to them. The rest remain in the corridor watching through the window and the open door. The prisoners firmly stress the negative aspects of the room, depicting it as an intolerable and undignified invasion of privacy. At times, during this stage in the proceedings, youngsters have been told to sit down on the lavatory, and some have been physically shoved. The first time the researchers were present, a boy who tried to refuse was brusquely commanded to sit. He had been pointed out in advance to the prisoners by the personnel as particularly hard-headed. A boy described his experience with this part of the confrontation: "And then one of them says: 'Sit down on the loo!' It was a kind of concrete loo. 'Sit down on the loo!' I didn't do it, just looked at him. Then he grabbed me and threw me down on it." Such descriptions were given in several other interviews.

Next, they move down the corridor to a cell with a bed. It has belts stretched across it. The same two inmates who took care of the lavatory cell handle this. They lead the youngsters inside the cell and start talking. "This is where you end up if you can't take it anymore. Nothing at all helps," explains the inmate generally doing the talking now. The men in uniform are all powerful. There is no use screaming. This has nothing to do with rehabilitation, it's storage.

Based on interviews and reports on the confrontations at Ullersmo, it is safe to state that episodes have taken place in which youngsters have been laid on this bed, either voluntarily or against their will, and have had the belts fastened around their hands and feet. This particular time this doesn't happen. A girl describes an episode that took place when she visited Ullersmo. The prisoners, she says, tied one of the boys to the bed while she and the others watched. Asked whether she thinks the boy let them do this voluntarily, she says:

> You know you don't dare resist much with the four prisoners there, them being locked up for murder and lots of things like that. So he lay down. I remember it 'cause they said: "You, lay down there!" And then they tied him. The four of them tied him. I could see he was frightened, clearly.

The element of compulsion during this part of the visit varies. Several youngsters told us the prisoners did nothing more than graphically describe how being locked up in these cells was experienced.

Neither inside the lavatory cell nor in this cell is there any particular show of aggression. It is a solemn affair, demanding complete attention from the youngsters. This, however, is an aspect of the late Ullersmo project. There is evidence in interviews and reports that even this part of the visit has been, for a substantial part of the project's history, marked by very aggressive tactics by the prisoners.

The five youngsters are presently divided into two groups. The two girls and the boy marked as particularly vulnerable are asked to go with two inmates to a cell down the corridor. One of these inmates is the one who has admitted to killing while under the influence of alcohol. The other one is the prisoner normally talking to girls during confrontations. The other two boys go to the neighboring cell with the two remaining inmates. The two inmates are, respectively, one of the seniors and the man having his first participation this day. The doors are closed, so there is no seeing what goes on, and listening is hampered by the narrowness of the gaps between the door and the door frame. These doors have not always been closed like this.

Standing very close to the doors, it is possible to catch fragments of the conversation inside. As before, the inmates do most of the talking. Emerging from the cell where the two boys are placed are statements like this, made by one of the inmates: "This is your life, boys, may be your life." He stresses the fact that there are so many foreigners at Ullersmo, as did the officer at the beginning of the visit. They bring "all their cultures" there. And some of them are quite fond of young boys. Inmates at Ullersmo "use" youngsters, he says, both for "pushing drugs" and for sexual abuse. The two inmates alternate in talking. There is no shouting, no loud voices. The exchange is generally soft spoken, almost inaudible. At one point, however, an inmate raises his voice: "Ah, man! Use your head!" And a little later: "Well then, mightn't it be time to reconsider a few things?"

The boy and the two girls in the other cell are subjected to a slightly different set of statements, but it is quiet and fairly grave here as well. "Will you remember what has happened here?" a prisoner asks one of the girls. She: "Ending up in prison is hellish!" He asks her how long since she got into trouble. At the age of thirteen, she answers. Actually, she wants to get out of it, but it's hard. "You can't easily break with your old gang." "Are you going to waste more time?" he asks her. "Will you go on like this?" Then they start talking of drug abuse. One of the inmates shows something to the three youngsters. From the sound of it, it is the pinpricks covering much of his arms—he has been on heroin for many years. "This isn't what I want. And worst of all, my parents support me. They sincerely hope I'll make a choice, they have been waiting for that for twenty years," he explains. Then he directs his attention back to the three youngsters: "You have just begun. Very soon you're gonna be adults. Learn to stand on your own two feet!"

They go on appealing to the youngsters to take the chance they have been given at M. The prisoners are well aware, they say, that youngsters believe that adults don't have a clue as to what really goes on. They are wrong: "Approach the adults at M if you wanna run away. Listen to them!" One of the inmates leaves, walking down the corridor into a small exercise yard. He lights a cigarette and remains there until the others arrive. The other inmate ends up the session inside the cell like this:

> We're so different. All have their complexes. You need help, safe zones around you before you try on your own. That's what M is. This is no place for you to end in. Myself, I haven't dared open up but hope I may get help to do that during my sentence. There's a chance for you that you have to grab hold of. Trust the adults a bit. Think about it. It's your responsibility, no one else's!

The two groups emerge from the cells and drift down the corridor toward the exercise yard. A couple of the prisoners speak to the youngsters. An inmate states: "Whatever you do, there is no blaming others anymore." He quietly admonishes the young to use their own minds: "Hell! Think for once!" Another inmate inserts: "As for some kind of middle of the road: Forget it! Either it's go-go-go, or else it's nothing." They are in the yard for just a few minutes.

Generally, the latter part of the visit taking place in the security cells is described by youngsters as more low-key than the first part in the dining hall. Comparing the two, youngsters use phrases such as "more relaxing," "an altogether different atmosphere":

> The prisoners calmed down a lot. They sort of walked together with us and the officers and personnel, talking quietly to us, describing things happening inside the prison and so on. They were more calm then. The talk was more, you know, easy. They weren't as agitated as before.

Most youngsters, like the boy just quoted, stress the element of conversation inside the security cells. "I could ask a question," says one, "and then he answered it." "The prisoners were calmer, more sensible [inside the security cells]," says another. It is clear from interviews and observations that during this part of the visit the prisoners generally open up more to the youths, revealing more of their personal lives. One girl says of this that she "came closer to them, got to see more of the real prisoner inside. They were very understanding, really, and I got to see something very, very gentle in them." Others describe how prisoners were moved to tears during these conversations. A girl told us that one prisoner's eyes were filled with tears as he gently touched her cheeks.

Nevertheless, quiet conversation hasn't always been the rule during the stay in the security cells. On several occasions inmates have transgressed the lines previously agreed upon with the officers. Several youngsters, as does the following boy, described how prisoners grabbed them and held them up against the wall.

> They started throwing us around, you know, up against the wall, holding us by the collar. At least this is what they did to me. I can't quite remember what they said but they did try to scare me. They said: "Do you really wanna end up here?" And then they said: "If ever you come here again we're gonna beat you every day." Such stuff. There was more of that for a while. They were really mean, threw me against the wall. Though afterwards they started telling me that I should watch after my mother and don't fool around no more. You know, in that manner.

Information from several interviews, with personnel as well as with youths, confirm an episode in which one prisoner "pulled" a boy inside a cell. The prisoner "yelled" at the boy until one of the officers had to intervene. Another participant says he resisted the prisoners: "One guy slapped me and then I slapped him. We ended up on the floor, rolling 'round and sort of fighting, until finally the other prisoner separated us." This episode too is confirmed by other participants. While such scenes are exceptions to the rule, they are informative as to the very real lack of control on the part of the officers and personnel present: acts presumably ruled out in advance nevertheless occur.

The inmates leave together with one person from the juvenile institution, one researcher, and an officer, heading for a meeting room. It is time for a summary of the confrontation. The youngsters, with the remaining institutional personnel, an officer, and the other researcher, head for another meeting room.

Two hours have passed since they entered Ullersmo. Reaching the meeting room, the group with the youngsters is seated around a table. The officer conducts the meeting, first asking them how they experienced it. A boy answers: "Tough!" (Which in Norwegian carries connotations both of excitement and of unpleasantness.) "Haven't you heard it all before?" the officer demands. One of the girls replies that "it's a whole lot different hearing it from them. And it's quite another matter to see it, to face those who live here." "Were you scared?" asks the officer. At first there is no answer. "Were you afraid?" One of the boys now replies: "At first, yes." Another boy refers to the salt and pepper pots that were swept to the floor. The officer turns to the subject of drugs, asking whether they really believe there are a lot of drugs inside Ullersmo. He answers the question himself, saying that it all depends on money. "If you have money, you will get drugs, as much as you like." One of the girls wants to know how much it takes before they intervene to stop a fight. He replies that they do this rather frequently but that such events often take place where there are no officers, outside the view of cameras, in the tunnels or the stairways. "Do you regret coming to Ullersmo?" he asks. Several say no. "I hope you keep in mind what has been said. This is the way it is. Was it very different from what you had expected?" he asks. They answer simultaneously: "No!" The girl who has until now been quiet—she sat near the pots that were swept to the floor—gets the last word: "It sounded a lot worse, what the others [youths at M who had visited Ullersmo before] said. It wasn't too bad." The five youngsters and their company now walk back to the reception area where they entered a little over two hours ago.

Meanwhile, an officer, the inmates, one of the researchers, and one of the personnel from the institution are meeting. All agree that this time it was "good." They got close to some of the youngsters, who opened up. There are remarks about the higher than usual number of drug abusers. An inmate comments on one of the girls, says it seemed as if she did not get it. "She's gonna weigh on the system for a while." One prisoner remarks that they did not "push it" with the other girl. Another one injects that he did not want to use what they had been told about the youths just before the confrontation to get her talking. He might have ended up saying to her that her brother had wanted to sell her for drugs. Had he said something like that, he maintains, it would have been revealed that the personnel from M had told him that she lived with her brother. They snicker good-heartedly over one of the boys. He is a funny guy, they agree. The two other boys are not mentioned. Finally they touch upon a girl whom they met before. She was one of the first to visit. A lot has changed for her. They all agree that the way she is now is impressive. The representative from M is asked to give her their regards.

A couple of other aspects of the confrontation are briefly reflected upon. Attention is directed at the researcher. What is his impression? The changes in set-up are referred to. Much of what was shown on TV has been changed, claims the officer. "The whole project has evolved," he says. Signals "from outside" have been listened to. They talk about the attempt to establish a separate ward for the project. So far they have not succeeded. There is a discussion on the question of recruiting additional prisoners to work on the project.

Someone cracks a joke about one of the participating inmates who has been too often on leave from the prison. He has become too soft-spoken, the others tease. The researcher asks whether this may come from the presence of the two researchers. The officer denies this, insisting that it has been a gradual change. The inmates, however, agree they are a bit hampered by it. Some of the spontaneity disappears when the researchers are present. The meeting disbands. Youngsters, institutional personnel, and researchers return to M.

Back at M supper is served. During the meal, there are no references to the recent visit to Ullersmo. One among the personnel nevertheless remarks to the researchers that the other youngsters are very curious. Shortly after the meal, a boy who visited Ullersmo on a previous occasion remarks to another who has just returned that they didn't have to do this or that: "lift and hold the ashtray," "surrender your shoes," or "give them your cigarettes." He seems quite preoccupied with the fact that the five youngsters who just returned had not been forced to do the things he had to do. He speaks quite loudly, his voice being heard even in the next room. He is cut off by one of the personnel; being told that this is something he may talk about at the "gathering" which will soon be taking place. At this gathering all residents and personnel do as the evening before—and every evening at M—form a circle in the living room. The time is half past ten in the evening. The one heading the visit to Ullersmo is in charge of the meeting. He addresses each and every youngster who was at Ullersmo in turn, starting with the girl who had seemed to take it most seriously during the visit.

"The whole thing was enormously good," she attests. Most got something to think about, and she has become more certain of "what she has started on." The other girl talks about "a very fine set-up" that made her "realize where it might all end." "I've learned a lot. It scared me quite a bit, the things I understood from what they explained." The boy who went with the two girls into the security cell expresses similar views: "I was scared but I learned a lot." The three refer to the prisoners as "experts," people who know exactly what they are talking about. "It's quite something else when they say it," adds the boy. One of the other boys describes the experience as "informative and interesting." "It really got to me, the terror of having to stay inside those walls year after year."

The dialogue continues, now including the other youths who are allowed to pose questions. "Were all the boys in the same room?" asks one. The answer is no, though one of the girls that returned from Ullersmo a couple of hours prior to this meeting has forgotten who was in the cell with her. "Was the prison as expected?" asks the leader of the gathering. "No," says one of the boys. "It was nicer. They had a volleyball court, a swimming pool. The place was nicer than I had expected." The girl who couldn't remember who was in the cell with her states that it looked "boring," "square." She would "go crazy from staying there for thirteen to fourteen years."

Associations keep coming, the subjects thus changing. Various boys and girls interject remarks on salt and pepper shakers, on claims that prostitution is inevitable, of having to stand alone in front of the inmates. There is talk of a youngster who went to Ullersmo on an earlier occasion, and who "got a real rubbing." Inmates laughed at him. Prior to this, leading representatives of M had pointed him out to the researchers as one of the "worst" they have ever had, close to incurable.

Toward the end of the gathering, a boy who has been to Ullersmo before talks of doors they had to open and hold while inmates passed through. Another boy, he too a former visitor to Ullersmo and one who received rough treatment after having been pointed out as particularly difficult, maintains that in their case inmates opened the doors for them. "We were a little tougher, you see." He laughs. The gathering lasts fifteen minutes. Afterward, the youngsters go to bed.

Later, having done the rounds to say good night, the personnel congregate as usual in the living room. This time conversation focuses mainly on today's visit to Ullersmo. A researcher refers to one of the girls, the one who had just talked about her regret and fear listening to the stories told by the inmates. Did she not open up now? The personnel disagree. She "overplayed" it, they claim. The one responsible for the visit is unsure whether she "took it in." "We will have to wait and see," he concludes.

"Do you arrange for meetings with youngsters to talk about the Ullersmo project," asks a researcher, "or do you talk of it only when it occurs coincidentally?" The answer is both. Generally, conversations with youngsters take place as part of everyday work at the institution. If anyone among the personnel notices a special need to talk with one of the youngsters, then a meeting may be arranged. "Talking together is more important than getting the work done," says one.

"Has the project changed since the broadcast a year ago?" asks a researcher. The one responsible for today's visit—and who has been to Ullersmo on numerous occasions—says no. What was shown on TV might as well have happened today. However, another staff member feels that it has softened. The meeting dissolves. Researchers spend the night and stay for breakfast the day after.

Day 3: Follow-up

Breakfast: Personnel and youngsters dine together, mixed at a long table. "Will there be references to the Ullersmo project here as well?" wonder the researchers. The subject is never touched upon. As the personnel said the evening before: The visits to Ullersmo are mentioned only "when the topic comes up naturally." This way of doing things is confirmed both by observation and in numerous conversations and interviews. M has no regular meetings or dialogues in which the visits are made the subject.

Notes

[1] R. J. Lundman, *Prevention and Control of Juvenile Delinquency* (New York: Oxford University Press, 1993), p. 166.

[2] This was visible to us upon reading the string of reports published around 1980 (e.g., R. Lewis, *The SQUIRES of San Quentin: An Evaluation of a Juvenile Awareness Program* (Sacramento, CA: Department of Youth Authority, 1981); J. van Zandt, *Menard Correctional Center Juvenile Tours: Impact Study* (Carbondale, IL: Greater Egypt Regional Planning and Development Commission, 1979); J. C. Yarborough, *Evaluation of JOLT as a Deterrence Program* (Lansing: Michigan Department of Corrections, 1979); as well as C. Lloyd, *To Scare Straight or Educate? The British Experience of Day Visits to Prison for Young People* (London: Home Office, 1995).

chapter ten

Through the Eyes of the Beholders

Aspects of the Confrontations

The Ullersmo project, for a substantial period of time, was defined by close social interaction and a feeling of community among officers, prisoners, and to some extent institutional personnel. Common goals and understandings made for this rather unusual phenomenon. There was a unified belief that the job done was valuable and even indispensable.

It is very clear from the material gathered that the primary product of the Ullersmo project, its confrontations, represented a variable practice, at least when it came to the experiences of those subjected to this treatment. The confrontation described in the previous chapter represents a well-established pattern at Ullersmo. This particularly applies to sequence and contents, though less to level of aggressiveness and intensity. One item on the agenda was the preparatory description of the participating youngsters given in advance by personnel to prisoners. This information affected how they were treated by the prisoners. Based on this and seen from the point of view of those responsible for the project, this information should have been considered a highly important differentiating factor affecting how each youngster was treated and how each confrontation was conducted. The prisoners achieved, so to speak, "closer hits" with than without this information.

It is clear, however, that this kind of pre-information had served to produce action-driving preconceptions that influenced prisoners when faced with youngsters who were considered to be especially trying. The prisoners thought of them as "cheeky," "troublesome," or "hard" in advance and treated them accordingly. The "cheeky ones" ended on the lavatory; "the troublesome ones" had to hold an ashtray stretched from the body for a large part of the confrontation; "the hard ones" were forced to carry a rag on their head crossing from the dining hall to the security cells; and so on. The researchers personally witnessed youngsters, who were pointed out in advance as being particularly intransigent, receiving a lot more attention during a confrontation than the others.

Institutional personnel obviously did not believe that the advance information supplied to the prisoners produced exaggerated images and unreasonable special handling. On the contrary, their general understanding was expressed by the deputy leader at one institution: "It's a little up to yourself whether they yell at you or not. You prepare the ground for it yourself." This does not seem to be correct. Few youngsters were able or found it expedient to be "cheeky"—to behave negatively toward the inmates at a confrontation. The path they walked in the short-lived contact with the prisoners was a narrow one, and they were not looking to make waves. There is substantial reason to conclude that it was the pre-understandings of the inmates that defined their actions toward the youths, rather than any cheekiness on the part of the youths. Depending on the information supplied in advance, confrontations were a changing event.

As a social phenomenon the confrontation became defined both by the momentary relationship that developed between youngsters and prisoners and by the instructions given by institutional personnel. An inmate explained:

> Sometimes we had to get more rough in order to make people really break. There's always someone supposedly tough, some would-be leader of the pack. Those are the people the weak ones look up to. Then, if we go for the strong one and he breaks, then all the others will come as well. For, you know, they are the leading figures . . . You notice how the attitude's supposed to be tough, the cheekiness of the guy, hands in his pockets and so on. Immediately when the tough one weeps a bit, then there's no fun there for the others anymore. Then they realize the seriousness of it all. The tough one supports them; that's obvious.

Pre-understanding was an important action-driving element in that momentary relation that defined a confrontation. Obviously, however, the general mood and motivation of the prisoners on any particular day had a significant effect. There were, of course, days in which inmates were not at all inclined to spend a lot of energy. Sometimes one inmate dominated the performance, at other times another inmate.

Thus the reasoning as well as the dominant behavior changed from confrontation to confrontation.

That in itself went a long way in turning the project into an ever-changing phenomenon. There was, however, another form of variation, that which is processual and discernible only across months and years. This processual variation, or process of change, redefined the project from "more" to "less" confrontational, or from "harder" to "milder"—in the terms of those involved. We return below to the involved person's own understanding of these terms. At this point it suffices to state that the modus operandi of the Ullersmo project underwent continuous, though slow, change ever since its inauguration.

One example of this change is how the program evolved from the beginning when the celebrity drug criminal (who was central to the "pilot project" of the Ullersmo project) was merely "an element" in the confrontations. He took part no more than "two or three times," as Nyborg put it. He "talked just a bit" but was never an integral part of the work inside the prison. Another element, introduced at first but then left out, were systematic attempts to humiliate the youngster who had taken on the role of leader in each group of visiting youngsters. Referring to an episode mentioned above, one inmate described this aspect of the Ullersmo project like this:

> There is no doubt a string of elements that . . . Yeah, there was one guy once. He was given a floorcloth to carry on his head, had to hold it there while we crossed the yard. We wanted to portray him as a clown, him being a so-called leader. It was OK in a way, he turned into a clown, all right. But it didn't work. The others just laughed.

On another occasion a short boy, he too identified as a leader, was forced to stand on a chair in the dining hall. The purpose was the same: humiliation. This method too was discarded. Taking the youngsters to the security cells was introduced long after the project was established. It remained, but changed. There was no longer the roughness that defined it initially. The founder remarked: "We felt that if there's only the constant attack, then that may work for some time, but after a while all you achieve is closure." The same man noted that there had been occasions when prisoners had gone out of the dining hall to fetch accompanying personnel when youngsters started "reacting too seriously." After 1994 (the year of the TV presentation) the part taking place in the security cells had been toned down. It had become "milder," as he termed it. The actual verbalizations changed as well: coarse and frequent curses became less coarse and less frequent.

The following are other elements that were introduced over the years and kept: incessantly clicking shoes (done by one of the inmates) to create unease; circling the youths for the same purpose; temporarily confiscating shoes from a youth to instill a sense of helplessness; abruptly and loudly sweeping salt and pepper shakers to the floor, ostensibly to get attention, but actually to produce fear and increase the general tension of the situation; displaying weapons confiscated inside Ullersmo; and confiscating and using cigarettes. Each of these elements and others that were introduced and kept originated as improvisation, brought in by a new prisoner to the project. Every prisoner had his own particular way of doing things, and new ideas were tested. "We see what there's any strength in, and what there's no use in repeating," said one inmate.

Generally speaking, the confrontations at Ullersmo seemed to have been changing continuously over time, from relatively "mild" to considerably "harder" and back again to relatively "mild." Added to the examples of change mentioned above is the element of follow-up conversation between inmates and officers just after the group of youngsters left the prison. This too was introduced along the way, kept for a time, but then disappeared.

Whose decisions were behind the changes? Asked who was responsible for the initiative to "dampen the project" an inmate responded unequivocally: "None of that came from the outside nor from the officers. We are the ones running the project!" Inmates were unanimous in this. One of the others was asked: "The design of it, is that a mutual thing between inmates and officers, or is it you who have defined and made the project?" His answer:

> I've never been told how to behave out there. That goes for others as well. We've been given certain limits to relate to, but those we've placed ourselves when we've seen . . . It's hard when you're out there, working with kids. You hear your own words . . . and then, afterwards, you notice it. That's when you notice it, and you think: Oh, hell!

The officers had "absolutely no control over what goes on out there," he said. They were "in the box." He stressed the fact that the officers "have never tried to rein us in." "Have you ever lost control of a confrontation?" he is asked. He dismisses it with light laughter: "No, I don't think so. If ever one of us takes off, someone gives him a kick on the calf or something similar to it." The founder of the project was asked whether they ever had been forced to remove a prisoner from a confrontation to calm him:

> No, I've never done that, 'cause we've always told them in advance. I think too, that many of the prisoners far supersede the so-called professionals when it comes to understanding and sensing when there's

a youngster having trouble. They've been told to remove their attention immediately. I have seen that this has happened.

Nevertheless, there were cases when inmates "took off" in frustration or anger when confronted with certain youths—or in an attempt to "reach in," as they say. Some of this seemed unknown to the officers. They did not report it. Some examples are: holding youths up against the wall inside the security cells (there are three or four confirmed instances); or when their language crossed the limits of permissibility, such as calling girls "sluts," who before the confrontation were diagnosed as victims of sexual abuse. An inmate explained episodes of escalation in this way:

Prisoner: It goes without saying that from time to time you run into youngsters who are really recalcitrant, who won't bother listening to you and sort of just laugh at you. There've been many such episodes, and I know of inmates who have physically shaken some guy down there. In anger—but fully aware of what he did. That's very . . . nothing like that has happened for a long time. There's nothing like that anymore, no. And it wasn't frequent before either. Of the kids who've been here I know of only three who have been manhandled like that.

Researcher: In the security cells?

Prisoner: In the security cells, yes. No, twice in the security cells and once up here in the dining hall. That's right.

Researcher: What happened, on those three occasions?

Prisoner: That I don't know. We heard about it afterwards. I wasn't present when it happened. We heard screams. I had just finished my session in the neighboring cell, and stood out in the corridor and heard it. But I . . . I thought it was just the screaming. There was no beating or anything, just grabbing of the shirt, lifting against the wall. That's how it was told.

Two aspects are worth stressing at this point. First, that these events did not define the project as such. They remained exceptions to the rule of painstaking self-restraint in combination with *seeming* loss of control. Second, the events show how limited the control of the officers was, their lack of actual knowledge as to the details of the project, and how great the possibility for abuse was. The nonrealization of these possibilities was due mainly to the fact that the inmates were permitted to improvise their behavior during each confrontation.

The image of a project defined by the inmates was put to Jan Kors-vold. He replied:

> But that's exactly what I mean. Of course there is mutual discussion
> between prisoners and officers, subsequent to a confrontation. Yes,
> we have told them that improvisation is OK. But it has to be within
> defined limits. A lot of the things you mention haven't been discussed
> in advance, they've just appeared. Some of it we've felt was good, oth-
> er parts not. That is how it has developed until where we are today.

There is no avoiding the image of an interactive project. The Uller-smo project was a social institution, enjoying the participation and influence of inmates as well as officers, and on a few occasions, client institutions. Regardless of the interactivity, the officers responsible for the project did not, in planning, founding, or in running it, have full control of the confrontations. Despite the fact that the officers—according to inmates as well as officers—did give feedback on the performances, the Ullersmo project developed very much in accordance with the experiences of the inmates as to what "worked" or felt right. That experience and those feelings have, as we have seen, changed over the months and years. Some inmates had defining and disproportionate influence, for intensification as well as for dampening. The inmates were given much rope and were highly aware of it. Interviews with them confirm this and the lack of insight and control on the part of the officers as to the many developments within the project.

Participants' Views on the Confrontations

First, we will discuss the *reasons* presented for the running or use of the project by, on the one hand, prisoners and officers at Ullersmo and, on the other, by institutional personnel; second, the *experience-based views* presented by the kids who have gone to Ullersmo are explored.

Prisoners and Officers

This section focuses primarily on the goals sought to be achieved by prisoners and officers in relation to the youths, and secondly on the driving forces behind the effort as related to themselves. Our point of departure is an episode during one of the confrontations when a boy participating was temporarily taken from the dining hall. One of the prisoners describes his understanding of the episode, explaining as he does this, what he hopes to achieve with the kids:

Poor sod! He was this tall [indicating a small person with his hand],
a little boy. But oh was he bullied around! It was necessary! No doubt
about it. He was one meter and forty-five tall, slight but one crafty
little bastard. The power he wielded over the other kids was frightening to behold. We were very careful. I for one simply considered
him some kind of china doll. As I got eye contact with him, however,
looked into those eyes—there's a long way into those eyes! I told the
others that it was no use going careful this time. It took a long time,
a really long time, before he broke. Poor one. He was placed on top
of a chair standing, got verbally attacked. That was funny to see, him
becoming as tall as the others only when on top of that chair, just
slightly above the ones he controlled. He couldn't take it, broke there
and then and was led out. As I hear it he's gone to h. . . . He couldn't
hack it—not because he broke there and then. He told the personnel
it had done him really good being at Ullersmo. But he was so sly, pre-
tending to listen, seemingly honest when he said he'd understood.
Inside his head it was another matter altogether.

Several aspects stand out in the above quotation, first among them
the explicitness of the prisoners' intentions. They started out being careful, based on instructions given to them by accompanying personnel.
Yet, when faced with the youth, they rapidly developed another understanding, expressed in the phrase "there's a long way into those eyes!"
With this new understanding their methods got rougher, leading them
to deviate significantly from the instructions given by the institution.
Their new understanding took approximately half an hour to establish,
leading directly to an effort to make the boy "break."

Continuing, the prisoner talks about the general goal of this kind
of method. It isn't, he says, to achieve a complete breakdown. There's
simply no sense in proceeding with them if they break completely, he
claims. "Then there's nothing more to accomplish. We're not chasing it,
making people cry. There is no sense in that in and of itself. But when
they cry they're as open as can be—which is when it's important to end
the whole thing." "Is it an opening you're after?" we ask. "Yes, of course,"
he says.

What I see is an infected wound. You have to open the wound, get
the shit out and then stitch it together before something else gets in.
The whole thing is a bacteria which it is very important you get rid
of. It's of utmost importance to end it when the wound is as open as
can be, to wrap it up inside the security cells where we can talk together, clean the wound, stitch it and "bye, bye!" Simply that—and
then follow up afterwards. It is very important you take care of the
wound. Follow-up is really important, the closing.

His use of the medical metaphor is striking. What he is saying, comparing himself and the other prisoners to "surgeons" responsible for life and death, is this: What they're dealing with is a "patient" inflicted with some very serious "illness," one that it takes a lot to "cure." The only "treatment" of any "help" is "opening the wound," removal of the "inflammation," and stitching up the "wound"; thereafter the "patient" should be in "intensive care" for a short period in order to fully "recuperate." The patient is a boy or a girl, the illness is crime and drug abuse or lack of knowledge expressed through the absence of realism. The surgery consists of verbal attacks, situational control, and a very firm lecture on the insufficiency and the plight of the youngsters. Further treatment consists in quiet conversation, after that it's the responsibility of the institution to follow up on the themes brought forth during the confrontation.

Other prisoners used different imagery to explain what they tried to achieve. Most often they said that they tried to make the youngsters "realize" what they were doing. This basically meant "throwing a bucket of cold water over their heads," "getting them to wake up," or "getting them to realize the true consequences of their actions"—all are phrases that combine to mean "make fully aware." The youths lacked knowledge or had the wrong knowledge. The prisoners were assigned the task of making them realize what that meant in sorrowful practice.

The phrases that describe the goals were not there from the beginning. Those inmates who first entered the project in 1992 were all slightly ignorant about what they were supposed to achieve and by what means. One of these early participants told us that initially he simply didn't know what they were supposed to tell, how to do it, or just what the effects should be. "We really didn't know much of what it was we tried to do in those days," he said. This was not the case toward the end of the project, at which point they were all unanimous in their desire, as they said, to "inform" kids about getting off the track they were on. Using their own degradation and experiences, the prisoners wanted to provoke a new way of thinking and then a change of course.

Did the youngsters have to be scared? According to the inmates, yes. The degree of scaring, however, and their views on the means to achieve it, varied. One inmate at first dismissed the necessity of scaring altogether. After a while he rephrased himself so as to become slightly more nuanced. It all depends upon the situation, he felt; who you're talking to and how receptive that youth is. "If we were to talk slowly and quietly all the time they would only get bored. It might work for half an hour, no more. The sudden raising of a voice is something a youngster will pay attention to and perhaps listen more carefully afterwards." His views were somewhat split. On the one hand he clearly believed in information and calm—which he demonstrated to us during confrontations. On the other hand, he stuck to the notion that "sometimes raising your voice is necessary" in order to make people listen.

The message itself was supposed to be scary. The effects applied were meant to amplify the information given. A certain measure of anxiety, even fear was something they all considered necessary, this prisoner said. Yet, they were not, according to their own statements, as focused on this toward the end as they used to be at the beginning. One inmate recounted how at the beginning they were all "a little too preoccupied with shouting and yelling," how they "banged the tables" and "threw chairs and tables about the room." "It was all in order to get attention," he explained. As the group matured these behaviors disappeared.

It's fairly straightforward "pedagogy": Knowledge simply sits better with the kids if it's conveyed together with fear. Fear, in other words, is supposed to be conducive to the whole process of learning. In addition, fear is, or so the kids were told, a fundamental aspect of prison life; and what better way to learn what prison is like than to experience that aspect of it directly. The experience of fear is also the "real" experience, closest to the life the prisoners are leading inside Ullersmo.

Inmates, as indicated, developed a view that the conveyance of fear should be *measured* and *controlled*. They moved, as one inmate phrased it, from the idea that all they had to do was to "scare the shit outta them" to a view substantially more moderate. Not all inmates wanted to "open" youths during confrontation; what they wanted was to inform, but with an element of fear especially in the initial phase of a confrontation. How did the officers see this? Do their views correspond to those of the prisoners, or are there significant differences? Let's look at this.

Korsvold reflected on the gradual development of many elements in the confrontations. "I can recall one episode in particular," he said, "where the inmates crossed the line. We dealt with it," he explained. The inmates "realized they didn't have to yell," that "the same may be achieved, if not more" by taking it more easy. It was toned down, he said, because "if you keep on yelling and stay on that level, the only thing you'll achieve is closed minds registering nothing of what's said." They lock up. Nevertheless, similar to the prisoners, he displayed a distinct readiness for the use of strong measures. The prisoners "should take action if there's a need for it, once in a while. They do it simply to get attention," he said. A salt shaker to the floor "on occasion," an ashtray swiped the same way, all were necessary from time to time. There simply is no sense in preaching alone; The youngsters won't listen if that's all you do. "The kids have to 'awaken,' and in order to achieve this, the sudden shock is vital," he concluded, avoiding the fact that shakers of salt and pepper went to the floor accompanied by yelling on a regular basis even in the latter period of the project. It was definitely not a "once in a while" thing. He continued: "The kids have to 'realize the consequences' of their actions, need to be 'confronted' with all the entailments." Nyborg, the founder of the project, expressed himself in exactly the same manner. There was, however, a nuance between them when it came to "shock" or "scaring." While the one clearly drew a line on the usefulness of scaring, the other was more unclear, seemingly attached to the element of scaring without having defined its exact usefulness.

It is clear that the officers and prisoners together developed overlapping understandings of the goals and contents of the confrontations. Their interaction was unusually close and frequent, as were comments and corrections going both ways. Together they developed a community whose contents and motivational force obviously must be rare in the prison context. Their mutual understandings and attitudes may be summarized in the following two quotations, both from statements made by prisoners working on the project. The first of these makes concrete the goals of the team as far as the youngsters go; the second is the very real driving force behind their work. They are highly interconnected.

> What we've wanted is for them to halt for a minute. They have to accept the fact that they're no more than 14, 15, 16, 17, 18 years old, that there are decisions that can only be made by adults. They have to realize that there's sense to such decisions, that they don't represent egoism or some kind of ego trip—which is what I thought when teachers or parents tried to talk to me. This is what we have to bring across. At the same time, when they've been out there taking heavy hits all alone we have to make them realize that such things take quite a lot, that you have to have a lot of guts to go and do a break-in all on your own. We have to give them credit for being fairly smart kids and being more grown-up than their age indicates. At the same time we have to impress on them that they are in need of help from grown-ups, that they have to halt a bit, reconsider for a few hours. We really have to convey to them that though a straight life may be boring, they should try it. That's what I try to impart.

Their rewards for doing this are indicated by the following, extracted from an interview with another inmate.

> The best and most important part of it is when there's response or when you get to hear afterwards that this or that kid has done alright. Such things warm even a cold heart—'cause you turn rather emotionally deprived from being locked up in jail. The best part of it is

when you receive signals that this or that kid is fine now. Such signals have given me vitamin shots that have made me into a warmer person. It's made it easier for me to stay here. I look people straight in the eyes and speak out about my problems. It's given me a lot. It is hard to explain it differently.

The positive effects on the prisoner are clear. These effects were in fact a recurrent theme in our conversations and interviews with officers and prisoners alike. The officers were crystal clear: The prisoners have benefited substantially from participating in the project and there is no doubt that this was an original intention of the officer who founded the project. In fact, it was a main motivational force behind the initiative. The founder said this: "The way I saw it, lots of inmates have substantial resources that they could use in a positive way, helping them, perhaps, to gain a little faith in themselves." Later he added, "I don't for a minute believe that incarceration turns a criminal away from crime. That may happen in a few cases, but incarceration is not a good solution or something that serves society well. The many that relapse into crime are proof positive of that." His reasoning was definitive: The prison does not rehabilitate people; on the contrary, people are being pulled down from being there. Even so, "prisons are obviously necessary." What is needed is far more differentiation, especially with respect to the "vast resources" of many prisoners.

Institutional Personnel

Before we describe the intentions and goals of using the Ullersmo project at the twelve institutions, the institutional personnel's view of the series of visits, their assessment of the balance between information and scare tactics, and their opinions as to effects of the visits, we present some notes on the characteristics of the twelve institutions. First, it is clear that the Ullersmo project was used primarily by *public* institutions, though there were a few that were private as well. Second, most institutions were residential, with congregate care of some sort. This applies both to institutions where the youngsters lived only for four to six weeks and to those where the youngsters lived for half a year or more. Third, the goals at the various institutions differed substantially. Some were dedicated to prevention, others were mostly concerned with diagnosis and preparation for later treatment, and yet others were explicitly treatment-oriented institutions. Some functioned simply as places to live, the youngsters having nowhere else to go. Fourth, the majority of these institutions seemed to share a general view of the conditions and needs of young and more or less maladjusted people. Expressions for this vary; several representatives referred to the importance of consequences of action, even to the so-called consequence pedagogy. It was clear from our investigations that several prominent users of the Ullersmo project were socially or professionally connected with each other and were communicating on a regular basis.

How then, did they express themselves as to the goals of the visits to Ullersmo? This is what one representative said:

> Realism, it's a lesson in realism in which the choices made by the kids in advance, before they came to us, are made visible to them together with the way they're headed and the real consequences. Everyone doesn't necessarily end up at Ullersmo, but there's no doubt that if allowed to continue, many do find themselves in a variety of county jails. Being as active as they are with regard to crime and drugs, there's a very real possibility that Ullersmo will be their final station. That's right. And that's why they're simply allowed to face people who have been in the same situation they are in, and who have used the very same arguments they do now: "Prison ain't that bad. I can do a year or two." Being locked up is kind of romantic, isn't it, for a group of kids. And they're allowed to see for themselves that it's not particularly romantic, that it is in fact the most humiliating situation anyone can be in, incredibly degrading.

Most representatives of the institutions argued like this, that the real goal of the visit to Ullersmo was to see that the youngsters were realistic with regard to crime, drugs, prison, and the consequences of their choices. The emphasis placed on each element varied; some personnel focused on prison. Others stressed the mere degradation the youngsters themselves would experience as a result of their aberrant actions—"their future." Some in this context referred to a *deromantization* of crime. Still others moved a bit further, describing the visit as an attempt to *awaken* the kids; they used phrases like "shaking them a bit" or "opening their eyes." Expanding on this line of argument, some even seemed to want to *punish* the kids. One representative was fairly explicit in this, comparing the visit to the act of "wolves shaking their puppies by the neck when they've been bad."

Only one representative explicitly told us that the intention was to *scare* kids, using the phrase "scare propaganda." Most said they did not intend to scare, which is of course a direct contradiction of those responsible for the project—the prisoners and the officers. Most institutions seemed to want to convey a sense of *realism* to the kids. What did they think of the visit afterwards? One representative, having participated only once, described his experience of the visit this way:

> I was scared. The context in itself was very confrontational. Yet the whole thing seemed very professionally set up by the prisoners. There was no senseless yelling or screaming, rather a kind of role

playing in which each prisoner used a lot of his own identity. I am sure there was a large element of self-help in it for them. They'd set it in context, had given it a structure connecting to the reasons the kids were there. I hadn't thought it was *that* confrontational, which was why I hadn't stressed this element when I prepared the kids for the visit. I guess that was my greatest mistake, being as I am very focused on the importance of honesty in these matters. What we're talking about, you know, is a very rough experience lasting an hour and half. Obviously the kids jumped as much as me. Imagine how it is being put in that room with these people in front of you. Me, I was on the sideline, and much more experienced too.

Other representatives used words such as "frightening," "strong," "shaking," "rough," "direct," "hard confrontation," but also "very right" and "extremely realistic." One representative who had been to Ullersmo several times said that he doubted the project the first time he took youngsters there. The first impression was "brutal." Talking about this a year before it was closed, he said that the project had improved. The inmates were doing a better job, were more secure, and their descriptions of prison life were more realistic. Another representative felt the project had "mellowed" and become more "nuanced." The prisoners were "using more of themselves now" even though the basic principle was the same. Their "tools" were generally the same as before. Both representatives stressed the changes that had taken place in the security cells.

"Was your first visit as expected?" we asked all representatives. Most claimed the actual contents of the visit came as a surprise to them. One said this:

He: No, the whole thing was a lot stronger than I expected, or else I wouldn't have reacted.

We: Did anything in particular surprise you?

He: No, he'd explained that they were to be placed in a hall alone with these prisoners. I knew that. But the words they used, and the thing when they demanded that the kids polish their shoes, holding ashtrays, picking up used cigarettes from the floor, when they wiped those salt and pepper shakers off the table, the kids having to pick them up too. Those were the things that were . . . The kids got so afraid. I had believed they'd tell it a bit more, not careful but . . . describe how things were at Ullersmo. In a way they did that too. That's what they do but as I said before, I think the kids get so afraid they cannot listen.

One other representative said "the amount of scaring surprised me"; another said that "the whole thing was worse than I'd imagined . . . rougher . . . more confrontational and threatening." Some felt the visit was "unnecessarily rough," stressing their worry that with this level of intimidation the youngsters may not have been able to listen and absorb what was said.

Others had thought, however, that it was going to be worse than it actually was. The message was presented in "an honest way." It is clear, then, that the various representatives differed substantially in their assessment of the visits they had been on. Significantly, their comments on the contents of these visits were indicative as well of their views of maladjusted youths in general. The limits on what was allowed to take place during a confrontation were not standardized, but were determined in process. The nature of the limits varied a lot between the various institutions. Some reasons for this are touched upon in our next chapter.

Was it all about *scaring*, or was *informing about reality* the most important goal? This question introduced the present chapter. We've seen now that the institutions generally stressed informing as the main goal *before* they went to Ullersmo. Was this what they got? One representative said this:

> I felt they went about it a little too hard, that the worst part of the scaring wasn't really necessary. The boys were sufficiently scared without having to be yelled at or manipulated, without having to tie the prisoners' shoelaces or lifting that ashtray. The whole thing was a bit too militaristic. That frightened me a bit, I felt it wasn't necessary. Having to face the inmates was scary enough, knowing what those people had done. The worst yelling was unnecessary. I do not believe the scare program in that form is any good. It could have been some kind of normal explanation of how they'd fared, rather than all the ghastly stuff the prisoners had gone through compressed in two hours.

Contrary to this, another representative stresses the fact that the Ullersmo project uses "explanation" and not scaring.

> They really do throw a light on it and manage to present a logical explanation for it. They start with their childhood, the thing becomes whole. Had others tried to talk about this it wouldn't have sounded natural. They're the only ones capable. It wasn't scaring. It was rough, of course, and close to scaring in that way. It's rough but at the same time they express both sympathy and empathy with the problems these kids have. This makes it something the kids have to bring with them.

The two representatives quoted above had only one visit each to Ullersmo. One who had been to Ullersmo several times felt the project had changed:

> The project used to be a little harder. They did step on it a bit more before, alright. Now there's the part where the prisoners are a bit more explanatory, calm, matter-of-fact, admonishing—yet have retained some of the stronger measures. It used to be little but those stronger measures. Presently the procedure is more nuanced, a mixture of press and release. The prisoners converse more with the kids now, like in the security cells. That conversation wasn't there before. The prisoners like it that way, to be able to spend some time explaining, having the kids on their own for a minute. They feel there's more in it for them too that way. It varies though, from time to time, depending on what group we bring. All in all there's more conversation and nuances than there used to be.

There's more conversation than before, he said, and greater variation as to the use of scare tactics. The cause for variation lies partly with the youngsters but also with utilizing new inmates in the project. We know as well that the personnel accompanying youngsters to Ullersmo were able to influence the contents of each confrontation to some degree. Time, a changing group of inmates, different youngsters, and personnel initiative were all sufficient to give the representatives interviewed fairly varied impressions of the visits.

How then do the representatives consider the effects of the visit when it comes to prevention of crime and drug abuse? Do they feel there were any preventive effects? A representative who had been to Ullersmo on several occasions felt the effects had been clear:

We: Would you please describe the effects the visit to Ullersmo has had on the kids you've brought?

He: There's been a drastic decrease in the number of reported crimes. We knew these kids very well, had been in close contact with them. It worked very well. At present most of those who participated have turned 18 [the legal age of adulthood in Norway], so there's not much follow-up we can do. I can't tell you how they've fared as to crime; I guess some have had some small lapse. Many are unemployed and haven't managed to adjust and go to school. I would be surprised if none had had some relapse.

We: Could you point to other positive effects of the visit, other than reduced crime? Anything else?

He: Some have had their eyes opened and are less withdrawn. They speak of things in another way than they used to before the visit. That didn't happen overnight but they sure did become easier to talk with. They could converse, which they couldn't do before.

We: Are you aware of any negative effects from the visit?

He: I haven't seen any negative effects, can't recall anyone harmed from it or their behavior becoming worse.

We: Is it possible to separate the effect of the visit to Ullersmo from the other things you've done for them here?

He: Yes. The effect of the visit to Ullersmo, amongst other things, has been strong when it comes to keeping them off drugs. All, I say all, are certain that they won't ever go to Ullersmo. Some have been in deep trouble from alcohol, pills, etc. The visit helped a lot in reducing that.

We: Why do you think so?

He: Their reactions got a lot stronger inside there. They were told by people having that problem very close, what kind of hell they've been through and are still in, how they've ended. They're there sentenced to fifteen years. I believe that has made an impression on the kids.

We: So you believe the Ullersmo project prevents drug abuse and crime?

He: Yes, as long as the aftercare is sensibly laid out. We've proved it's possible now—but whether they'll be free of drugs and not engaged in crime in ten years I can't say. I'd be surprised if they all were, for they come from very rough backgrounds.

We: How, exactly, are the kids you brought at present?

He: We took seventeen all in all. A year ago we did a summary. Two had gone slightly astray. Three or four, I think, still have some problems. We do have some shining examples. But to believe you should be able to turn it all and make them into lawyers, no I don't believe that. Our goal, I think, must be to get them off drugs and lead them away from crime, to help them find themselves a place in society. There are examples of this.

When you read the above remarks closely, it is clear that the representative's reasoning is inconsistent on several occasions. He believes firmly in the concrete and direct positive effects of the project with regard to drug use as well as to crime reduction. Nevertheless, he stresses the fact that the changes didn't happen overnight. He also feels they've "proved" that the Ullersmo project prevents crime, but states too that there's no knowing the situation in ten years because the youths' previous lives have been so bad. In this interview, as in many others, the

desire for it to work has a profound influence on the interpretations of
its results.

How do other representatives feel about this? Most, as with the
representative quoted above, were certain that the project had more
positive effects than negative ones. Asked to provide specific examples
of the positive effects, references were generally to less crime, the tearing
down of misconceptions and romantic ideas of prison, opening of eyes,
less drug abuse, return to school, and on the whole kids who were easier to talk to. Paradoxically, even though all but one felt that the project
had more positive than negative effects, not all could point to *specific*
positive effects. The one who pointed to negative effects describes these
as "imitation of the prisoners" by the youngsters. This view was mentioned by one of those positive to the visit as well.

One demonstration of how the effect was viewed was whether an
institution returned to Ullersmo after the first visit. Four institutions out
of a total of twelve went to Ullersmo twice or more. Among the eight that
went only once, the representatives of seven said they would be prepared to return to Ullersmo. Their not doing so came from a lack of
appropriate kids. How can it be that institutional representatives who
could not point to unequivocal positive effects of the project still wanted
to go? Several factors influenced this attitude. First, the will simply to
act, to do *something*, was strong. This and other projects available on
"the market" all came under consideration. As one representative said
it: "I honestly believe in taking the measures possible." Faced with the
absence of accurate results, some representatives argued that the Ullersmo project could be properly understood only within the larger context
of the total rehabilitative effort: It's "part of a whole." One said:

> I'm among those who believe in the influence of things on each other.
> Consequently, if you're going to work with kids such as these,
> harmed and harmful as they are, you have to work in many areas
> simultaneously and hope that the total effort changes their behavior.
> You can't use just one measure and think that's enough to change
> the behavior. You need several activities, more than one conversa-
> tion, and numerous supportive situations to make the total effect
> positive. I can't claim that the Ullersmo project was the most impor-
> tant influence on these boys but I do believe it to be one important
> piece in the puzzle, at least for those boys.

One of the critics, Sturla Falck, has made an ironic point of this
readiness to use whatever means are available: "When treatment per-
sonnel/helpers experience impotence, they don't give in but try everything—which is good and commendable, but only to a certain limit."
Efforts such as the Ullersmo project may far cross the line: "Impotence

and lack of measures can't legitimize any action at all." We return to these and related considerations in the next chapter.

Several representatives argued on behalf of the Ullersmo project because it represented an option separate from the rest, from the general crop of projects whose effectiveness is considered highly doubtful. "I believe it works," said one, "so I think it's good." Lots of other projects were "too kind," she said, that's why they don't work.

The Youngsters

As the media generally would have it, the kids who visited Ullersmo belonged to a group of "worst cases" deep in crime and drug abuse. This was more or less confirmed by those responsible for the project at Ullersmo: The kids coming were supposed to be particularly troublesome when it came to drugs and crime. But were they?

One hundred and forty-four kids went to Ullersmo from 1992 to 1996. The majority were boys—one hundred ten as compared to thirty-four girls. We interviewed thirty-eight of them based on a random selection, twenty-eight boys and ten girls, whose ages at the time of participation varied from between thirteen and nineteen years (which is the same as those who were not interviewed as well). Most were between fifteen and seventeen years when they visited Ullersmo. As for criminal background in our sample, most spoke of burglaries, car or motorcycle theft, and peddling illegal substances. Six of them said that they'd done nothing worse than petty theft in stores or breaking a window. Two said they had never been involved in any sort of crime. As to drug abuse prior to participation, fourteen told us they had used drugs on a regular basis, the particular drugs ranging from cannabis to heroin. Ten others had experimented with drugs but didn't use them regularly. Fourteen had done no more than drink alcohol on weekends.

Their experiences are presented here, organized around the following issues: Did the youngsters feel they obtained a better understanding of "reality" through visiting Ullersmo? Did they see the confrontation as more focused on "scaring" than on "informing"? Was their experience of the visit positive? Were they less prone to crime or drug abuse after the visit than before? As mentioned previously, the officers who ran the Ullersmo project claimed that it should absolutely convey "a real image of the life of crime, drug abuse and prison," and this view was shared by institutional personnel. "Truth" or "reality" were keywords in many of the interviews with this group. In accordance with that, one of the youngsters, a girl, said the following:

Being at Ullersmo, that's reality. That's how it is. Those are the actual people talking to you, sharing with you, not someone reading from some book or who's just been to school. That's how it is.

Not all the youths, however, felt that the image presented to them was the *real* one. Several described the confrontation as a "play." Others felt that being at Ullersmo wasn't as bad as the prisoners tried to convince them it was:

Obviously they exaggerate a bit. Scare tactics. The way they talk, people are being stabbed in the back every day. That's not true. It ain't possible. They sort of presented it as horrifying, people dying every day. I didn't exactly see that as a true description.

The experience of realism during these visits varied. Some kids simply stated that they were presented with "reality," while others felt it was little more than "scare tactics." The actual contents of the confrontation and the relative stress on crime and drug abuse were experienced differently by the kids. Some felt that the confrontation covered both issues, yet others felt that it was all about crime and not at all about drugs. This variation is probably due to the fact that each confrontation represented an improvisation based on information from personnel and on the actual meeting itself.

Almost all the participants we interviewed stated they'd been scared at Ullersmo. Actually *what* scared them, however, differed. Some stressed the things they saw and the information given to them by the prisoners as scary. Others said the prisoners themselves scared them—they didn't know what would happen next, if the prisoners would hurt them. Several maintained that both aspects were equally frightening. One named some specific aspects: "Their eyes and the way they looked at you, their language and the things they said they'd do to us if we didn't do this or that, and what would happen inside."

Not all, though, were scared during the visit. A girl described her experience like this: "You know, it ain't all who're scared by that stuff. You get more . . . You're young, you know, you might be busier with how handsome one of them is—'cause he really was." Several girls expressed themselves in the same manner, describing how infatuated they were with certain prisoners. There is one case in which a prisoner answered letters from a girl he met during a confrontation, and then met her outside the prison and engaged in a short sexual relationship with her. She wanted some kind of "Bonnie and Clyde" relationship he told us. Most kids didn't attempt to go that far; several did, however, express themselves in a manner that indicated that prisoners functioned as models or heroes. This went for girls as well as boys.

Some even spoke of the visit to Ullersmo as an exciting experience. It seems likely to us that the way the visits were referred to by the young-sters who visited all the institutions increased the element of excitement for those who had not yet gone. Youths who had been to Ullersmo talked of the visit in ways that turned it into some kind of daredevil's challenge. Their references were often exaggerated. Several youngsters who had been told of the confrontation by former participants said that it wasn't as bad as they had been led to believe and had expected. One girl claimed that the others expected those who returned from Ullersmo to be scared. "You were supposed to display this emotion," she explains. The visit was considered a "test of courage," she said. Asked what exactly it was she meant by this, she referred to the fact that all the youngsters "had" to go through it. The personnel started talking about the impending visit as soon as a youth arrived at the institution. "You get to be a real part of the group only after you'd been to Ullersmo," she main-tained.

Most youngsters stressed that they felt the actual experience of vis-iting Ullersmo had been *positive* for them. Several thought that other kids should go too. A girl said to us: "I hope you're able to make it so that others may go the way I went." She said this is because the visit was so "educational." Another youth described his view this way:

> I think it should continue, 'cause it helps. It does. Had they only come and talked quietly, had they not been physical and scared you in there, you wouldn't give a damn about it afterwards. But you don't forget things like that, do you? So it's very good. You know, you're supposed to be frightened inside Ullersmo, to make you stay away from trouble. That's what I think.

While many youngsters claimed the visit was positive *per se*—most did not believe it would have any effect upon their behavior. Some couldn't see the point in their going to Ullersmo: "I can't see why I had to go. There doesn't seem to be any point to it. It was a waste of time." Others reflected upon the "benefits" of the project this way: "If you could have saved money by closing the Ullersmo project and making a place for the elderly in hospitals, I would have closed the project. Because I think that's a better way to spend money."

All in all, twelve of the thirty-eight youngsters interviewed by us felt that the Ullersmo project had a positive effect on them. The rest saw no positive effect of the project with regard to themselves. They were nei-ther less criminal nor less prone to abuse drugs.

Conclusions

Interviews and observations confirm that the officers and prisoners who were responsible for the Ullersmo project had established congruent views of its contents and goals. In short, they wanted to "open" kids to information relevant for a reconsideration of their choices. Fear was a necessary ingredient in this. Representatives of the twelve user institutions had a slightly different focus, stressing the need for realism with the kids, generally to be achieved with the help of graphic displays of the consequences of their actions. Few were explicit as to the necessity of fear in this, though most in hindsight recognized the prominence of this element in the confrontations. The representatives were highly diverse in their comments on the various measures taken during confrontations, thus mirroring distinct differences in the views of what measures may be allowable when working with very troublesome youths. Most representatives felt the effects of the visits were positive.

The kids on their part differed in their reflections on the putative realism of the presentation. Two general views crystallized, one that dismissed this part of the presentation and one that accepted it. Most told us that they were frightened during the visit, though the stated cause of this fear varied: for some the message and the prison itself was the most scary, for others the measures taken by the prisoners, or the threat of the prisoners themselves, gave the greatest cause for alarm. Not all were scared. Some girls were infatuated with one or more prisoners and quite a few seemed to see them as heroes or models afterwards. So most kids felt the visit to Ullersmo was positive, but paradoxically the majority said it didn't change them.

chapter eleven

The End of Scared Straight in Norway?

We begin again in the United States, whose methods have been influential in Norway as well as other European nations. Historically, U.S. society's handling of juvenile delinquency has been characterized by a pattern of interpretation and action regularly repeating itself.[1]

In this cyclical pattern, the criminal justice establishment and the general population seem to share three main notions that are constants. There is a feeling that (1) the crime rate is too high, (2) present policy makes matters worse, and (3) changes to this policy will improve the situation. One consequence of this myopic formula is an ever-changing repertoire of experiments, models and methods, and treatment facilities. The underlying "root causes" of the (perceived) increase in crime are, however, never addressed: these include urbanization and the attendant ills of an industrial society, especially the dissolution of traditional social control in the family, kinship group, village or small town.[2]

Seen from the other side of the ocean, the United States looks at present to be implementing an array of "get tough" policies. The media regularly carry reports of chain gangs, imprisonment and—unsurprisingly—variants of Scared Straight. One of the latest reports, found on the Internet, tells how juveniles from the Washington, D.C., area are taken to operating rooms and a "trauma center" at Prince Georges Hospital in Maryland. Here they are exposed to "live" victims of gunshots, stabbings, and various other forms of violent crime. Maryland has, we are told, the fourth highest rate of violent crime in the United States. The director of the hospital wished to take evil by the root by showing youths the consequences of drug abuse and street violence. "It's a no-lose proposition," says the founder of the program, costing nothing but the time of those involved.[3] It is fairly obvious where the confrontational programs fall in this: They are part of a large but mixed bag of attempts at firm treatment and/or punishment.

Although the United States is resorting to more harsh measures to deal with crime, newspapers in Norway carry reports that crime has already declined. Their source is the FBI (e.g., Federal Bureau of Investigation, press release October 13, 1996). Thus, it is not really clear from media reports if the levels of crime are high or low, or if levels of some types of crime are high while others are low. It seems obvious, however, that the deciding factors in people's understanding of what actions to take in relation to crime are more closely related to their personal convictions and their perception of *crime rates* than to the *actual* levels of crime. The media's influence on perceptions of crime is as strong in Norway as it is in the United States.[4]

Let us imagine for a moment that those believing there is indeed a dramatically higher crime rate among juveniles are right, or at least that there exists a group of juveniles particularly afflicted with drug abuse and crime. For the sake of argument, let us accept that most treatment has failed. What then, can be done—what *must* be done? There are, as far as we can see, two general approaches available: one that might be labelled the "complex" approach and another the "cut-through" approach.

Contrasting Approaches

The complex approach takes a long time, is relatively expensive, and is difficult to implement. Its foundations are expressed by social scientists and criminologists in words such as these: "Delinquent behavior results from a host of complex and deeply internalized psychological, social and psychosocial causes."[5] "For over half a century the contours of inner-city delinquency have been well established. In any city, delinquency rates are highest where infant mortality rates are also high, life expectancies short, jobs hard to find, education poor, and hope scarce."[6]

In brief, this view of social conditions and the behavior of the individual is concentrated on the underlying social causes, stressing the idea that for the behavior of the individual to change, the social conditions must change with it. In other words, in order to change the juvenile delinquent you will have to change the living conditions that give cause to his or her behavior—at least if the aim is for lasting change. You will have to strive to attain slow and tailored solutions emphasizing each juvenile's situation and personality. Quick fixes aimed at large and diverse groups are meaningless.

At a distance, what we are faced with is a "phenomenon" labelled juvenile delinquency and drug abuse. It stays a "phenomenon," however, as long as our focus is on the category and not on the individual, as long as the individual remains hidden. This changes when the figure behind "car theft" becomes a person, or "the child care client" turns into a real live boy. This is the point at which cut-through approaches, thus labelled because they push aside societal complexity and the demands for changing this complexity as a condition for real treatment, become relevant. Therefore, let us use the following imagined but entirely plausible example to have a closer look at the reasoning behind the cut-through approach. Imagine for a moment there is an officer at Ullersmo who has been involved with the Scared Straight project and has also been helping kids in the neighborhood. In doing so, he is bound to come across a boy somewhat like this:

Let's say this boy is fifteen years old and has been abandoned by his father and is neglected by his mother. For a year or two the boy has been smoking marijuana. He's a loudmouthed kid, though for someone as experienced with teenagers as the officer whose position we have taken, the glimpses of insecurity in the boy's eyes and behavior are easy to see. The boy has already committed crime, but this has not yet become a fixture in his behavior. At present he is staying at a live-in group home mostly against his own will. Faced with this boy, all talk of "processes," "modern urbanity," and "divorce rate" is irrelevant to the officer. What is at issue is this particular troublesome boy, grinning shamelessly, running at full speed toward the ranks of the hardened criminals. At least that's how it looks. The boy is in deep trouble. The officer has neither the time nor the inclination to ponder the problems of "society." He can't, even had he known of it, risk trusting the hope that this boy will grow out of it—the so-called "maturation effect." His task is the boy at hand, going, as it seems, downward at high speed. The imperative, which is how he sees his task, is to change the boy now.

This is the logic of the cut-through approach. Its starting point is the individual, the flesh-and-blood person right in front of you. Its elaboration is the grouping of youths understood to share some characteristic problems. There is little attention paid to "social causes," other than a certain amount of lamentation when it comes to lack of control and the general decline of civil standards. The reality of the boy or girl at hand represents a moral imperative that has to be tackled head on. And how do we do it? By attacking the seemingly fundamental problem: the youth's lack of insight into the real consequences of action. Delinquent youngsters have to be told what they can't realize on their own. What better tool to use, then, than those who have already made tragedies of their lives, the prisoners?

This reasoning takes teenagers behind the walls of Rahway, to confrontations at Ullersmo, and into the bowels of prisons in the United States, Norway, Great Britain, Australia, Denmark, and elsewhere.[7] Given their skills of interpretation, "our" officer and a host of others can find support and rationale for their experience-derived views in theories of behavior modification and the so-called "pedagogy of consequence," etc. "Common sense" is transformed into "scientific treatment," making the confrontations not only possible but even sensible.[8]

The officer sees that "his" boy must be brought to understand the realities of life, prison, and crime. Otherworldly do-gooders and meddling welfare officers are of no use; neither are the lofty thoughts of criminology professors or pedagogues. The conviction that scaring helps—must help—is held firm no matter what professionals may say. Finckenauer claims, "Altering or redirecting [delinquent behavior] by psychological shock therapy seems to run counter to much of what we know about human behavior."[9] With this statement, it seems as though Finckenauer hasn't really comprehended the choices with which authorities in the justice system are faced, or at least he has lost his common sense—so the officer may reason. *He*, not I, has misunderstood, he thinks, as have the head of the institution, the police officer, and the action-minded child-care official. The professor in his ivory tower can't really understand the ways of the world and of criminal youths. He can't fully realize that the only proper approach to hardened juveniles is prompt action, and that only in this way can we make them assume responsibility for their actions and for themselves.

Could he, our hypothetical officer, and the other adherents of the cut-through approach be right? Our answer, and that of most evaluators, has been and is no. The theoretical and research material used to substantiate the wide rejection of the various confrontational approaches is covered elsewhere in this book. It shall not be repeated here, though it constitutes an important part of our evaluation project. Let us rather point to a few traits common to confrontational approaches as well as to a number of other cut-through measures. The common characteristics are:

1. A *linkage* between "real-life" experiences and "reality orienting" knowledge. The idea seems to be that those best suited to the communication of crime- and drug-prevention information are the ones closest to that reality. With Project DARE they are police officers, with confrontational approaches they are prisoners. A former prison director ran a shock incarceration facility we visited in

Texas. His staff was to a large extent former soldiers hired from a private company.

2. The fixing of *limits*. With shock incarceration, limits are close to total, being achieved by the use of locked doors, constant surveillance, the use of co-"students," military drills, and punishment. At confrontations that same fixing of limits is short-term—locked doors inside prison, guards, prisoners, verbal control, etc.—but its effects are supposed to last. There is an attempt, so to speak, to raise "fences" in the minds of the youths, which will function to prevent unwanted and destructive behavior from occurring long after the confrontation has taken place.

3. *Deterrence*. This element is highly variable. At some projects youngsters are scared half out of their wits. The project at Rahway very early seemed to have turned in this direction.[10] Other approaches, such as shock incarceration, deal more with the stimulation of anxiety through the production of knowledge. There is an attempt to convince youngsters of the "reality" of their degradation and probable future, not unlike that taking place in campaigns against drunken driving and tobacco smoking. The Ullersmo project had some of each. There was an attempt to instill fear and anxiety through information as well as by concrete measures.

4. The responsibility is directed straight and heavily at the *individual*. Not society, the gang, the family, the father or mother, but the individual is held responsible for his or her present situation. It's the individual's rationality, common sense, will, and ability to express sorrow and avoid criminal behavior that is appealed to. Nothing else. According to a brochure produced by M (the most prominent among the users of the Ullersmo project), "In the end, it is the kids' own will, own courage and own action it comes down to if the necessary change is to be achieved." M uses the peer group, fellow residents and surroundings, though to a highly variable degree, but there is no intervention into the original social environment of the juvenile. The gang, the family and the neighborhood—they are all set aside. The fundamental approach is a request to *that individual* for rational behavior.

A wide array of projects is based on these four elements, all related to the Ullersmo project and to JAP. Some utilize classrooms: Individuals who had belonged to a gang, correctional officers, repentant criminals, police officers, or others visit, lecture, and try to "talk straight," generally with an edge meant to instill some anxiety in the youths. Other projects are based on short- or long-term stays at institutions. Some institutions make use of the wilderness. Youths are driven to exertion and their limits are tested, all as part of an attempt to reorient them.

Others are militarily-oriented, such as shock incarceration. Youngsters are subjected to regimes similar to or worse than an ordinary drill school for recruits. Again an attempt is made to impart new attitudes, replace unacceptable social conduct, and instill resistance to temptation and degradation. Yet other projects are, like JAP and the Ullersmo project, based on youngsters visiting prisons. Within the latter category the variation is very large, as Lundman and Finckenauer and the present book show.[11] Nevertheless, the kinship of these programs can be identified in several ways: by looking at participants (prisoners and presumably delinquent juveniles); examining the scene (the prison); or assessing ideology or understanding.

Some critics understood the Ullersmo project primarily as an anomaly within an otherwise well-functioning system. The origins of the project were attributed to stray individuals who entered the scene more or less coincidentally, representing nothing but themselves, rather than to reactions based on perceptions of crime. Were they right—was the Ullersmo project really that unique in Norway, so unlike the U.S. pattern? We believe not.

The Ullersmo project was—and this is vitally important—only *one of several related means* ("treatments") employed by the institutions who took to it. Understanding one particular institution's use may be possible by reference only to some personality or social entrepreneur working there, to the personal qualities of that person. However, understanding the use by many institutions of the Ullersmo project is not possible through such personalized explanations. The use of the Ullersmo project sprang not primarily from personal preferences. It represented a more general trend. Our material clearly indicates that the particular modus operandi of the Ullersmo project is best comprehended as a *symptom* of strict attitudes toward delinquent behavior, rather than as a unique occurrence within a child-care system otherwise very differently constituted.

The Ullersmo project was one expression, among a string of others, of a profound determination to *act* rather than wait, to *intervene*— as in the case of the good Samaritan—rather than pass by and neglect. This determination is found with skilled and unskilled individuals working in prisons and child-care institutions, and with various categories of publicly and privately employed youth workers. Those involved with the Ullersmo project, as well as our other sources, pointed our attention to a widespread tolerance in many circles for strong and unorthodox measures. The measures are limited by little other than imagination. *You may* send youngsters on an exhausting hike through the wilderness; ship them to an islet in some fjord; subject them to gatherings with crass though partly directed attacks by peers; remove their freedom of movement and confine them to an institution out in the countryside; keep them from contact with presumably disruptive relatives or friends . . . Or you may: take the youngsters to Ullersmo for a confrontation with people sentenced for murder and the smuggling of drugs, prisoners alternating between yelling, criticism, comfort and encouragement, who put them on a bench and strap them with belts, hold them up against the wall, force them to polish the prisoners' shoes, confiscate the youngsters' tobacco, etc. There are differences in expression but not in fundamental reasoning. Hard on hard. It's imperative that adults make youngsters reconsider and take responsibility for their own lives. The design of the Ullersmo project was imported, though adapted. The soil in which it was planted was fertile.

Choice of Approach

Earlier in this chapter we introduced the idea of two general approaches to the prevention of juvenile delinquency. We called one "complex" and the other "cut-through." The first takes a long time, requires patience, is laborious and is devoid of firm guarantees as to its eventual results. It is geared toward social causes as well as to the compound nature of each youngster's problems. Generally, this is where one will find researchers and evaluators. The other approach, represented by the Ullersmo project and JAP, is quick, cheap and generally accompanied by firm convictions as to effectiveness. It is founded on personal experience and gut feelings; it is particularly appealing to people rich from practice as opposed to study.

Which way is to be chosen? Reflecting on this choice, Anne Schneider writes:

> Even if criminal behavior might be reduced substantially through changes in social institutions that provide greater opportunity for individuals, such changes are viewed as too indirect and expensive when compared against the simpler solutions of increasing the severity, celerity, or certainty of punishment.[12]

Even in Norway, a country well known for its egalitarianism, there are profound disagreements on the relative weight of individually oriented as opposed to social solutions. Schneider's comment, although about the United States, is also applicable to the situation in Norway. Norwegian collective traditions and social democracy are strong. Nevertheless, there has been little effective resistance to the individualist, and in some instances, harsh measures introduced lately.

However, with the disintegration of the Ullersmo project, at least this individualist measure has not taken root. The choice to abandon the project did not come about unhesitatingly, despite the clarity of our conclusions. Some of the reasons for this will become clearer in the next section on the ethical aspects of the Ullersmo project. With this we move further into the world of polar opposites.

Ethical Aspects

Imagine for a moment that the Ullersmo project and its ideas really work. That despite the conclusions of Finckenauer and many others, these projects actually deter crime. Are they then defensible? Most critics in Norway have answered no. Some of their views on this follow. (Names are kept but actual references left out, being of little use to an international audience. The translations are ours.)

The criminologist Sturla Falck was among the most vocal. Referring to Lundman, whose book *Prevention and Control of Juvenile Delinquency*[13] is his primary reference, he states unequivocally that the genre of projects represented by the Ullersmo project is, at best, without effect in preventing juvenile delinquency. At worst, these projects cause an increase in crime. Scared Straight, meaning the Ullersmo project, he says, "far crosses the limits." Any measure taken against juvenile delinquency has to be ethically warrantable. "Not always do the ends justify the means." There just is no "go ahead" for any kind of project. The project is indefensible, he concludes. It should be stopped immediately. Interestingly, Falck supports the notion of juvenile visits to Ullersmo in the form of a "seminar or a forum for discussion." No harm comes from knowing about prison and prisoners, he says. But this knowledge should not come from "threats, aggressive behavior, or cursing."

Of equal clarity, though a bit less crass, are the remarks of Professor Thomas Mathiesen. He argues along the same lines as Falck (and Lundman, on whom most critics drew). Mathiesen, however, focuses even more on the ethical aspects. Obviously very disturbed by "shaking breaches of fundamental principles in the decent treatment of people," he states that the project far transgresses the limits of the permissible. You cannot do whatever you feel will work in the name of effectiveness, he argues. The treatment given to the kids in this project "sets aside basic values of human integrity and dignity." Effects aside—about which he states that nothing is known—the project is immoral under any circumstance. These views have a wider aim than Falck's, crossing over into a general critique of society. The present zeitgeist (or spirit of the time), in which cost effectiveness has become a supreme measure of the value of all programs, has but one example in the Ullersmo project, he claims.

Professor Nils Christie, mentioned in chapter 8, argues along the same lines: "This kind of treatment of criminals represents a breach with our humane traditions." Christie believes it should be discontinued at once.

Ulf Jansen is head of one of Norway's most disputed and nontraditional drug treatment facilities. As with the people responsible for the Ullersmo project, his opinions are based to a large extent on years of practical experience; however, his point of view differs from theirs. The "shock therapy" at Ullersmo is totally indefensible, he states. He is "in despair" over what he has seen, arguing that the use of terms like prevention and pedagogy are nothing more than "a cover for abuse." What happens at Ullersmo is best likened to "Gestapo methods," and is of no value whatsoever. It becomes slightly difficult to recognize the project when Jansen starts using terms such as "visions from a chamber of horrors and the darkest cellar." His primary goal seems to be distancing his own more or less controversial project from the Ullersmo project. In order to achieve this, any nuance is left out: The Ullersmo project is a form of treatment "torpedoing the value of human beings."

Finally, let us have a brief look at an article written by two professional representatives of the practice field, the psychologist Erika Lofwander and the pedagogue Gro Knutsen. This article appeared in direct reaction to the TV presentation. Their argument is mainly ethical, and their skepticism is signalled in the title: "When Coercion Becomes Abuse and Is Presented as Treatment." Their examples are, as with the other critics, taken from the United States and Denmark. "These things take time," they say. There is no reason to believe that quick fixes are effective even though they may look to be so at first glance. "How far may someone go before the integrity of the young is abused? . . . Certain treatment communities believe that the end justifies the means." The real basis of the Ullersmo project, they claim, is the so-called "black pedagogy," which is based on the idea that obedience achieved through coercion is "a virtue." This is a concept very far from the truth, they say. What is needed is belief in the developmental potential of the youngsters, as well as child-care workers who have been taught "patience and the skill of noticing small but certain and visible successes." The Ullersmo project—and the use of it by the institutions—represents a kind of "professional prostitution" against which every sensible professional has to speak out. The authors assert that it simply is not true, as some would have it, that the alternative to the Ullersmo project and black pedagogy is "letting them die on the streets."

So much for the critics of the Ullersmo project. The essence of their criticism seems to be this: The project is morally indefensible whether it works or not. There seemed, at the time of this debate, to be little hope of establishing a bridge between supporters and critics. Few critics seemed able—or willing—to give credit to the dedication and beliefs of the supporters.

On the other side of the fence, defending the project, there were very few professionals to be found. We will have a look at the arguments of one, psychiatrist Stein Ikdahl, who was affiliated with the institution M. Ikdahl's main contribution to the debate was given at a conference arranged by M in May 1995, with a paper titled, "From Psychotherapy to Consequence Pedagogy."

To Ikdahl, as to the personnel at M, the principles of the so-called consequence pedagogy provide a sufficient foundation for working with juvenile delinquents. Ethical considerations are constantly moderated by goals, they say. The ethic is fundamentally target-oriented, pragmatic, and situationally dependent. "Coercion" versus "no coercion" is not an issue. The reasoning behind certain choices in dealing with youngsters is centered on the *responsibility* of the people charged with the treatment of the kids. There is a moral rejection, not of the use of coercion, but of not using it when that would probably help.

Other supporters of the Ullersmo project rarely have the kind of professional background that Ikdahl has, or use the kind of language he does. Nevertheless, their views, though phrased differently, are more or less the same. The most important expressions used to defend the Ullersmo project are these three:

1. "If only someone had put us through shock therapy when we were young, we would most probably have ended up differently." This thesis probably is the most important of all stated by the prisoners themselves. Somberly looking out from photos taken inside the prison, the prisoners, the epitome of failed lives, use themselves and their sorrow as *the* proof of the effectiveness of the method. They basically say: "We know. We've been there, now we're here."

2. "If but one is helped . . ." Asked how he reacted to information that four kids who had just visited Ullersmo had fled, stolen a car, broken into a house, and gotten intoxicated, a prisoner replied: "That's sad. Of course. But . . . let's say we're able to help only one or two out of a hundred—I think that's a pretty good result after all." In this way weak results are upheld as being of some significance. The reasoning is rather biblical: If but one sheep is saved, then it is worth any effort on part of the shepherd. The individual is unique and must be rescued. *Not* doing so is morally indefensible.

3. "The results are what is important." Said one prisoner: "I believe it's the results of this whole thing that are important." As a consequence of this logic, results are relative and set aside the highly questionable aspects of the approach.

Principles of Assessment, Probabilities, and Proofs

Most evaluations of Scared Straight look-alikes have been based on true or quasiexperimental designs focused on behavioral modification.[14] Few have ventured far into the sociology of the various projects or the contexts in which they are situated. Reflections on these aspects have been for the most part incidental (Finckenauer 1982 being the obvious exception). This being the situation, our work represents a clear exception to the rule. It is based on participant observation, in-depth interviews, and rather wide-ranging literary studies. Our conclusions are based upon processual analysis and are the results of contextualization and assessment of probabilities rather than on "hard" evidence. We never tried to *prove* that the Ullersmo project was not up to the task. Rather, we sought for understanding through the gathering of data from a wide range of sources. Our answers are the results of careful weighing and interpretation of these data—the explanatory analysis of the far-flung and complicated history, sociology, ideology and experiences of the Ullersmo project and the varied group of actors who came together to produce the project. Our goal was to understand rather than obtain evidence, to contextualize rather than dismiss.

Most of our material has been presented in these four chapters. One part of it is, however, totally absent. Very important relative to our conclusions was the string of evaluations done mostly in the United States at the end of the seventies and the beginning of the eighties. Some of these have been briefly referred to above. In our original report, a substantial part of the text was devoted to presentation, discussion, and application of this material together with literature devoted to general discussions of crime and juvenile delinquency. As it is, our conclusions here may seem somewhat unfounded, but they are based on a larger body of material.

Our recommendation was that the Ullersmo project should be terminated. This was based on two considerations. First, the internal weaknesses of the project were manifest, severe, and seemed unavoidable. The project simply didn't function in the way it was supposed to. Information didn't flow as it should, events went out of control, and youngsters who should on no account have gone were taken to Ullersmo. The controlling mechanisms in the Ullersmo project were highly inadequate. Actions took place inside the prison that violated both the letter and certainly the spirit of the bylaws that regulate the treatment of troublesome youths in Norway, and ethical transgressions were numerous and highly serious. Interpretations and tweakings aside, this simply isn't the way troublesome or delinquent youngsters are supposed to be treated. Though the principle of discussion and compromise had been basic to our work from day one, there seemed to be no room for compromise on this fundamental issue nor for methodological adjustment in the project.

Second, we could find no evidence in the literature, neither in published evaluations nor in discussions with researchers, to support the idea that scaring and admonishing delinquent youths for two hours inside a prison helps their rehabilitation. Delinquency prevention and rehabilitation are difficult to achieve. Attempts are legion and success is hard to come by—in fact, truly impossible as the result of scaring and intimidation. The evidence for this in the literature to us seemed overwhelming.

Thus, the weaknesses embedded in the practices of the Ullersmo project as well as in the treatment method itself were demonstrated to us.

End of Story?

Our report was released in January 1997. The attention it received was formidable. The Ullersmo project was stopped immediately. The officers and prisoners who ran it expressed deep disappointment and doubts as to the contents of the report.

Could it happen again? Could there be another Ullersmo project in Norway? There seems to be no chance for any projects stating kinship with Scared Straight. Any project explicitly related to the project at Rahway or to the one at Ullersmo would most likely not be allowed to be established. What of others, then, projects drawing on the same fundamental understanding, focused on the relevance of "real experience," but applying other methods, such as boot camps, wilderness experiences or even Project DARE? Could such projects be established in Norway?

The head of one of the most prominent institutions responsible for sending kids to Ullersmo called us shortly after the publication of our report. In his original interview with us he had stressed the indispensability of the Ullersmo project for the institution's own work, and the informational material distributed by the institution explicitly stated the usability of the Ullersmo project for the rehabilitation of youngsters living there. Talking to us after our report was published, this same person was anxious to stress the opposite of what he'd said before. This was no surprise. Reinterpretation and change of mind is common in participant observation and processual analysis. What's more interesting is the fact that his fundamental belief in the ideas underlying Ullersmo were the same as they were during our interview a year and a half before.

In general, the response to our report serves to convince us that yes, the Ullersmo project is dead. But its relatives will keep appearing in Norway as they do in the states. The founder of the Ullersmo project has been back to the United States for yet another dose of inspiration and training, though with a focus on approaches other than Scared Straight. He still believes an awareness of experiences inside the prison are valuable to many people living outside of it.

Notes

1 See, for example, T. J. Bernard, *The Cycle of Juvenile Justice* (New York, Oxford: Oxford University Press, 1992), p. 3f.
2 Ibid., p. 6.
3 K. S. Taylor, "Urbane Woes: Scared Straight?" *Hospital & Health Networks* 6, no. 4, (1995): 54.
4 G. Cavender, "'Scared Straight': Ideology and the Media," *Journal of Criminal Justice* 9 (1981): 431–39.
5 J. O. Finckenauer, *Scared Straight! and the Panacea Phenomenon* (Englewood Cliffs, NJ: Prentice-Hall, (1982), p. 44.
6 R. J. Lundman, *Prevention and Control of Juvenile Delinquency* (New York: Oxford University Press, 1982). p. 245.
7 C. Lloyd, *To Scare Straight or Educate? The British Experience of Day Visits to Prison for Young People* (London: Home Office, 1995); P. O'Malley, G. Coventry and R. Walters, "Victoria's 'Day in Prison Program': An Evaluation and Critique," *Australian and New Zealand Journal of Criminology* 26 (1993): 171–83; C. Kiberg, "Unge lod sig ikke skræmme til lovlydighed," *Nyt Fra Kriminalforsorgen* 5 (1992): 6–7.
8 R. Ross and B. McKay, "Behavioral Approaches to Treatment in Corrections," *Canadian Journal of Criminology* 20 (1978): 279–92; Finckenauer, *Scared Straight!*, p. 44.
9 Ibid., p. 44.
10 Ibid.; Finckenauer, *Juvenile Awareness Project. Evaluation Report No. 2* (Newark, NJ: Rutgers University School of Criminal Justice, 1979); Finckenauer and J. Storti, *Juvenile Awareness Project Help. Evaluation Report No. 1* (Newark, NJ: Rutgers University School of Criminal Justice, 1979).

[11] Finckenauer, *Scared Straight!*; Lundman, *Prevention and Control of Juvenile Delinquency*.

[12] A. L. Schneider, *Deterrence and Juvenile Crime: Results from a National Policy Experiment* (New York: Springer-Verlag, 1990), p. 105.

[13] Lundman, *Prevention and Control of Juvenile Delinquency*.

[14] Finckenauer, *Juvenile Awareness Project. Evaluation Report No. 2*; J. C. Yarborough, *Evaluation of JOLT as a Deterrence Program* (Lansing: Michigan Department of Corrections, 1979); S. Langer, *The Rahway State Prison Lifers' Group: A Critical Analysis* (Unpublished doctoral dissertation, Kean College, Union, NJ), Department of Sociology; R. V. Lewis, "Scared Straight California Style: Evaluation of the San Quentin Squires Program," *Criminal Justice and Behavior* 10, no. 2 (1983): 209–26; T. P. Locke, G. M. Johnson, K. Kirigin-Ramp, J. D. Atwater and M. Gerrard, "An Evaluation of a Juvenile Education Program in a State Penitentiary," *Evaluation Review* 10, no. 3 (1986): 281–98; D. D. Cook and C. L. Spirrison, "Effects of a Prisoner-Operated Delinquency Deterrence Program: Mississippi's Project Aware," *Journal of Offender Rehabilitation* 17, no. 314 (1992): 89–99.

chapter twelve

Scared Straight Survives

The Norway experience just described is much more dramatically definitive than what has typically occurred in the United States. In the United States, Scared Straight has not disappeared, but rather has reinvented itself. This reinvention or partial reinvention of many Scared Straight programs mostly involved simply downplaying their scare tactics and calling what they now do "education." They emphasize that this is different from the traditional Scared Straight-type confrontation. Let us examine this claim.

If the goal of these programs is education, that would seem to pose several issues. One has to do with the medium and the message. Since the message—delinquency will get you into trouble—is one regularly delivered by parents, teachers, counselors, probation officers, and judges, it is obviously not new. It is the messengers (prisoners) and the medium (prison) that are different. The belief is that these messengers and this medium—being more harsh, more realistic, more graphic—will be more credible, and being more credible, will be more effective. However, the results clearly indicate otherwise.

Another issue is the intent of this education. If it is education, then to what end? Or perhaps is there no end? Perhaps the prison experience is meant as a kind of civics education—education that is its own reward and that has no particular utilitarian purpose. If these efforts to enhance juvenile awareness have no utilitarian purpose, then we should not expect nor look for effects upon behavior. Of course if that is so, then Scared Straight is not delinquency prevention.

But, you might ask, if the goal is not to prevent delinquency, what is the justification? What is the rationale? Is it just a sham to give the impression of action? Is it to make the various parties feel good that they are doing something about the delinquency problem? Is it to give prison inmates something to do? Is it to entertain them? Since it is hard to imagine that these motives are what program supporters have in mind, then there must be some purpose.

We are then back to asking just what that purpose is. What could it be except to try to change youthful attitudes and behavior? And if this education is intended to prevent delinquency, then we can ask if it works. With respect to that question, according to every scrap of information we have marshalled and presented, the answer is a resounding no!

Apart from an obfuscation of goals, the new brand of nonconfrontational "education" mostly looks to us just like the old (and now much maligned) scare tactics. Old wine in new bottles? Even more subtly, the same message is delivered, minus the screaming and four-letter words—but with the same set of assumptions. Unless these programs are all frauds, then no matter how you look at it, and no matter what you call it, those assumptions and their underlying philosophy still point to deterrence. There is a firm belief that this kind of mix of direct and vicarious experience of the consequences of deviance will change the attitudes and rational choices that lead to crime. There is an overarching belief in the myth that youth can be "educated" in this special way to make informed decisions regarding their behavior based upon the lessons and examples of the inmates who share their stories. It is just this philosophical assumption, and not simply the means by which it is delivered, that has been overwhelmingly refuted.

Obfuscation also rears its head in the form of the low threshold/cost effectiveness rationale. According to this argument, these programs are not doing any harm. Even if only one or a few juveniles may get something out of it, it doesn't cost anything, so what is the harm? There are a number of reasons why things may not be as benign as they are made out to be. First, that an aversive experience of this kind is not harmful to the young persons subjected to it is an untested assumption. The fact is we do not know whether it may be harmful to at least certain children. Second, to the extent that these approaches encourage even more harsh and frightening efforts at deterrence propels us further in a search for this particular "fools' gold" as a panacea for delinquency. Third, individually focused aversive efforts may divert attention away from pressing needs and may paper over a multitude of criminogenic factors that lie at the heart of juvenile delinquency. These effects are all harmful.

Our conclusion is that Scared Straight and other similar programs are failures. The endurance of many of them, however, is another matter—seemingly untouched by success and failure. This paradox results from two sets of factors that appear to operate in tandem. The first is contextual factors—factors related to the environment in which the programs exist. The second is policy as myth factors—factors having to do with the enduring, gut-level belief in deterrence by aversion.

- The first of the contextual factors is a political climate that demands that something be done about the juvenile crime problem and that this something be rough and tough. Tough means holding juveniles responsible and accountable and employing meaningful sanctions. Among other things, this political climate both encourages and is receptive to the myth that being an object of aversion is deserved and the fear of it deters deviance.

  Interestingly, Scared Straight-type programs may gain support from both ends of the political spectrum: On the one hand, they appear to be tough; but on the other, they are an alternative to even more punitive punishment.

- Next, there is an environment in which there is a perception that little else (especially treatment) works, an environment in which there have been cuts in rehabilitation programs for juvenile offenders. When the original Scared Straight program began in the 1970s, it followed on the heels of the "nothing works" debate sparked by the famous Martinson report[1] that spurred that conclusion. Not knowing what else to do, but being driven to do something, leaves people especially receptive to a cheap approach that talks "tough" about consequences and responsibility.

- Then there is the inertia of programs that once created have a way of taking on a life of their own. As we have shown, the ineffectiveness of Scared Straight led some programs to simply redefine their purpose. It is not insignificant that their new mission became education. However defined, this is a purpose that is not easily challenged. Not only is it ambiguous, but it piggybacks on the widespread belief that education (whatever it is) is good.

- Finally, there is the media climate that also helps perpetuate the myth. Whether in the form of mysteriously sourced success rates, or in tales of the one wayward youth who has turned his or her life around, the media's message is that it works. For a variety of reasons media may not be all that interested in the scientific evidence. Scared Straight programs play well on TV; they have visual appeal. They also lend themselves to sound bites.

A combination of these contextual factors, working in conjunction with what we want to believe or are programmed to believe, helps insulate Scared Straight from other information to the contrary. As we have repeated over and over, Scared Straight in all its forms represents faith in the mythical powers of deterrence. This faith is preserved in several ways.

- As witness the Norway example, the gap between practitioners and researchers may leave those practitioners who are the principal forces behind these programs ignorant of any research results. This is not entirely their fault, since researchers (especially academic evaluators) communicate their research more to the academic community than to practitioners. In any event, out of their ignorance, these practitioners have no reason to distrust their fundamental belief in repressive deterrence.

- There is also a rejection of science by those who know about but are suspicious of that which is rational-empirical, which is a product of the ivory tower. It is difficult to discern definitive results in programs that purport to change human behavior. The outcomes of programs are often perplexing to judge. Social science is complicated, conclusions are hedged, scientists disagree, results conflict. An approach based on common sense rather than on scientific data is often much easier to handle.

- Then there are those administrators and officials who do not try to find out, or do not care to find out, what information might be available to them. They ignore anything that does not support where they want to go. And where they want to go is with the sweep of public feelings and fears, thus being in the safe position of carrying out the will of the people.

The importance of our argument and our findings, we believe, goes beyond Scared Straight per se. Two of the most high-profile approaches for combating delinquency currently extant reflect much of the very same pattern we have just described. The philosophy underlying the enormously popular drug abuse education program called Project DARE reflects this belief in deterrence. It is based upon the idea that education—giving information that stresses consequences, with police officers as the credible messengers—will deter children from using drugs. The evidence is overwhelming that it fails to achieve that objective.[2] Nevertheless, Project DARE continues to thrive.

The same is true of juvenile boot camps. Using harsh, military-like treatment, these boot camps stress individual accountability and responsibility. Consequences and specific deterrence are big parts of their approach to juvenile offenders. Does this aversive experience deter further delinquency among their graduates? The best available evidence we have suggests it does not.[3] But as with DARE, boot camps too continue and multiply.

Because the belief in myths and panaceas dies hard, we expect Project DARE, juvenile boot camps, and yes, the progeny of Scared Straight, to live on.

Notes

[1] Robert Martinson, "What Works?: Questions and Answers about Prison Reform," *The Public Interest* (Spring 1974): 22–54.

[2] See, for example, Dennis P. Rosenbaum and Gordon S. Hanson, "Assessing the Effects of School-Based Drug Education: A Six-Year Multi-Level Analysis of Project DARE," *Journal of Research in Crime and Delinquency* 35, no. 4 (November 1998).

[3] See, for example, Michael Peters, David Thomas, and Christopher Zamberlan, "Boot Camps for Juvenile Offenders: Program Summary" (Washington, DC: OJJDP, September 1997). This report concludes that "[a]t this point in their development, boot camps do not appear to be the panacea that many hoped they would become" (p. 32).

Appendix A

NAME: _____

ADDRESS: _____

_____

_____

AGE: (Circle One)

12   13   14   15   16   17

SEX: (Circle One)

Male   Female

RACE: (Circle One)

Black   Hispanic   White   Other

I. ATTITUDE TOWARD PUNISHMENT OF CRIMINALS

This is a study of attitudes toward punishment of criminals. Following are a number of statements expressing different attitudes toward punishment of criminals.

Put a check mark if you AGREE with the statement.

Put a cross if you DISAGREE with the statement.

Try to indicate either agreement or disagreement for each statement. If you simply cannot decide about a statement you may mark it with a question mark.

This is not an examination. There are no right or wrong answers to these statements. This is simply a study of people's attitudes toward the punishment of criminals. Please indicate your own convictions by a check mark (√) when you AGREE and by a cross (X) when you DISAGREE.

_____ 1. A person should be put in prison only for very bad crimes.

_____ 2. It is wrong for the government to make any people suffer in prison.

_____ 3. Hard prison life will keep men from committing crime.

_____ 4. Punishment does not make some criminals any better.

_____ 5. In prison many men learn to be worse criminals.

_____ 6. We should not bother about the comfort of a prisoner.

_____ 7. A criminal will go straight only when he finds that prison life is hard.

_____ 8. There isn't any punishment that will keep men from committing crime.

_____ 9. Prisons make men worse than they were.

_____ 10. Only men who have committed several crimes should be punished.

_____ 11. We should use physical punishment in dealing with all criminals.

_____ 12. I don't know anything about the treatment of crime.

_____ 13. We should be ashamed to punish criminals.

_____ 14. Putting a criminal in a cell by himself will make him sorry.

_____ 15. It is better for us to be easy on certain criminals.

_____ 16. Only kind treatment can cure criminals.

_____ 17. Cruel prison treatment makes criminals want to get even.

_____ 18. No kindness should be shown to prisoners.

_____ 19. Many men who aren't very bad become dangerous criminals after a prison term.

_____ 20. If we do not punish criminals, we will have more crime.

_____ 21. Only by very cruel punishment can we cure the criminal.

_____ 22. Severe punishment makes men worse criminals.

_____ 23. A criminal should be punished first and then reformed.

_____ 24. One way to keep men from crime is to make them suffer.

_____ 25. We cannot make a good citizen of a criminal if we punish him.

_____ 26. Having to live on bread and water in prison will cure the criminal.

_____ 27. Cruel treatment of a criminal makes him more dangerous.

_____ 28. A jail sentence will cure many criminals.

_____ 29. Prisoners should be chained.

_____ 30. In order to decide how to treat a criminal we should know what kind of person he is.

_____ 31. Even the very worst criminal should not be mistreated.

_____ 32. It is fair for the government to punish men who break the laws.

_____ 33. Kind treatment makes the criminal want to be good.

_____ 34. We have to use some punishment in dealing with criminals.

II. SEMANTIC DIFFERENTIAL

The purpose of this study is to find out what certain words mean to different people. In filling out this form, please judge the words based on what they mean to YOU. Each page presents a concept (such as AUTOMOBILE), and a number of scales (such as good— bad, dirty—clean, and so on). You are to rate the concept on the 7-point scales which follow it.

If you feel that the concept is VERY CLOSELY RELATED to one end of the scale, you might place your cross mark (X) as follows:

AUTOMOBILE
good X : : : : : : bad

If you feel that the concept is QUITE CLOSELY RELATED to one side of the scale, you might mark it as follows:

GIRL
beautiful : X : : : : : ugly

If the concept seems ONLY SLIGHTLY RELATED to one side as opposed to the other, you might mark as follows:

AUTHORITY
clean : : X : : : : dirty

If you consider the scale COMPLETELY UNRELATED, or BOTH SIDES EQUALLY RELATED, you would mark the middle space on the scale:

APPLE
kind : : : X : : : cruel

This is NOT a test. There are no right or wrong answers. We want your first impressions. We want your honest impressions. Work rapidly. DO NOT GO BACK.

CRIME

good	:	:	:	:	:	:	bad
beautiful	:	:	:	:	:	:	ugly
clean	:	:	:	:	:	:	dirty
cruel	:	:	:	:	:	:	kind
unpleasant	:	:	:	:	:	:	pleasant
happy	:	:	:	:	:	:	sad
nice	:	:	:	:	:	:	awful
honest	:	:	:	:	:	:	dishonest
unfair	:	:	:	:	:	:	fair
valuable	:	:	:	:	:	:	worthless

LAW

good	:	:	:	:	:	:	bad

worthless	: : : : : :	valuable
beautiful	: : : : : :	ugly
unfair	: : : : : :	fair
clean	: : : : : :	dirty
dishonest	: : : : : :	honest
kind	: : : : : :	cruel
awful	: : : : : :	nice
pleasant	: : : : : :	unpleasant
sad	: : : : : :	happy

JUSTICE

worthless	: : : : : :	valuable
fair	: : : : : :	unfair
dishonest	: : : : : :	honest

	: : : : : :	
awful	: : : : : :	nice
sad	: : : : : :	happy
pleasant	: : : : : :	unpleasant
cruel	: : : : : :	kind
dirty	: : : : : :	clean
ugly	: : : : : :	beautiful
bad	: : : : : :	good

I (MYSELF)

	: : : : : :	
happy	: : : : : :	sad
nice	: : : : : :	awful
honest	: : : : : :	dishonest
fair	: : : : : :	unfair
valuable	: : : : : :	worthless

bad	: : : : : :	good
ugly	: : : : : :	beautiful
dirty	: : : : : :	clean
cruel	: : : : : :	kind
unpleasant	: : : : : :	pleasant

PRISON

awful	: : : : : :	nice
bad	: : : : : :	good
beautiful	: : : : : :	ugly
clean	: : : : : :	dirty
cruel	: : : : : :	kind
dishonest	: : : : : :	honest
fair	: : : : : :	unfair

happy   : : : : : :   sad

pleasant   : : : : : :   unpleasant

valuable   : : : : : :   worthless

POLICEMAN

valuable   : : : : : :   worthless

fair   : : : : : :   unfair

bad   : : : : : :   good

ugly   : : : : : :   beautiful

honest   : : : : : :   dishonest

nice   : : : : : :   awful

dirty   : : : : : :   clean

cruel   : : : : : :   kind

happy   : : : : : :   sad

pleasant : : : : : : unpleasant
          : : : : : :

PUNISHMENT

pleasant : : : : : : unpleasant
          : : : : : :

cruel : : : : : : kind
       : : : : : :

clean : : : : : : dirty
       : : : : : :

ugly : : : : : : beautiful
      : : : : : :

good : : : : : : bad
      : : : : : :

happy : : : : : : sad
       : : : : : :

awful : : : : : : nice
       : : : : : :

honest : : : : : : dishonest
        : : : : : :

worthless : : : : : : valuable
           : : : : : :

fair : : : : : : unfair
      : : : : : :

III.   ATTITUDES TOWARD OBEYING THE LAW

For each of the following statements indicate whether you agree or disagree by placing a cross mark (X) in the appropriate box.

1.   It's all right to take things which are covered by insurance.

Strongly Agree	Agree	Disagree	Strongly Disagree
☐	☐	☐	☐

2.   It's all right to keep things you find if they are covered by insurance.

Strongly Agree	Agree	Disagree	Strongly Disagree
☐	☐	☐	☐

3.   It's all right for a person to break the law; it is getting caught that is bad.

Strongly Agree	Agree	Disagree	Strongly Disagree
☐	☐	☐	☐

4.   A person should obey the law no matter how much it gets in their way.

Strongly Agree	Agree	Disagree	Strongly Disagree
☐	☐	☐	☐

IV.   GLUECK SOCIAL PREDICTION TABLE

Five statements are given in the following section. For each one, mark (X) the idea that seems the best way to describe most of YOUR LIFE AT HOME.

1. The discipline given to me by my father (or person acting for my father) was:
   - (   ) Very strict.
   - (   ) Strict, but usually fair.
   - (   ) Sometimes strict, sometimes easy.
   - (   ) Usually easy.
   - (   ) Very easy.

2. My mother (or person acting for my mother) gave me supervision that was:
   - (   ) Very helpful, with close watch over me.
   - (   ) Usually helpful, although sometimes she failed.
   - (   ) Helpful only when I asked for help or advice.
   - (   ) Most likely to let me do anything I pleased.
   - (   ) Completely useless, because she did not care what I did.

3. My father (or person acting for my father) usually showed that he:
   - (   ) Liked me a great deal.
   - (   ) Liked me about the same as he liked his friends.
   - (   ) Neither liked me nor disliked me.
   - (   ) Disliked me most of the time.
   - (   ) Did not want me around.

4. My mother (or person acting for my mother) usually showed that she:
   - (   ) Liked me a great deal.
   - (   ) Liked me about the same as she liked her friends.
   - (   ) Neither liked me nor disliked me.
   - (   ) Disliked me most of the time.
   - (   ) Did not want me around.

5. My family (parents, brothers, sisters) has made me think that we:
   - (   ) Stick pretty close together in everything.
   - (   ) Would help each other more than we would help friends.
   - (   ) Can be equally happy at home or away from home.
   - (   ) Would rather be with friends than with relatives.
   - (   ) Have almost nothing that we like to do together.

Appendix B

Code Number

County of Residence

I. INTERVIEW SCHEDULE

   1. Sex
☐ Male   ☐ Female
   2. Race
☐ White   ☐ Black   ☐ Hispanic   ☐ Other
   3. How old are you? _____
        When were you born? _____
   4. Do you go to school?
☐ Yes   ☐ No
  4a. (IF YES) What grade are you in?_____
  4b. (IF NO) What do you do with yourself?
☐ Full-time job   ☐ Part-time job
☐ Other   (WRITE IN) _____
☐ Nothing
   5. With whom do you live?
☐ Both parents   ☐ One Parent (WRITE IN)
☐ Other   (WRITE IN) _____

☐ No one
   6. What does your (father/mother/guardian) do for a living?
☐ White-collar job   ☐ Blue-collar job
☐ Other (WRITE IN) _____
☐ Don't know/no answer

THE FOLLOWING QUESTIONS ARE TO BE ASKED ONLY OF THE
JUVENILE AWARENESS PROJECT ATTENDEES

1. Who decided that you should visit the Lifers' project at Rahway
    Prison?
2. Why do you think that they decided that? (PROBE)
3. Did you want to go? Why or why not? (PROBE)
4. What did you think of your visit to the project at Rahway? (PROBE)
5. Do you think that the visit was helpful to you? Why or why not?
    (PROBE)
6. Do you think that these visits are helpful to other kids? Why or why
    not? (PROBE)

II. FOR JUVENILE AWARENESS PROJECT ATTENDEES

Assure Confidentiality of Information.
Emphasize Importance of Answering Fully and Accurately.
Assure that *Information Will not Be Given to Anyone.*

Think back! Think carefully! *Since you went on the visit to Rahway Prison,* have you done any of the following things:

1. Did things your parents/guardian told you not to do?

If yes, about how many times? Once, twice, three or four times, or five or more times?

☐ Once ☐ Twice ☐ Three or four ☐ Five or more

2. Did things other adults such as a teacher, the school principal, a policeman, etc.—told you not to do?

If yes, about how many times? Once, twice, three or four times, or five or more times?

☐ Once ☐ Twice ☐ Three or four ☐ Five or more

3. Driven without a license?

If yes, about how many times? Once, twice, three or four times, or five or more times?

☐ Once ☐ Twice ☐ Three or four ☐ Five or more

4. Committed any other traffic violations—such as drunken driving, causing an accident, careless or reckless driving, etc.?

If yes, about how many times? Once, twice, three or four times, or five or more times?

☐ Once ☐ Twice ☐ Three or four ☐ Five or more

5. Ran away from home?

If yes, about how many times? Once, twice, three or four times, or five or more times?

☐ Once ☐ Twice ☐ Three or four ☐ Five or more

6. Skipped school without permission?

If yes, about how many times? Once, twice, three or four times, or five or more times?

☐ Once ☐ Twice ☐ Three or four ☐ Five or more

7.   Bought beer, wine or liquor? Or, had someone buy it for you?

If yes, about how many times? Once, twice, three or four times, or five or more times?

☐ Once   ☐ Twice   ☐ Three or four   ☐ Five or more

8.   Drank beer, wine or liquor without your parents permission?

If yes, about how many times? Once, twice, three or four times, or five or more times?

☐ Once   ☐ Twice   ☐ Three or four   ☐ Five or more

9.   Taken anything of minor value—say under $2.00, such as cigarettes, candy, comic books, money, etc.?

If yes, about how many times? Once, twice, three or four times, or five or more times?

☐ Once   ☐ Twice   ☐ Three or four   ☐ Five or more

10.   Taken anything of medium value—say worth between $2.00 and $50.00—such as clothing, auto parts, liquor, radios, money, etc.?

If yes, about how many times? Once, twice, three or four times, or five or more times?

☐ Once   ☐ Twice   ☐ Three or four   ☐ Five or more

11.   Taken anything of major value—say worth more than $50.00?

If yes, about how many times? Once, twice, three or four times, or five or more times?

☐ Once   ☐ Twice   ☐ Three or four   ☐ Five or more

12.   Destroyed property such as by throwing rocks or sticks in order to break windows, or street lights or things like that?

If yes, about how many times? Once, twice, three or four times, or five or more times?

☐ Once   ☐ Twice   ☐ Three or four   ☐ Five or more

13.   Destroyed property by breaking up or helping to break up the furniture in a school, church or other public building?

If yes, about how many times? Once, twice, three or four times, or five or more times?

☐ Once   ☐ Twice   ☐ Three or four   ☐ Five or more

14. Stolen a car?

If yes, about how many times? Once, twice, three or four times, or five or more times?

☐ Once   ☐ Twice   ☐ Three or four   ☐ Five or more

15. Broken into another person's house, garage, shed or other building to try to steal something?

If yes, about how many times? Once, twice, three or four times, or five or more times?

☐ Once   ☐ Twice   ☐ Three or four   ☐ Five or more

16. Smoked marijuana or used some other sort of dope or narcotics?

If yes, about how many times? Once, twice, three or four times, or five or more times?

☐ Once   ☐ Twice   ☐ Three or four   ☐ Five or more

17. Sold marijuana or some other dope?

If yes, about how many times? Once, twice, three or four times, or five or more times?

☐ Once   ☐ Twice   ☐ Three or four   ☐ Five or more

18. Started a fist fight?

If yes, about how many times? Once, twice, three or four times, or five or more times?

☐ Once   ☐ Twice   ☐ Three or four   ☐ Five or more

19. Beat up on someone who hadn't done anything to you?

If yes, about how many times? Once, twice, three or four times, or five or more times?

☐ Once   ☐ Twice   ☐ Three or four   ☐ Five or more

20. Robbed someone by threatening them with a knife, or a razor or a gun?

If yes, about how many times? Once, twice, three or four times, or five or more times?

☐ Once   ☐ Twice   ☐ Three or four   ☐ Five or more

Index